THE WAR IN THE AIR

MAP CASE 5

THE WAR IN THE AIR

Being the story of the part played
in the Great War by the Royal Air Force

MAP CASE 5

Airship & Aeroplane Raids from
16-17 March 1917 to 19-20 May 1918

www.naval-military-press.com

Published by

The Naval & Military Press Ltd
Unit 5 Riverside, Brambleside
Bellbrook Industrial Estate
Uckfield, East Sussex
TN22 1QQ England

Tel: +44 (0)1825 749494

www.naval-military-press.com
www.nmarchive.com

In reprinting in facsimile from the original, any imperfections are inevitably reproduced and the quality may fall short of modern type and cartographic standards.

LIST OF MAPS

AIRSHIP RAIDS, 1917

1. 16-17 March 1
2. 23-24 May 7
3. 16-17 June 13
   21-22 August
4. 24-25 September 17
5. 19-20 October 23
6. 19-20 October 33

AIRSHIP RAIDS, 1918

7. 12 March 39
   13 March
8. 12-13 April 43
9. 5-6 August 53

AEROPLANE RAIDS, 1917

10. 25 May 57
    5 June
11. 13 June 60
12. 7 July 63
13. 4-5 September 65
14. 24th September 75
15. 25 September 81
16. 28 September 85
17. 29 September 89
18. 30 September 99
19. 1 October 109

20.	31 October	119
21.	6 December	129
22.	18 December	139

AEROPLANE RAIDS, 1918

23.	28-29 January	149
24.	29-30 January	159
25.	16 February	169
26.	17-18 February	175
27.	7-8 March	185
28.	19-20 May	195

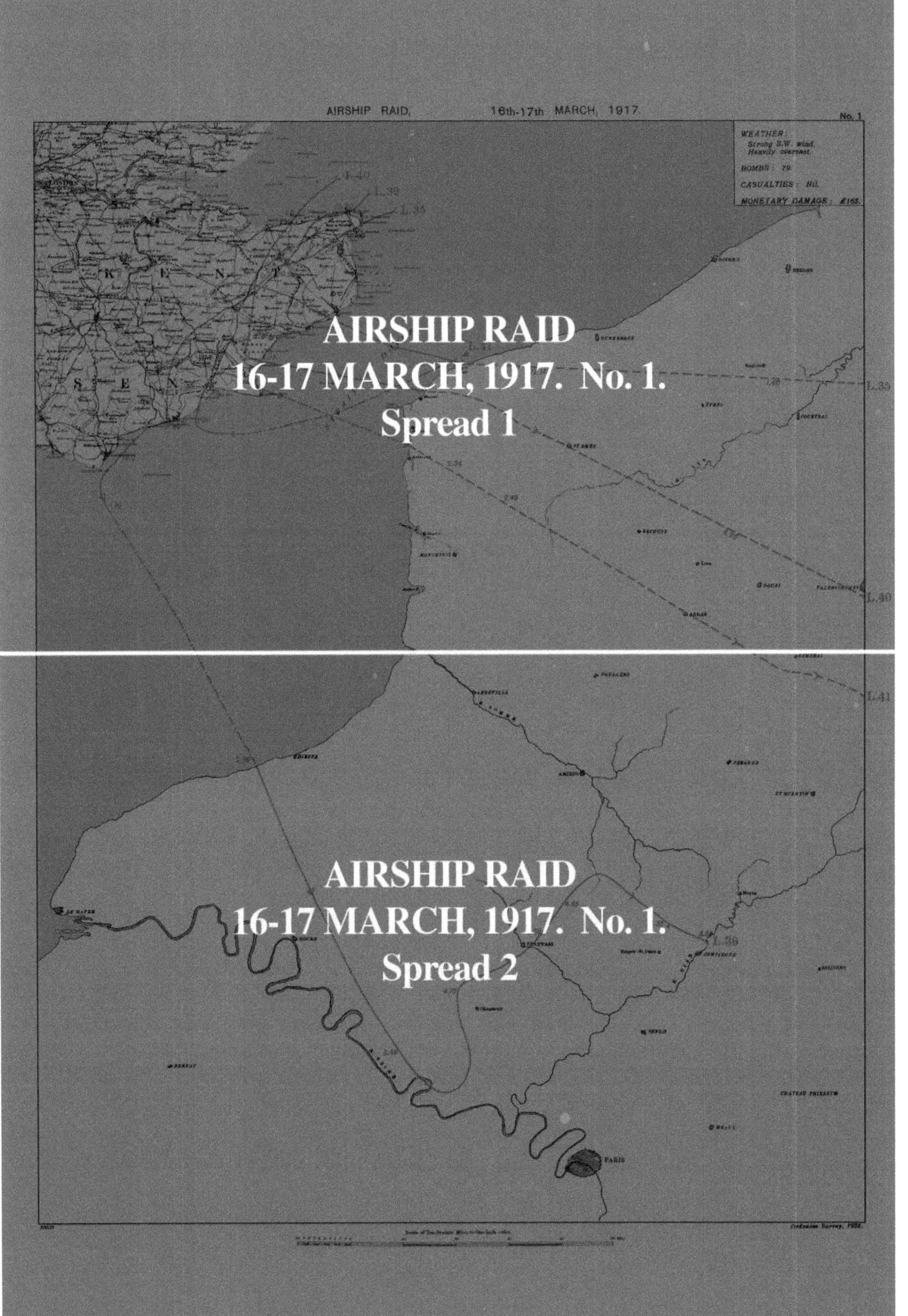

Spread 1

AIRSHIP RAID,

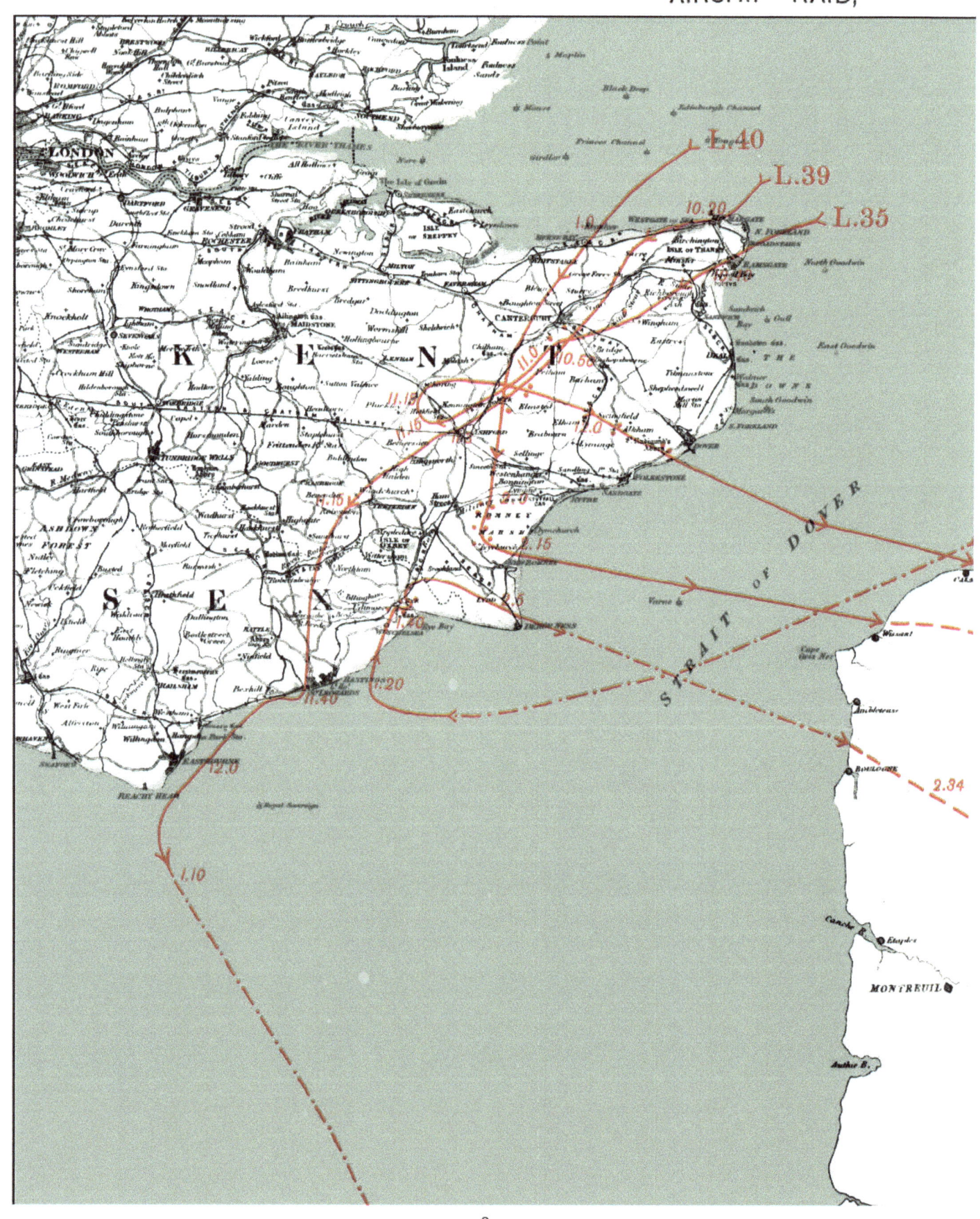

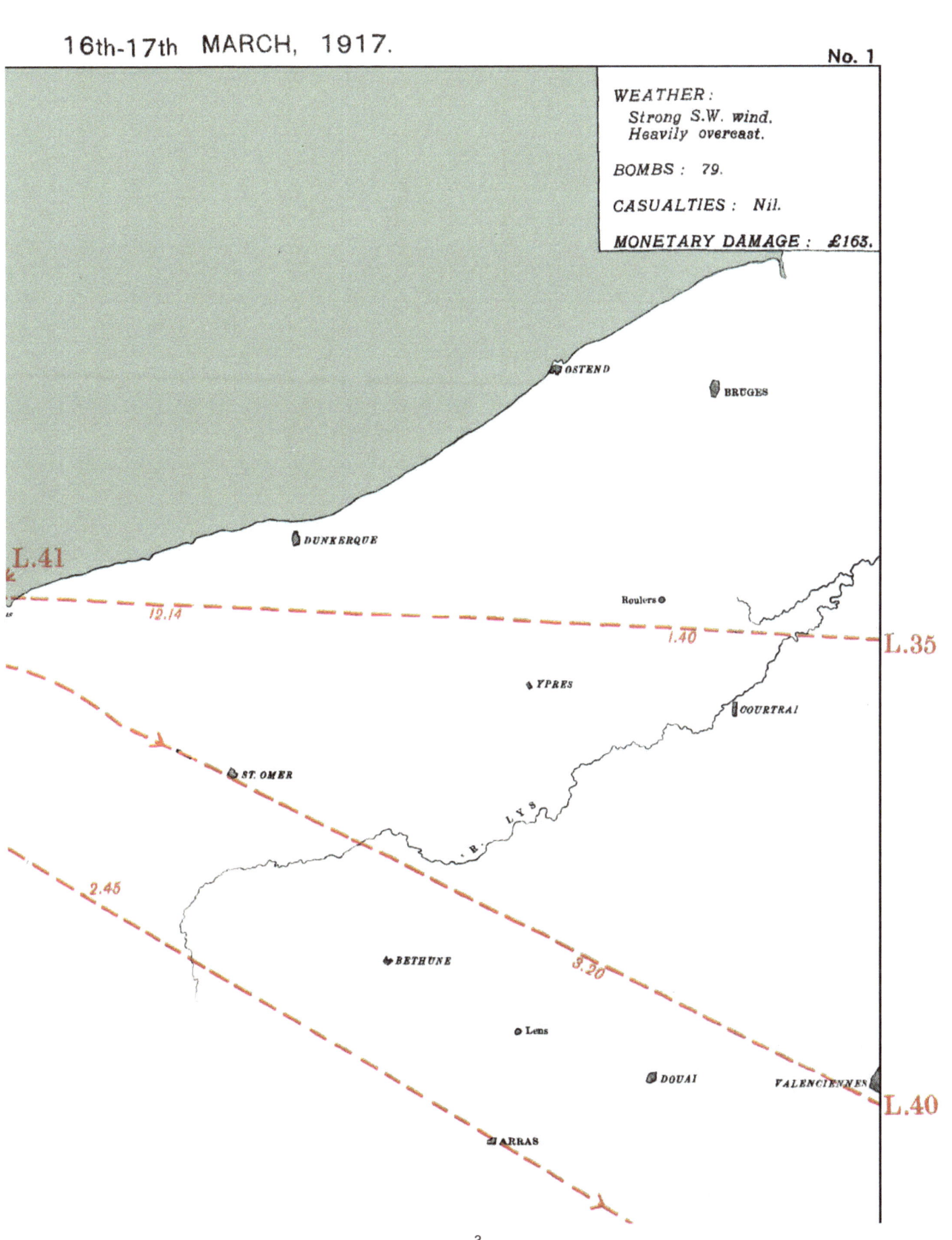

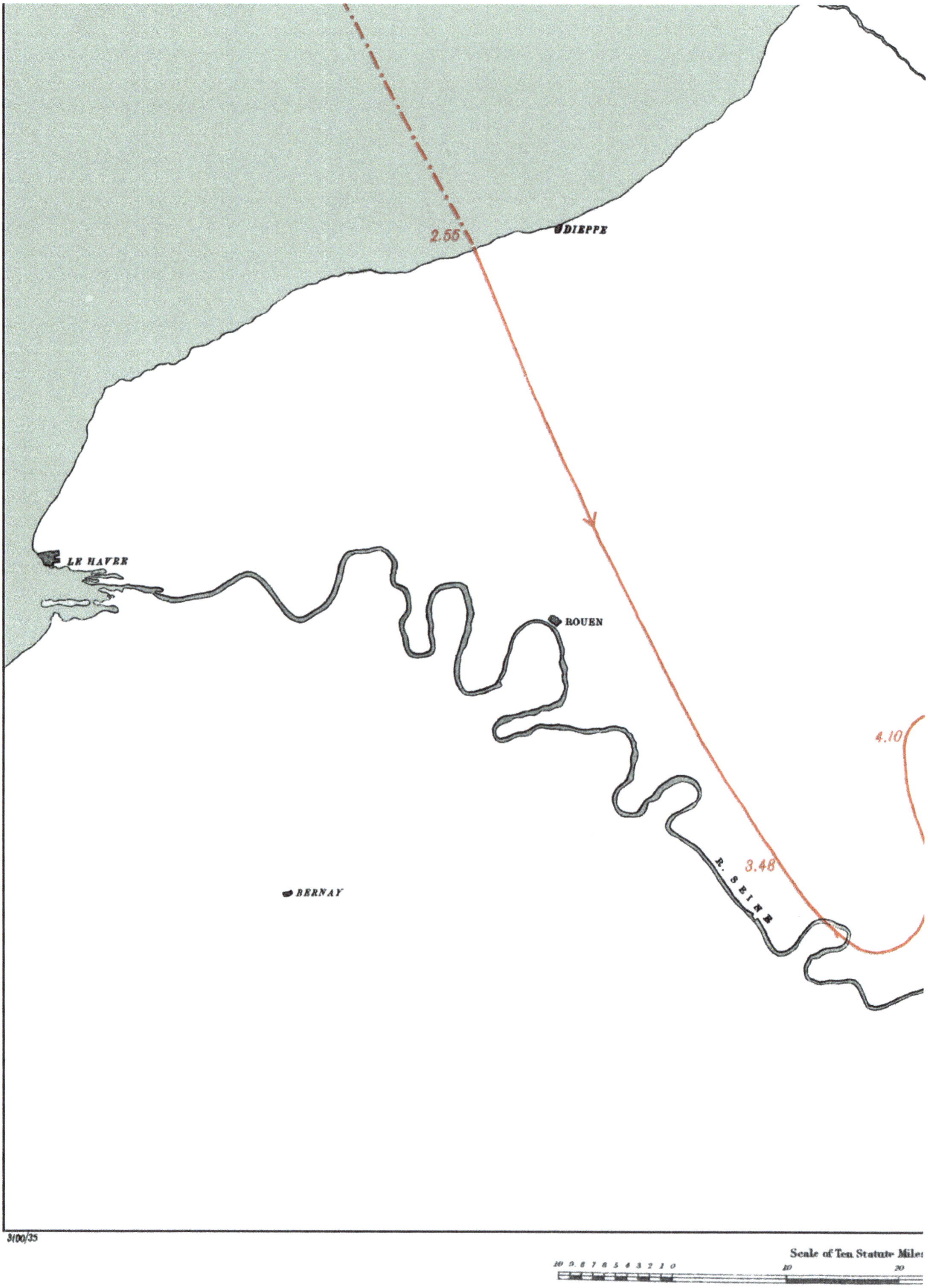
2.55
DIEPPE
LE HAVRE
ROUEN
4.10
R. SEINE
3.48
BERNAY
3100/35
Scale of Ten Statute Miles
10 9 8 7 6 5 4 3 2 1 0
10
20

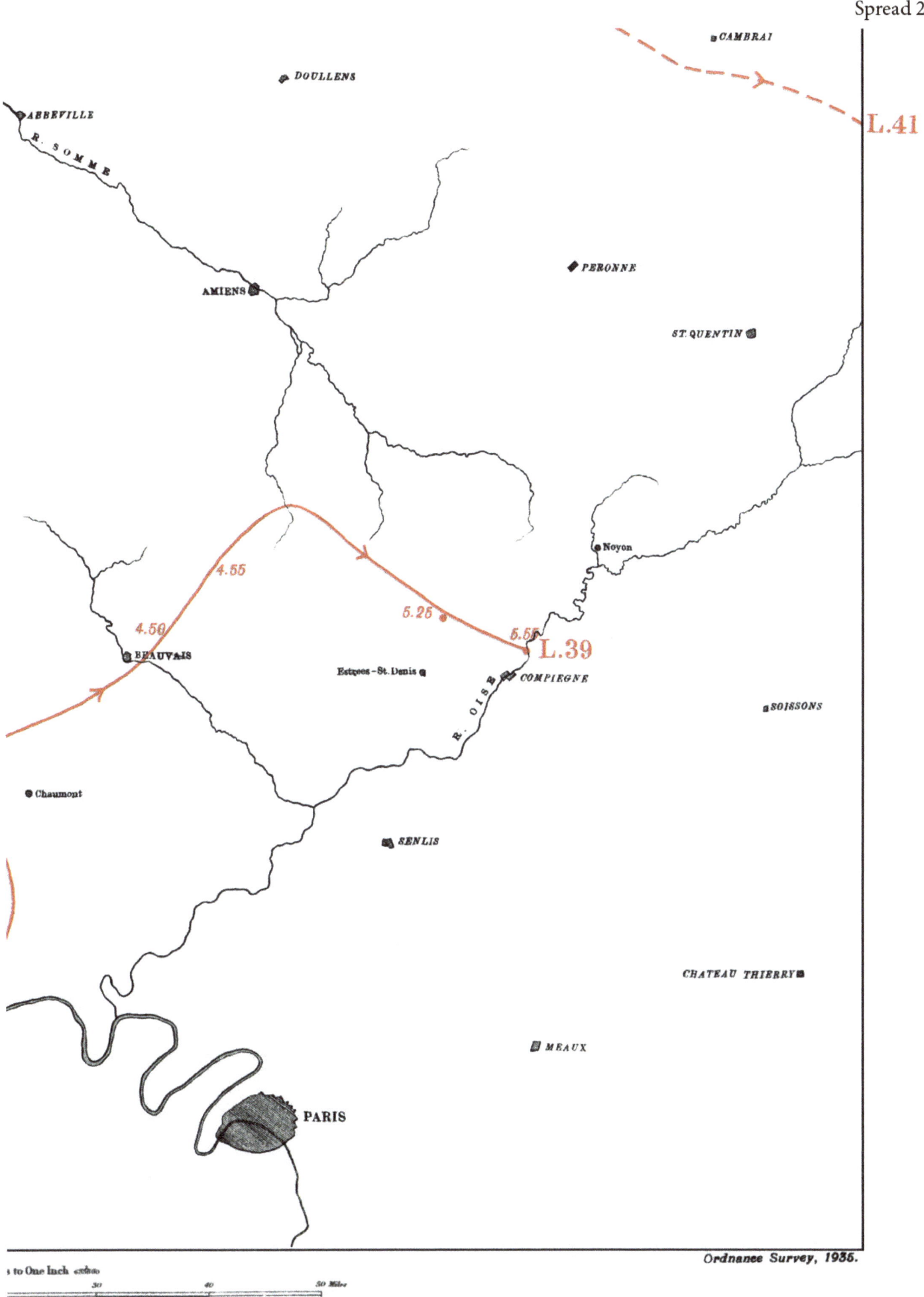

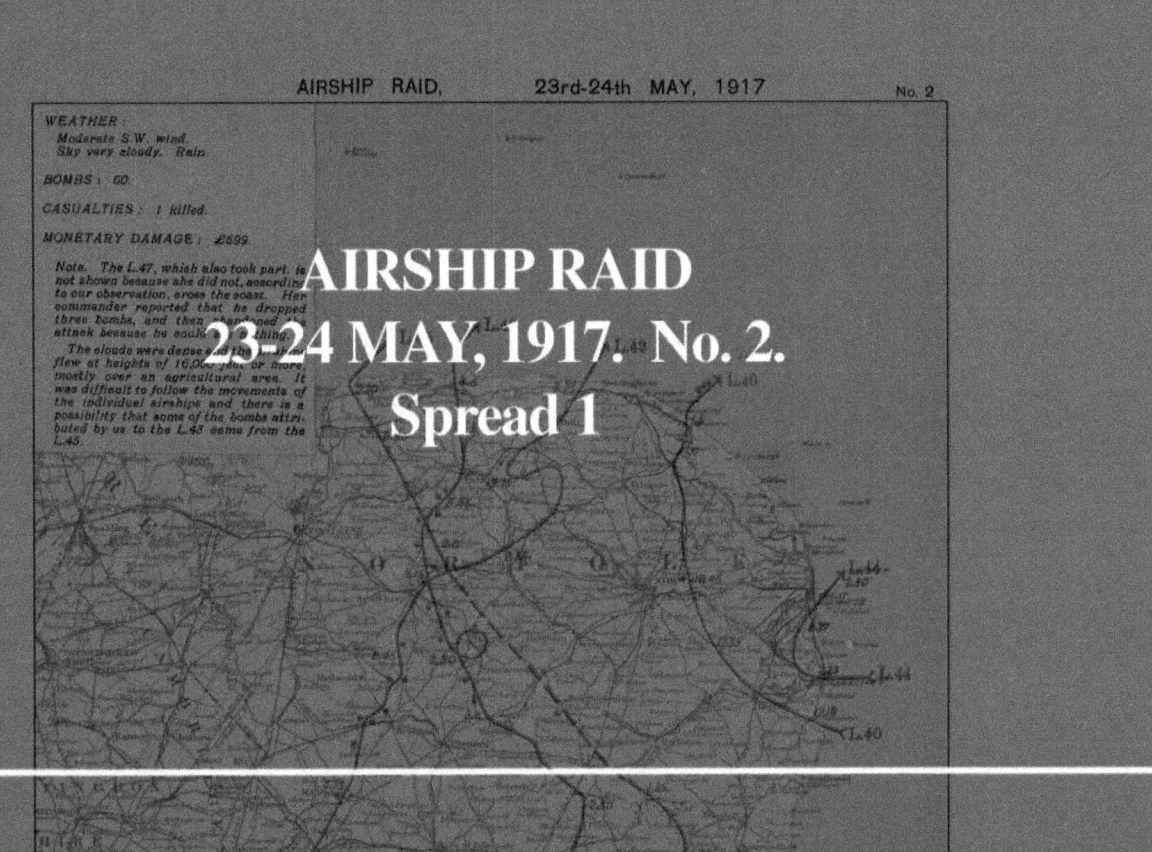

AIRSHIP RAID
23-24 MAY, 1917. No. 2.
Spread 1

AIRSHIP RAID
23-24 MAY, 1917. No. 2.
Spread 2

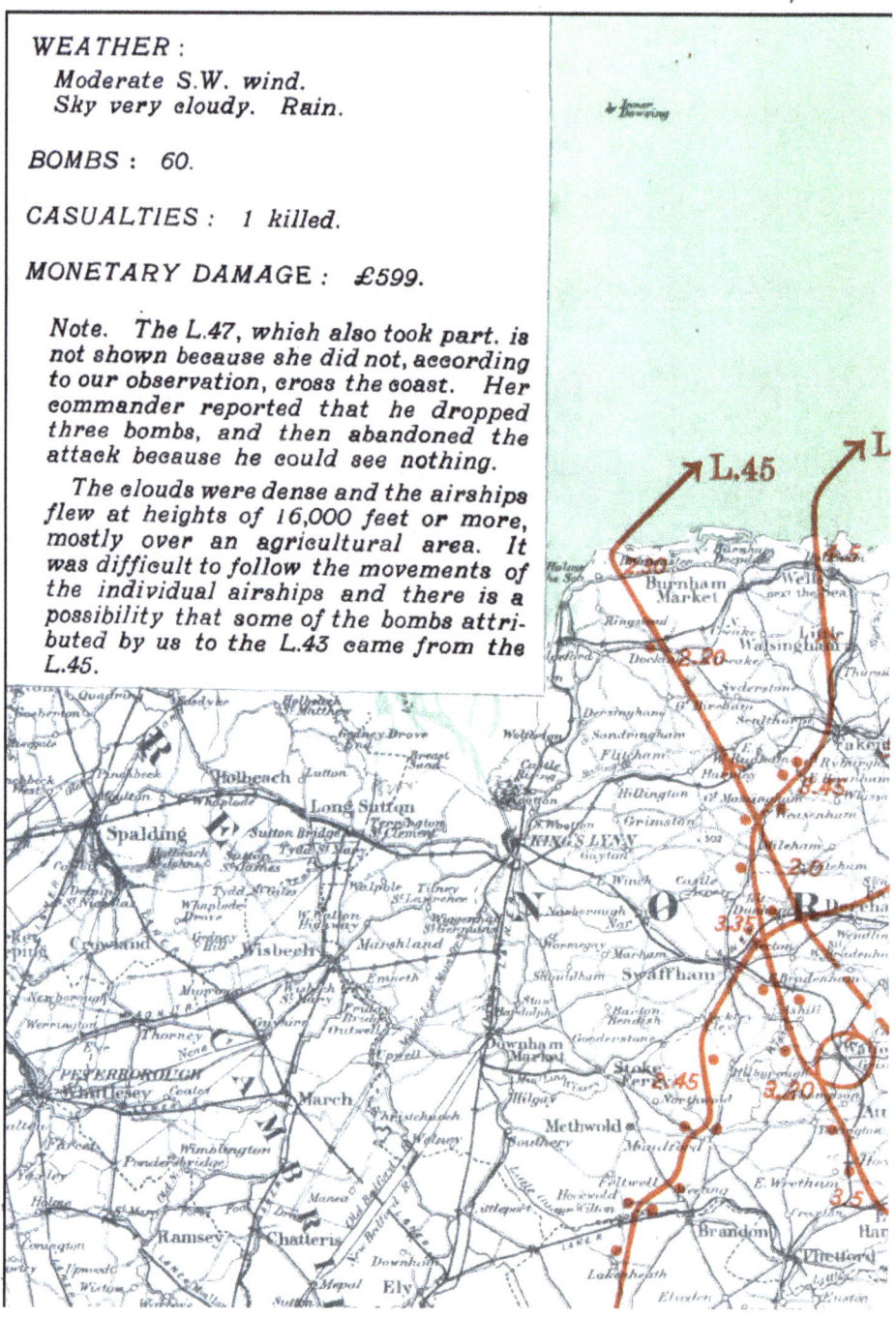

AIRSHIP RAID,

WEATHER:
Moderate S.W. wind.
Sky very cloudy. Rain.

BOMBS: 60.

CASUALTIES: 1 killed.

MONETARY DAMAGE: £599.

Note. The L.47, which also took part, is not shown because she did not, according to our observation, cross the coast. Her commander reported that he dropped three bombs, and then abandoned the attack because he could see nothing.

The clouds were dense and the airships flew at heights of 16,000 feet or more, mostly over an agricultural area. It was difficult to follow the movements of the individual airships and there is a possibility that some of the bombs attributed by us to the L.43 came from the L.45.

23rd-24th MAY, 1917   No. 2

Spread 2

AIRSHIP RAID
16th-17th August and
21st-22nd August, 1917. No. 3.
Spread 1

16th-17th June 1917

WEATHER: Wind light. Fine and clear.

BOMBS: 41.

CASUALTIES: 3 killed, 16 injured.

MONETARY DAMAGE: £28,159.

21st–22nd Aug. 1917 — No. 3

WEATHER: Strong, S.W. wind, low clouds.

BOMBS: 29.

CASUALTIES: 1 injured.

MONETARY DAMAGE: £2,272.

Note: According to German records, bombs were also dropped by L.42, L.44, L.45, L.46 and L.47. Although the map shows only L.41 as coming overland, it is possible some of the others crossed the coast and that at least one went some distance inland. No bombs, however, other than those indicated have ever been traced.

Ordnance Survey, 1935.

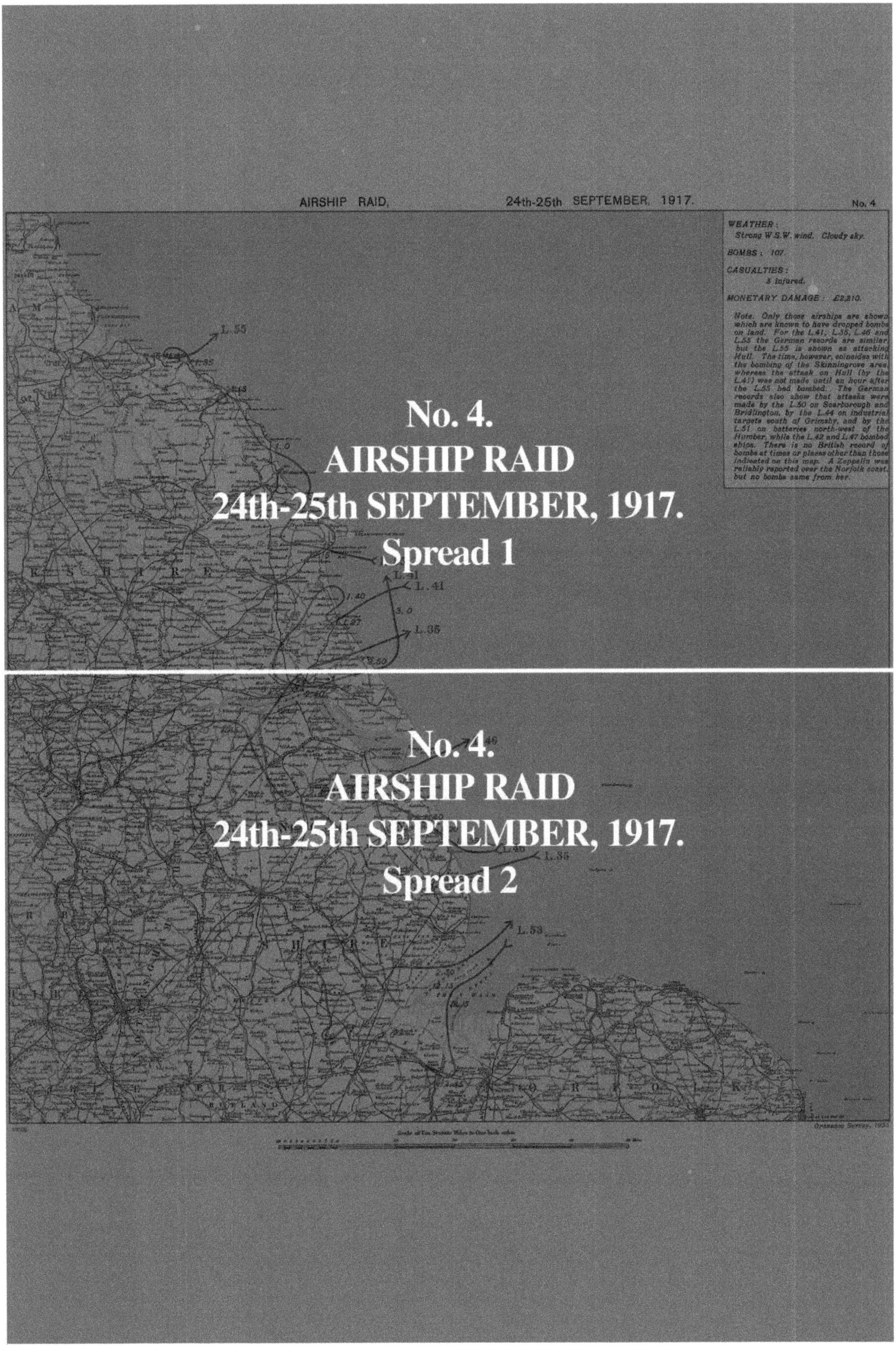

No. 4.
AIRSHIP RAID
24th-25th SEPTEMBER, 1917.
Spread 1

No. 4.
AIRSHIP RAID
24th-25th SEPTEMBER, 1917.
Spread 2

AIRSHIP RAID,

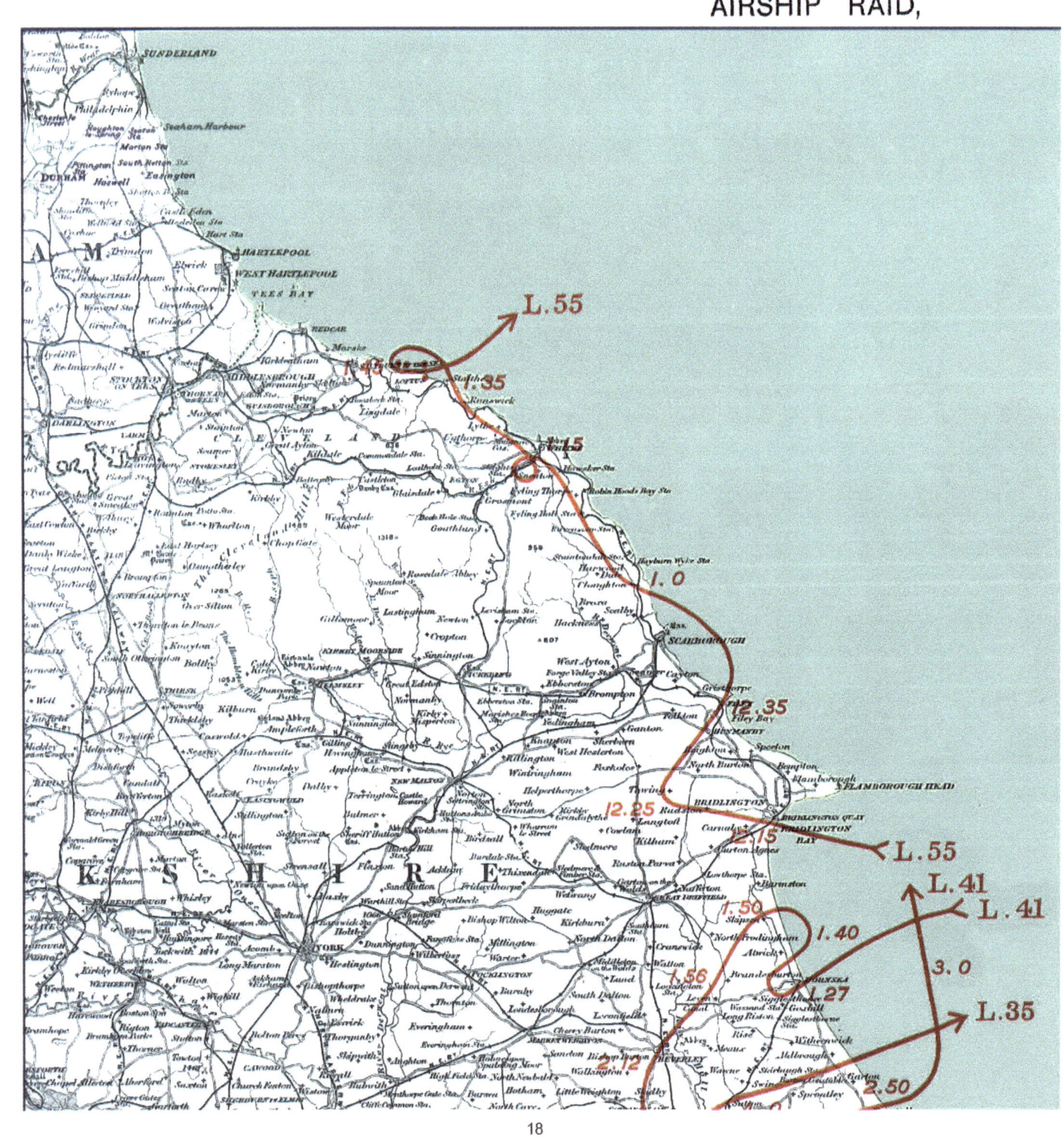

24th-25th SEPTEMBER, 1917.

No. 4

WEATHER:
Strong W.S.W. wind. Cloudy sky.

BOMBS: 107.

CASUALTIES:
3 injured.

MONETARY DAMAGE: £2,210.

Note. Only those airships are shown which are known to have dropped bombs on land. For the L.41, L.35, L.46 and L.53 the German records are similar, but the L.55 is shown as attacking Hull. The time, however, coincides with the bombing of the Skinningrove area, whereas the attack on Hull (by the L.41) was not made until an hour after the L.55 had bombed. The German records also show that attacks were made by the L.50 on Scarborough and Bridlington, by the L.44 on industrial targets south of Grimsby, and by the L.51 on batteries north-west of the Humber, while the L.42 and L.47 bombed ships. There is no British record of bombs at times or places other than those indicated on this map. A Zeppelin was reliably reported over the Norfolk coast, but no bombs came from her.

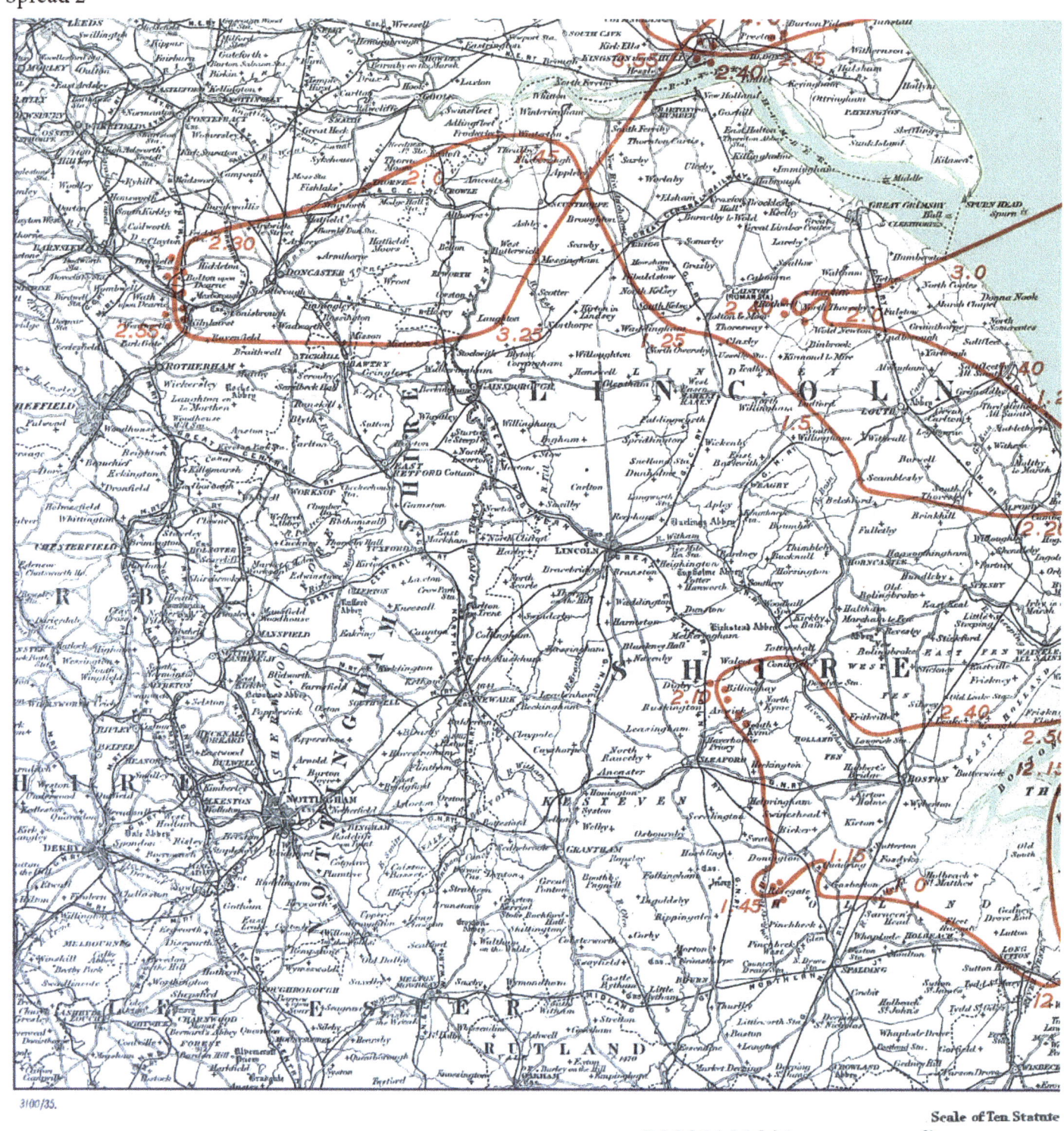

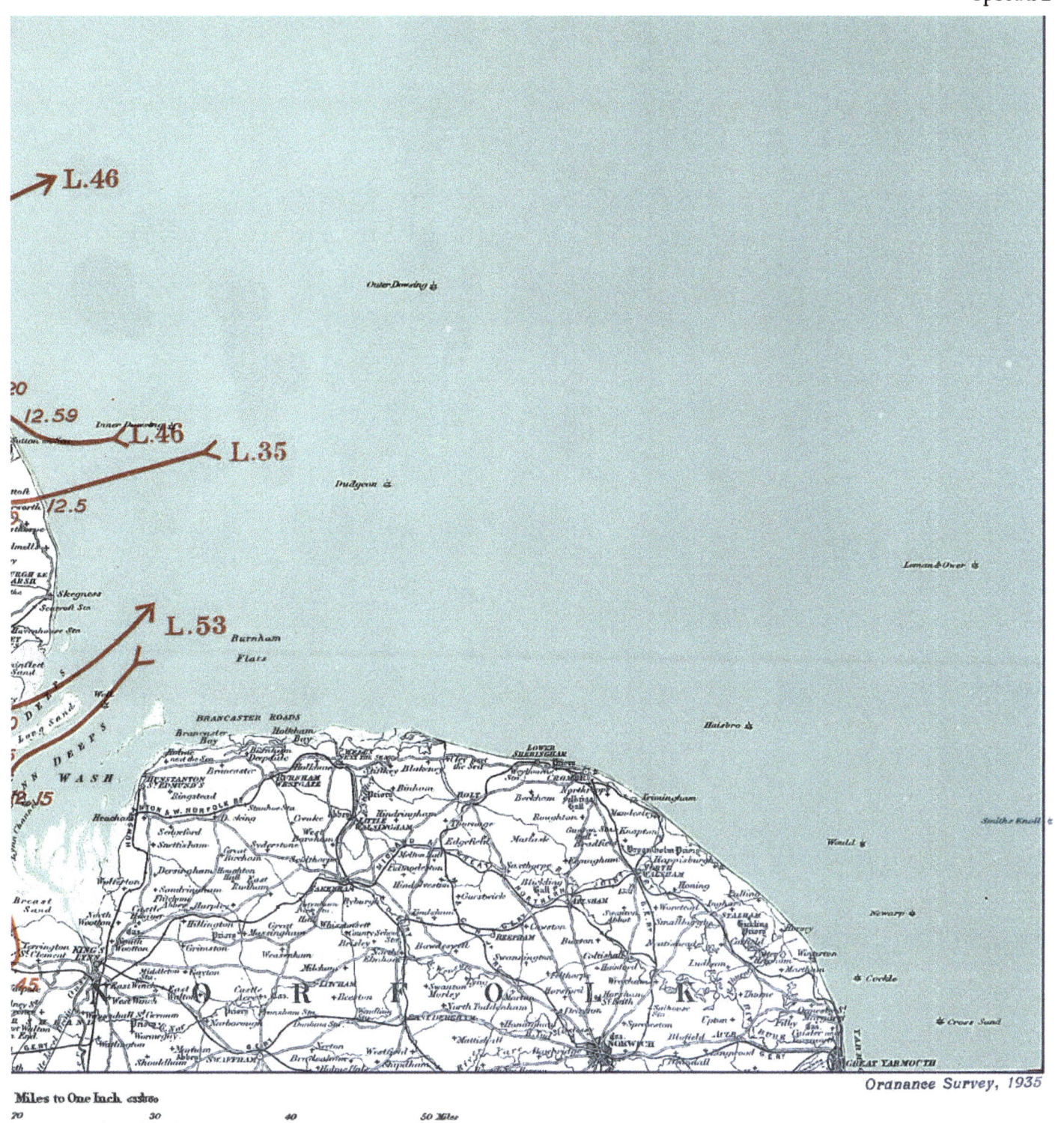

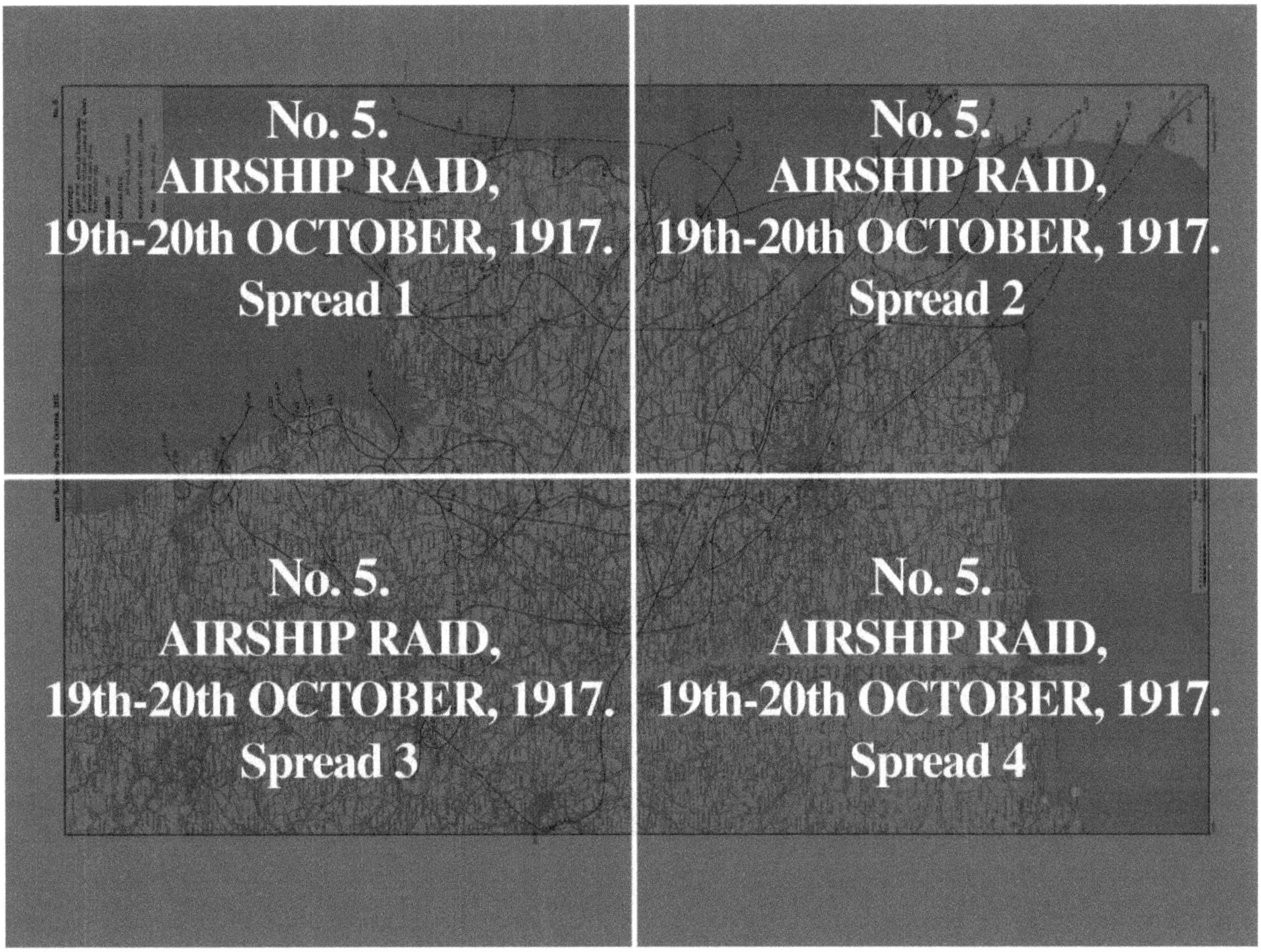

No. 5.
AIRSHIP RAID,
19th-20th OCTOBER, 1917.
Spread 1

No. 5.
AIRSHIP RAID,
19th-20th OCTOBER, 1917.
Spread 2

No. 5.
AIRSHIP RAID,
19th-20th OCTOBER, 1917.
Spread 3

No. 5.
AIRSHIP RAID,
19th-20th OCTOBER, 1917.
Spread 4

19TH-20TH OCTOBER, 1917. No. 5

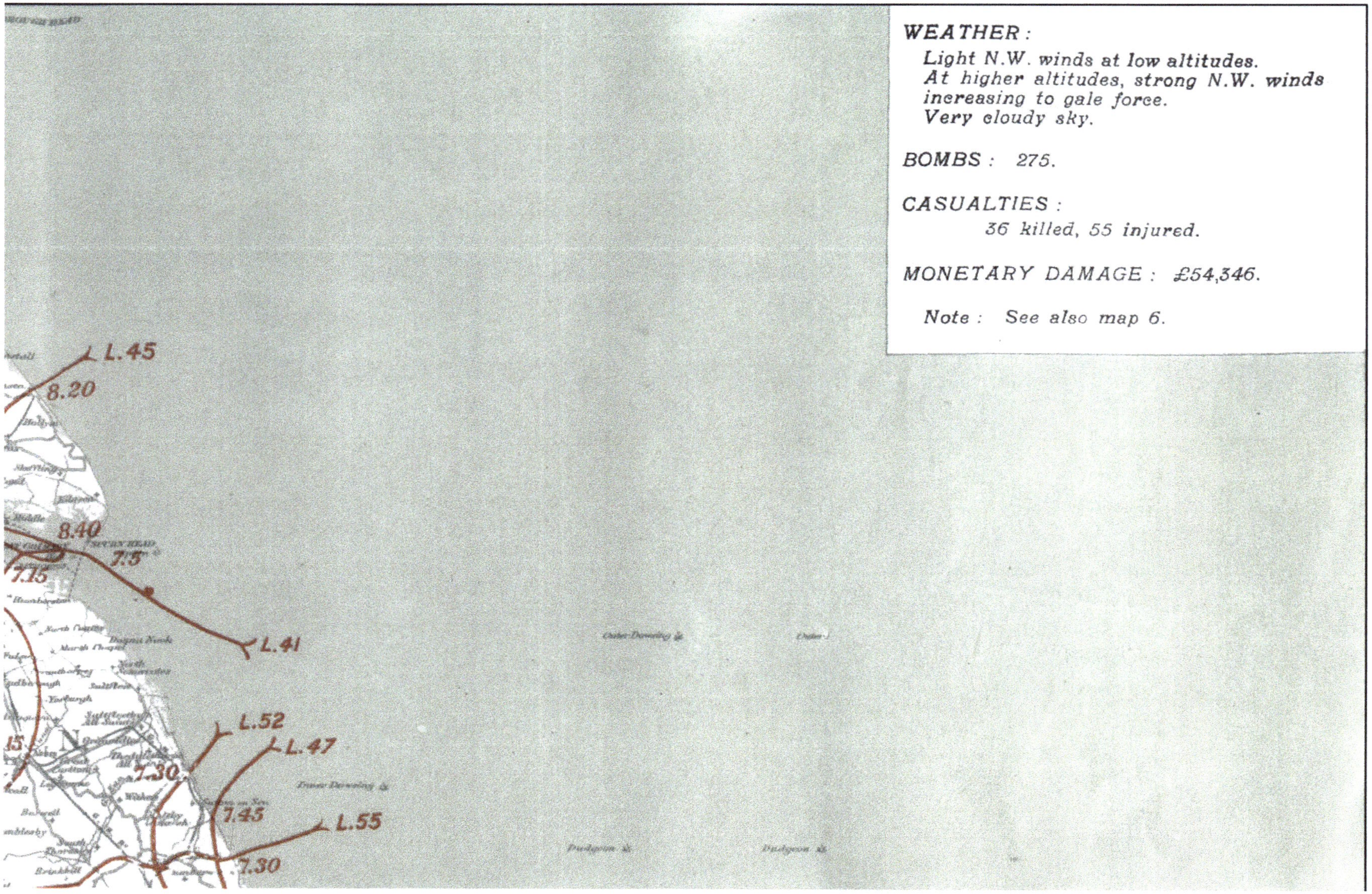

WEATHER:
Light N.W. winds at low altitudes.
At higher altitudes, strong N.W. winds increasing to gale force.
Very cloudy sky.
BOMBS: 275.
CASUALTIES:
36 killed, 55 injured.
MONETARY DAMAGE: £54,346.
Note: See also map 6.
L.45
8.20
8.40
7.15
7.15
L.41
L.52
L.47
7.30
7.45
L.55
7.30

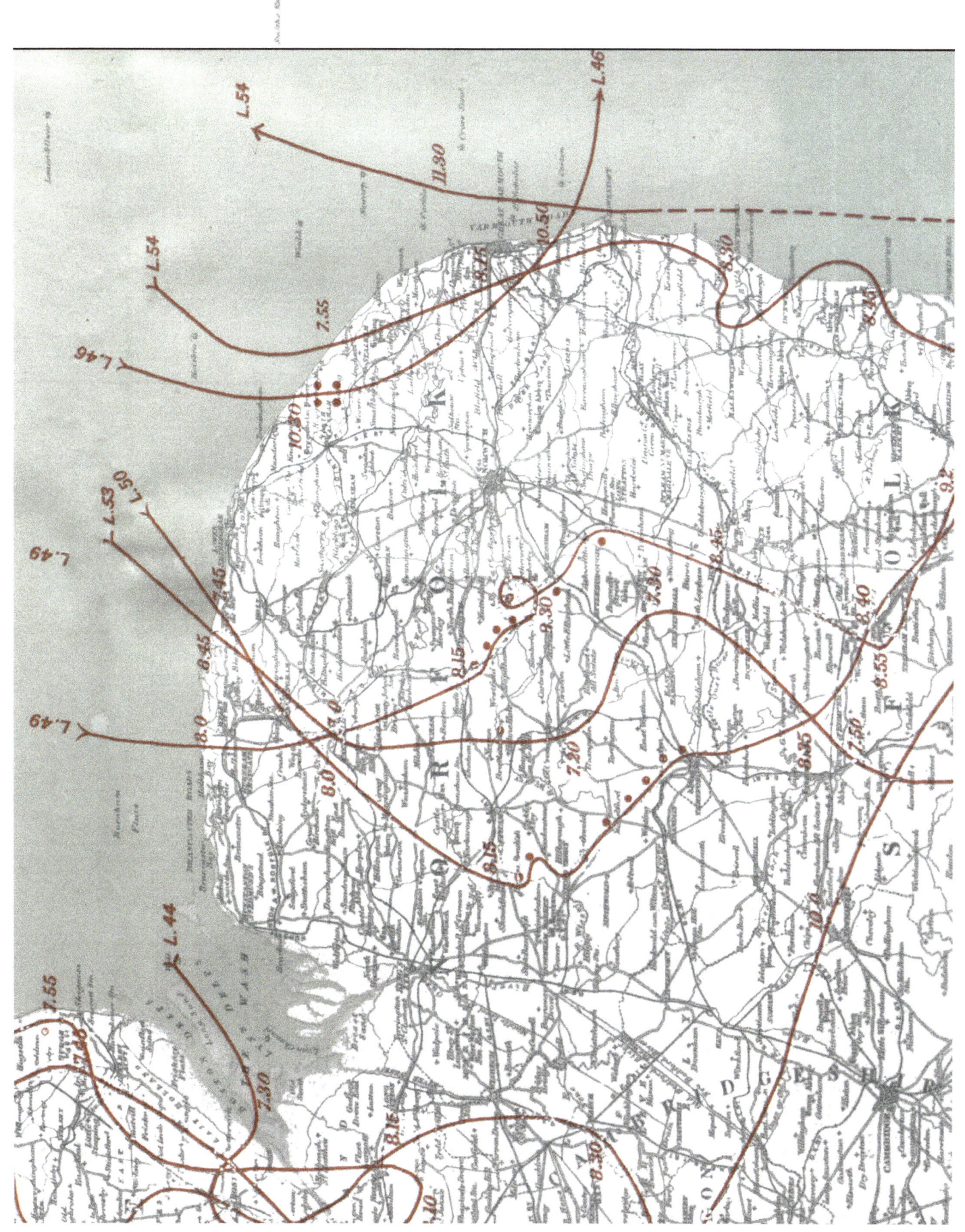

Spread 2

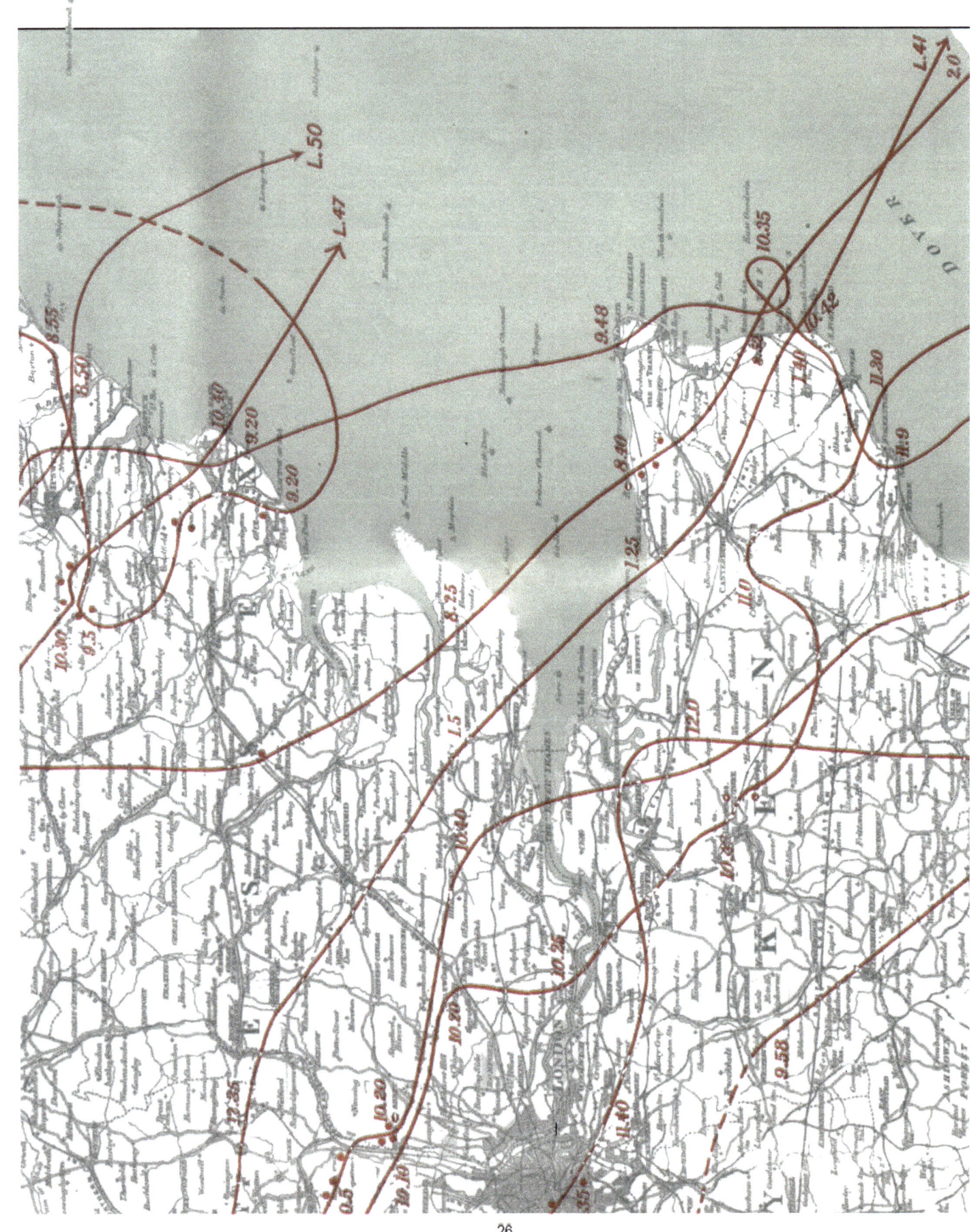

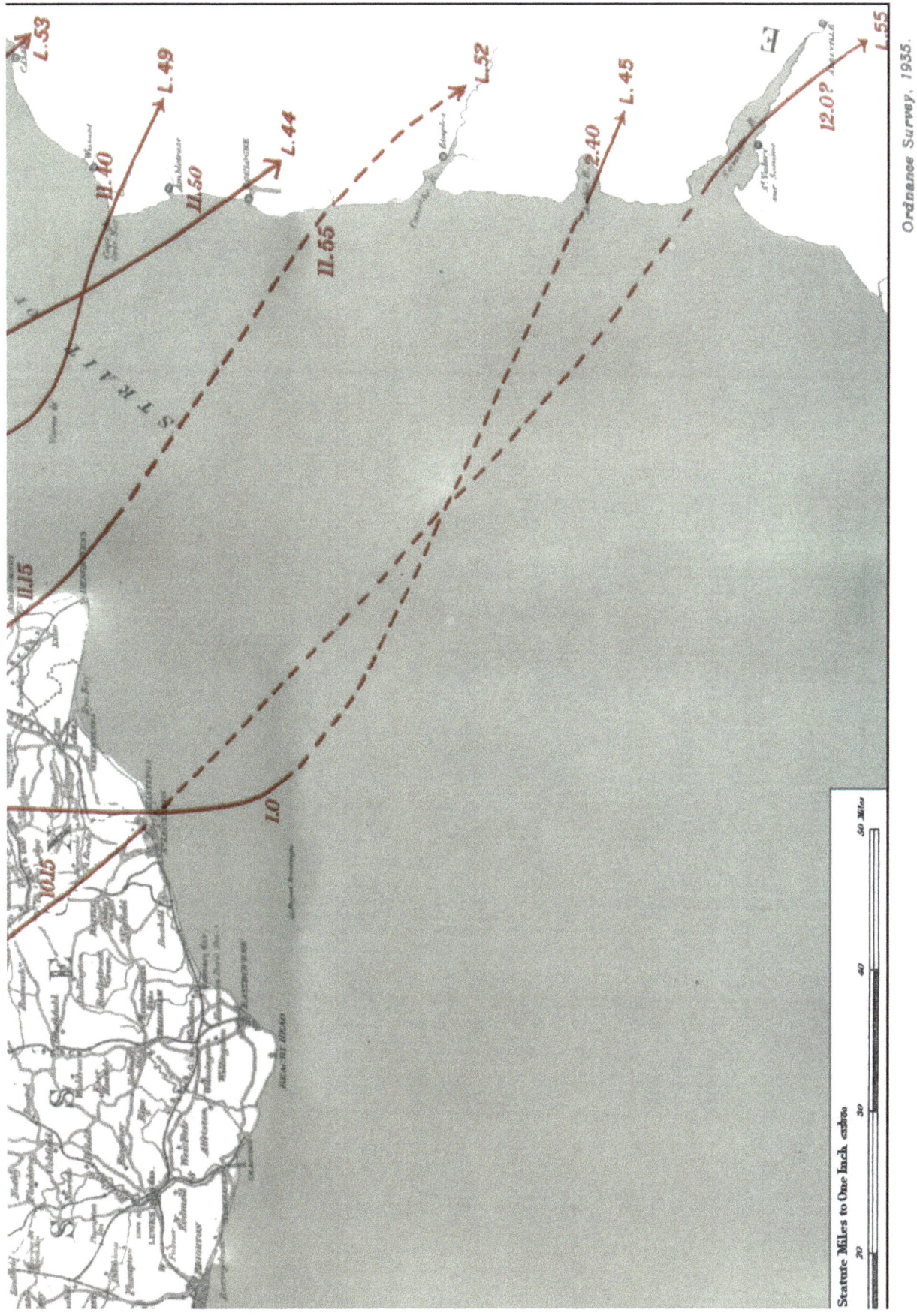

Spread 3

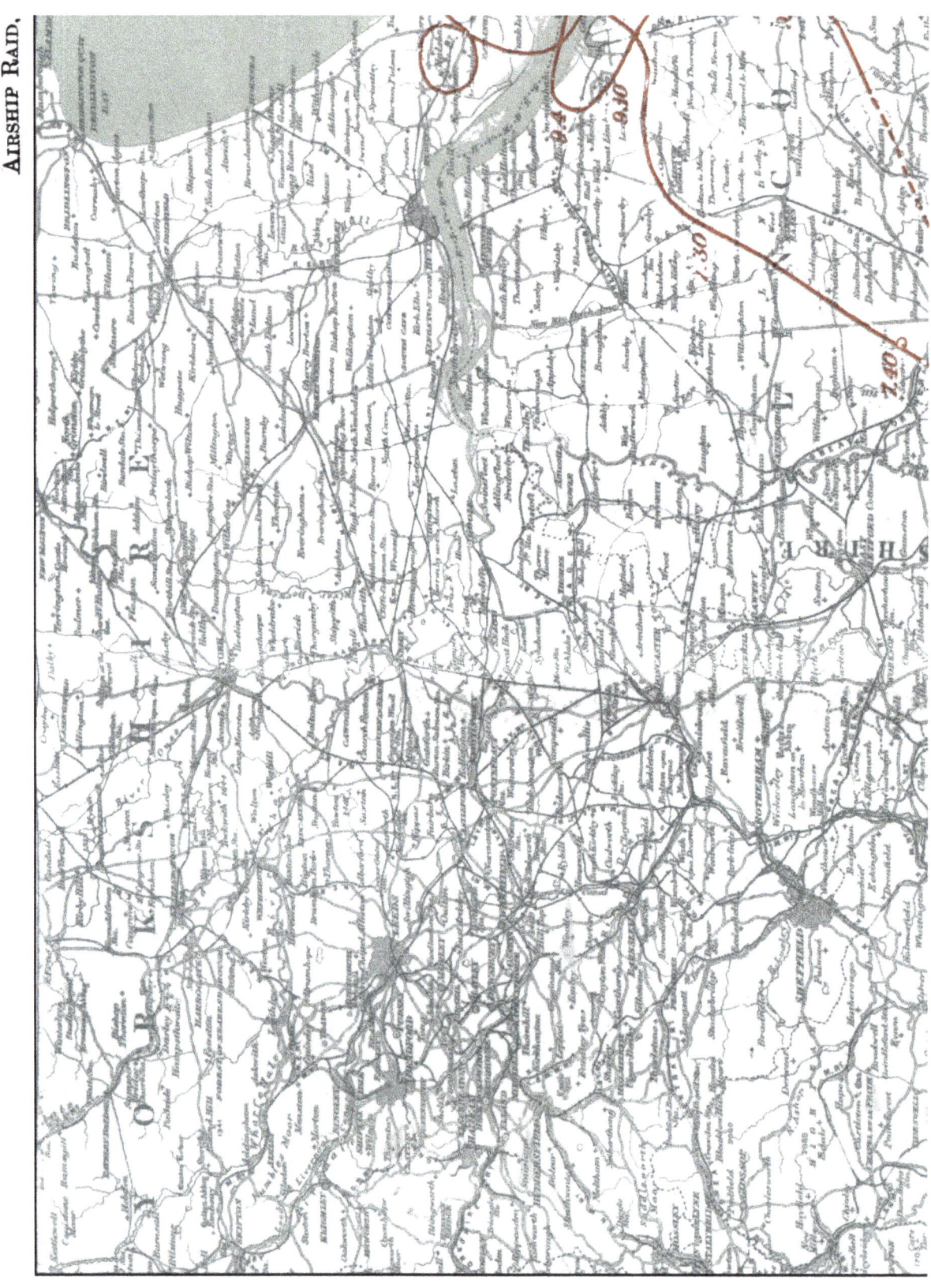

Spread 4

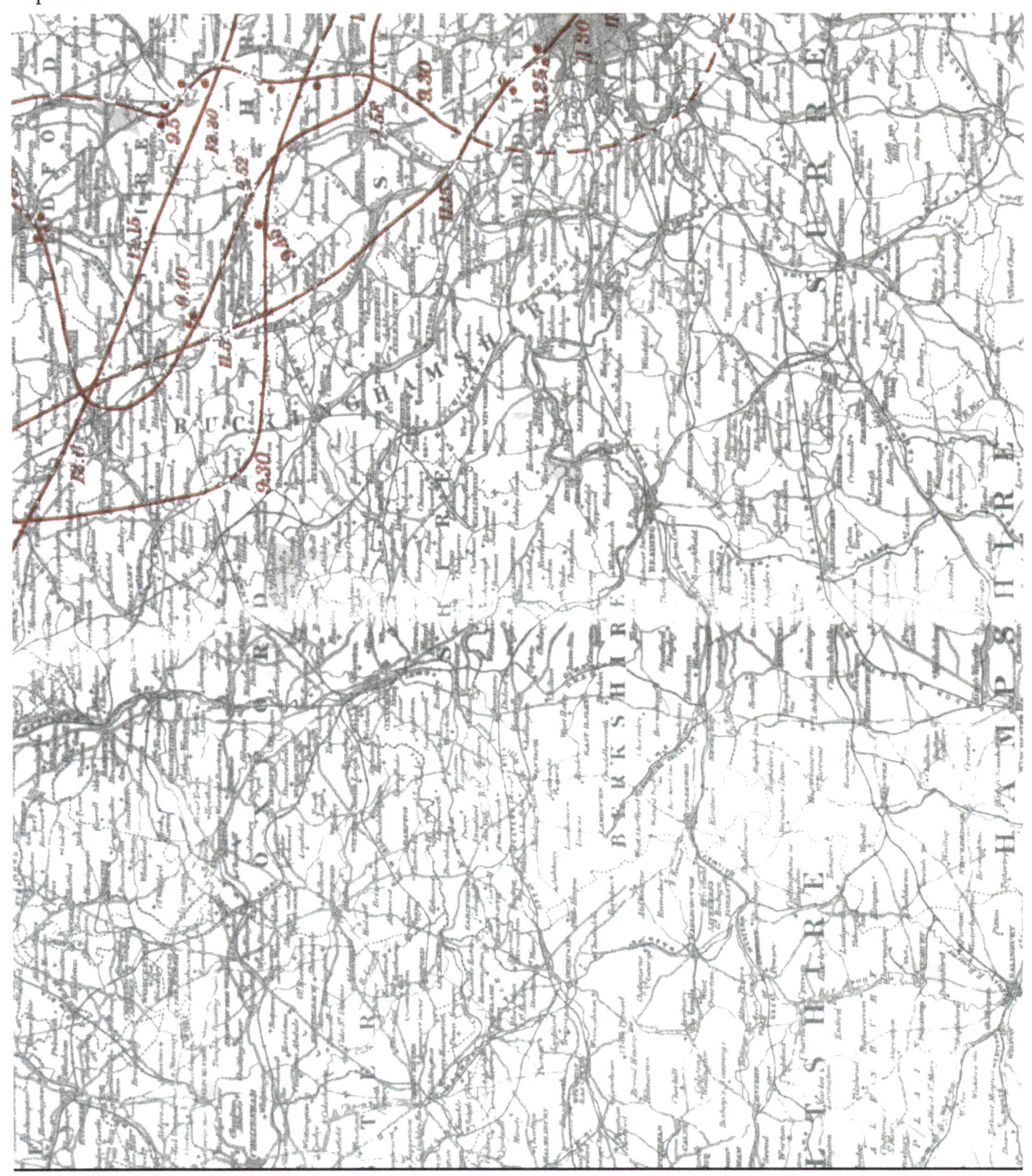

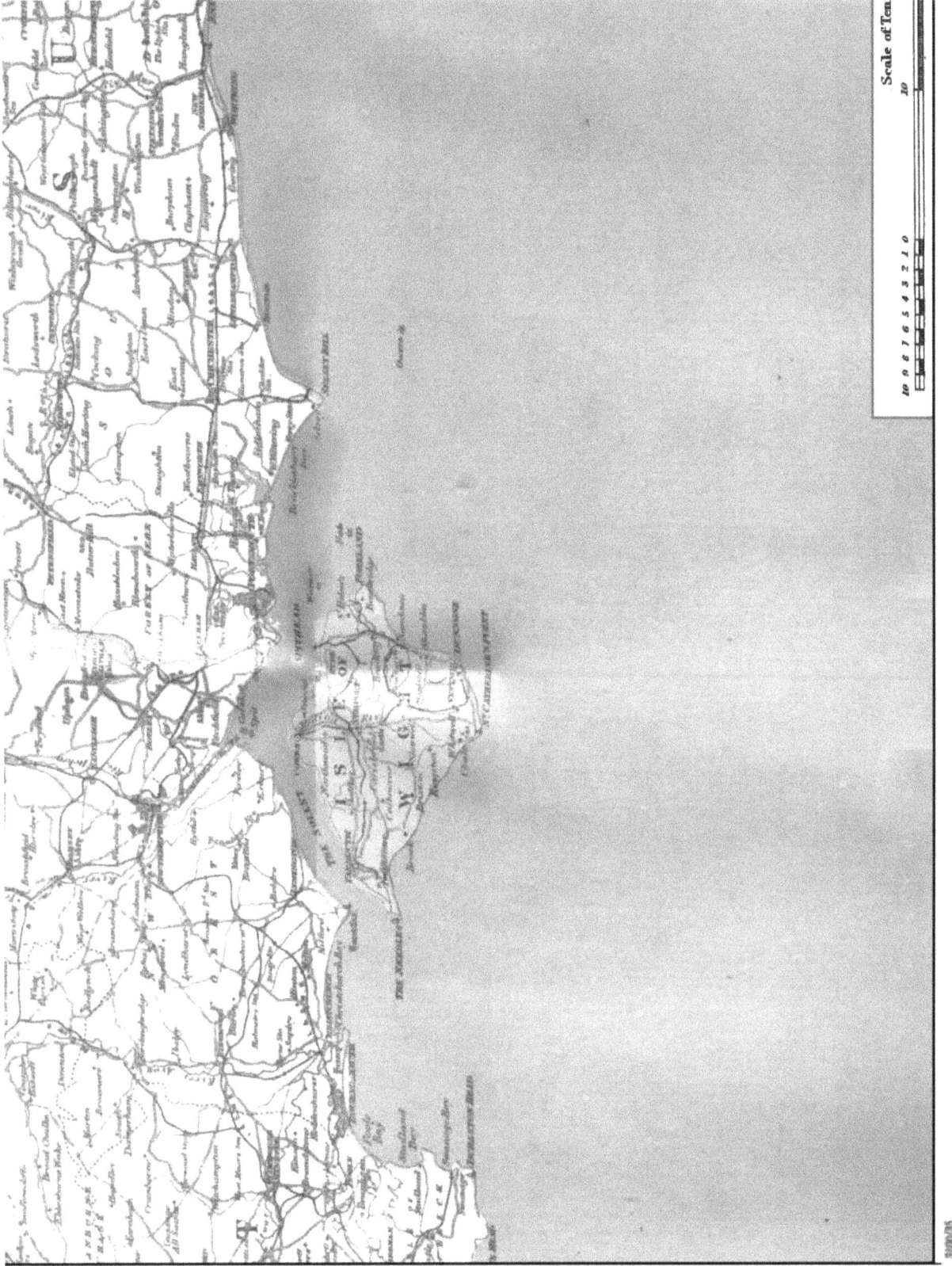

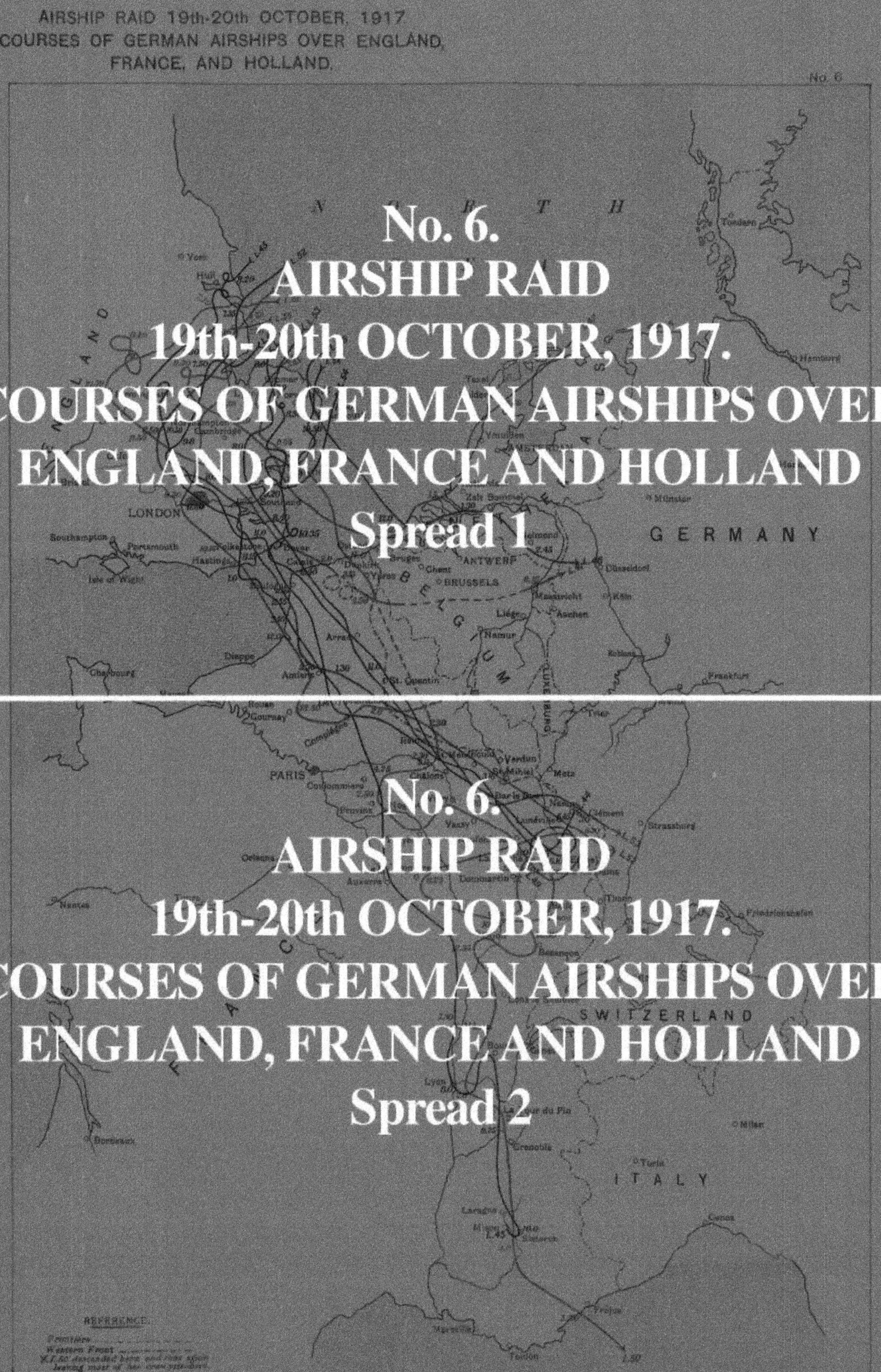

No. 6.
AIRSHIP RAID
19th-20th OCTOBER, 1917.
COURSES OF GERMAN AIRSHIPS OVER ENGLAND, FRANCE AND HOLLAND
Spread 1

No. 6.
AIRSHIP RAID
19th-20th OCTOBER, 1917.
COURSES OF GERMAN AIRSHIPS OVER ENGLAND, FRANCE AND HOLLAND
Spread 2

AIRSHIP RAID 19th-20th OCTOBER, 1917. COURSES OF GERMAN AIRSHIPS OVER ENGLAND FRANCE, AND HOLLAND.

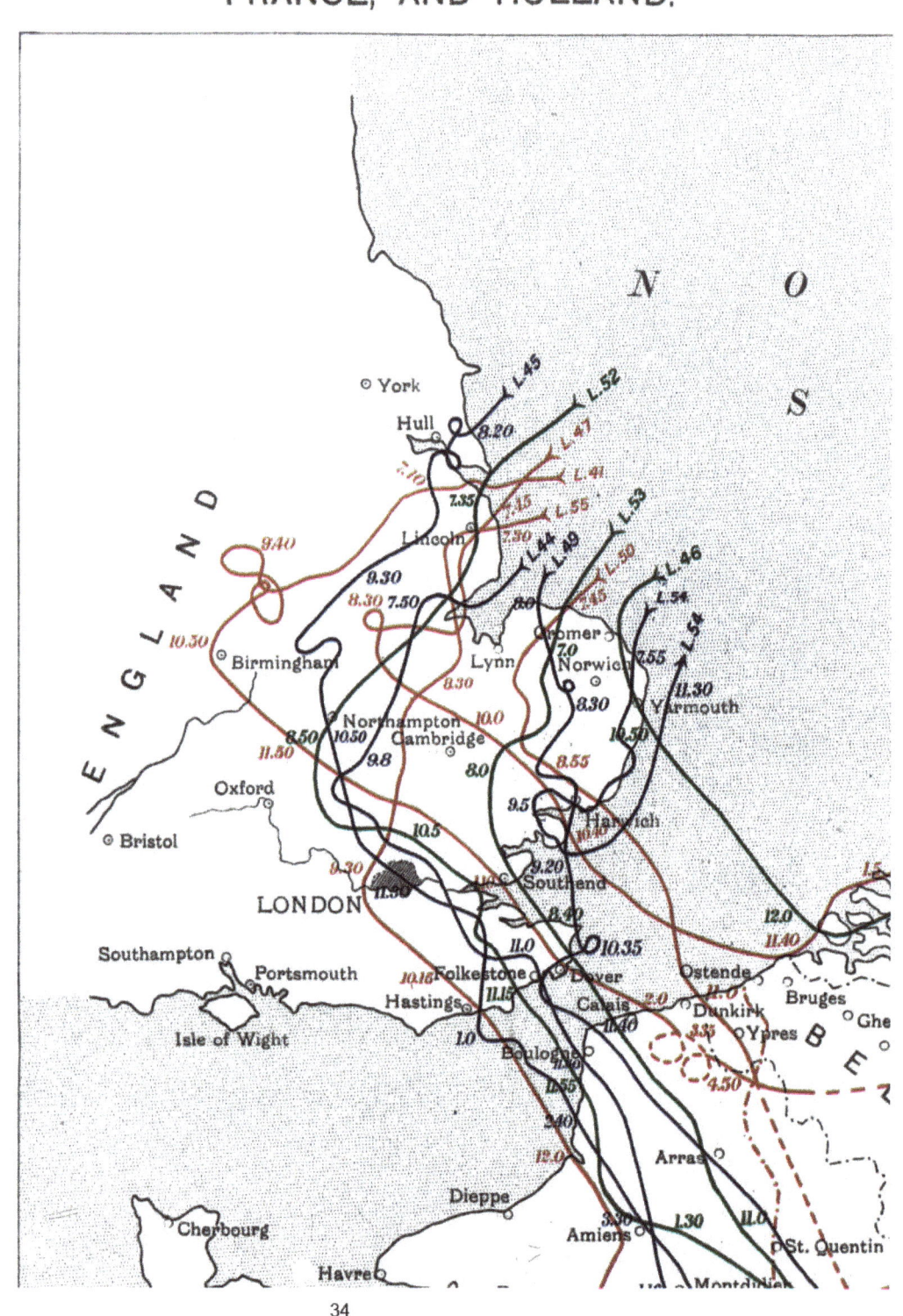

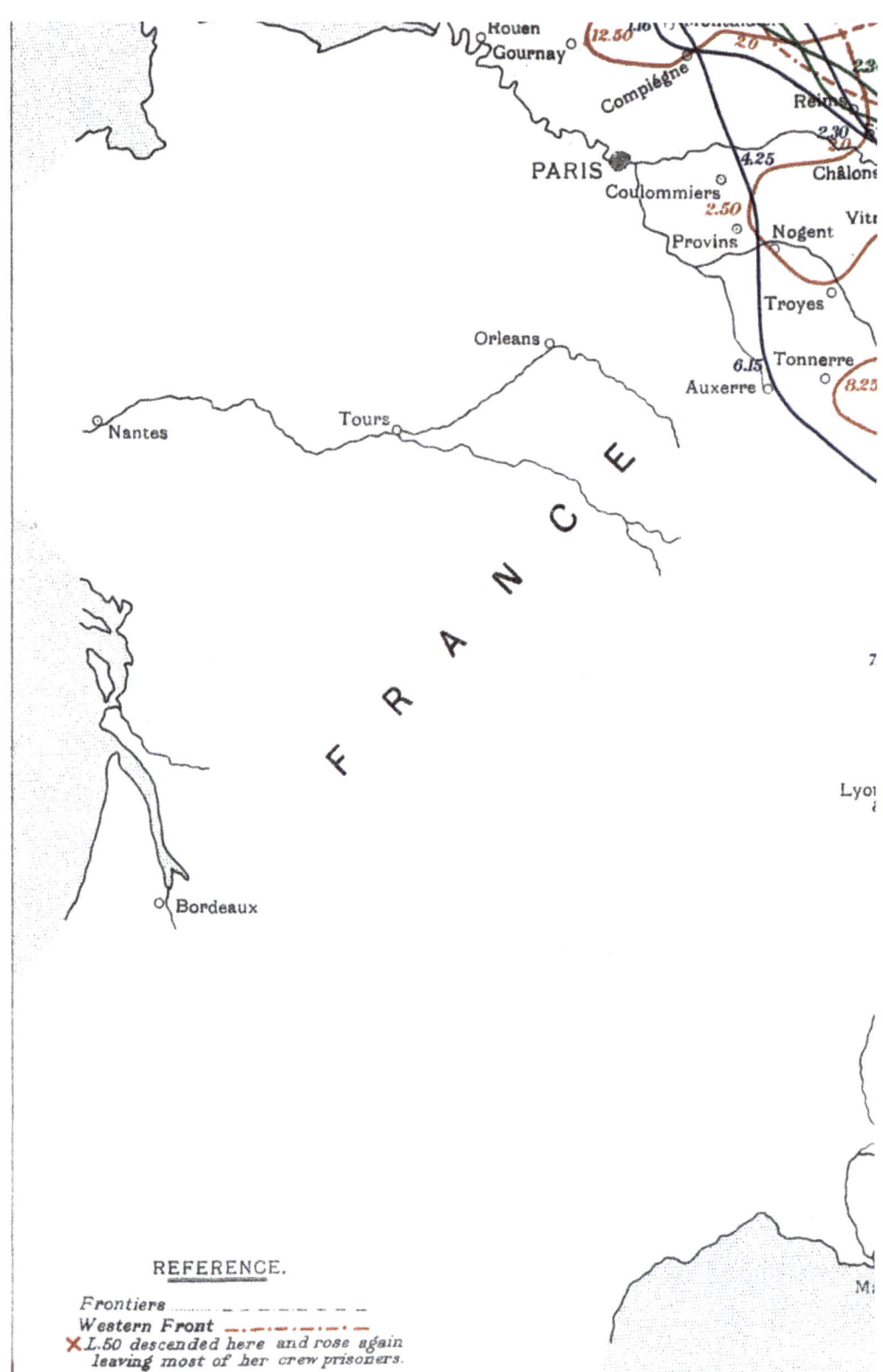

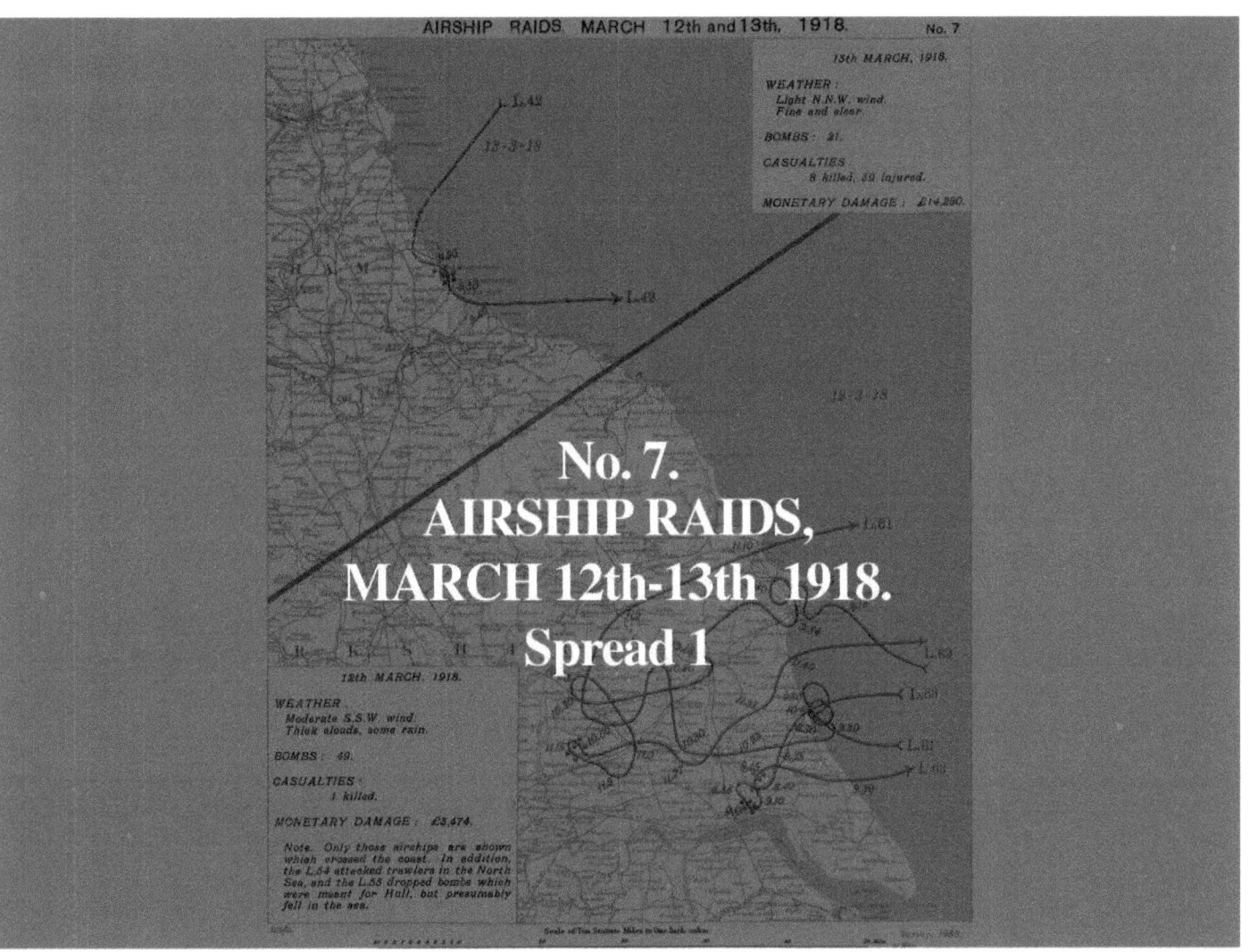

AIRSHIP RAIDS, MAR

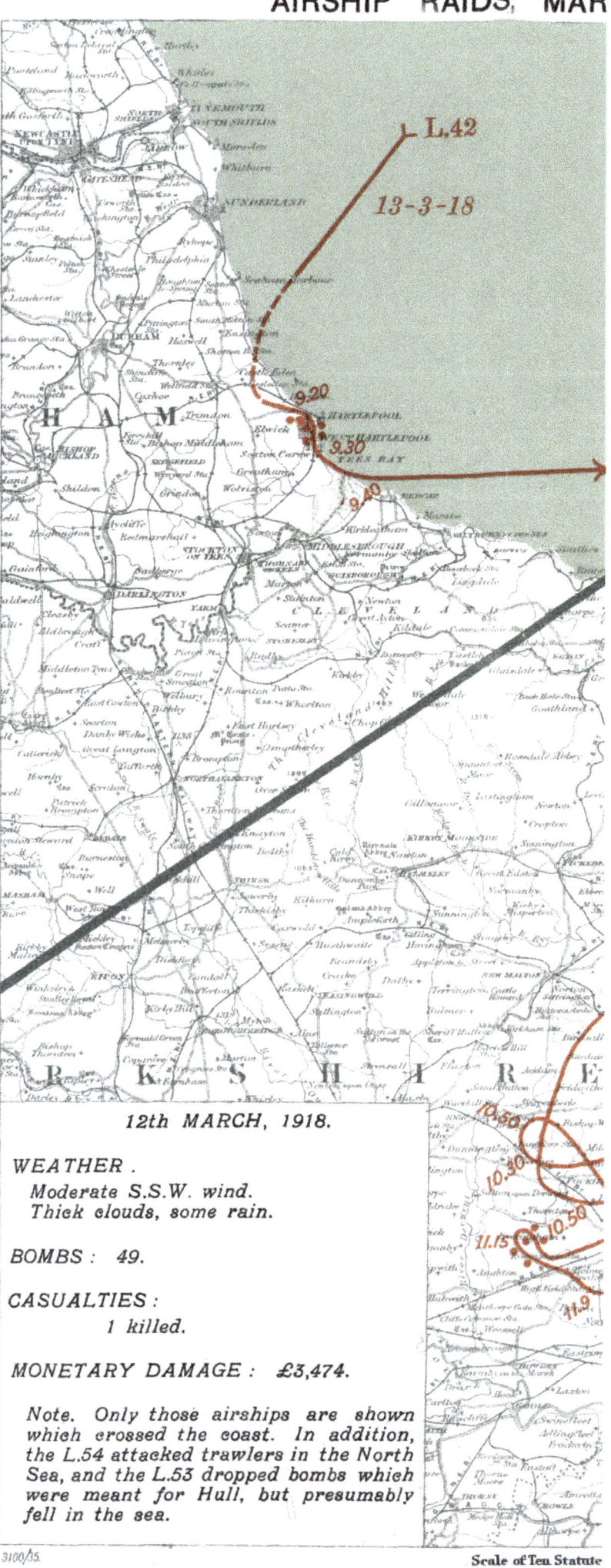

12th MARCH, 1918.

WEATHER.
  Moderate S.S.W. wind.
  Thick clouds, some rain.

BOMBS: 49.

CASUALTIES:
  1 killed.

MONETARY DAMAGE: £3,474.

Note. Only those airships are shown which crossed the coast. In addition, the L.54 attacked trawlers in the North Sea, and the L.53 dropped bombs which were meant for Hull, but presumably fell in the sea.

CH 12th and 13th, 1918.　　　　　No. 7

13th MARCH, 1918.

WEATHER:
　Light N.N.W. wind.
　Fine and clear.

BOMBS: 21.

CASUALTIES:
　8 killed, 39 injured.

MONETARY DAMAGE: £14,280.

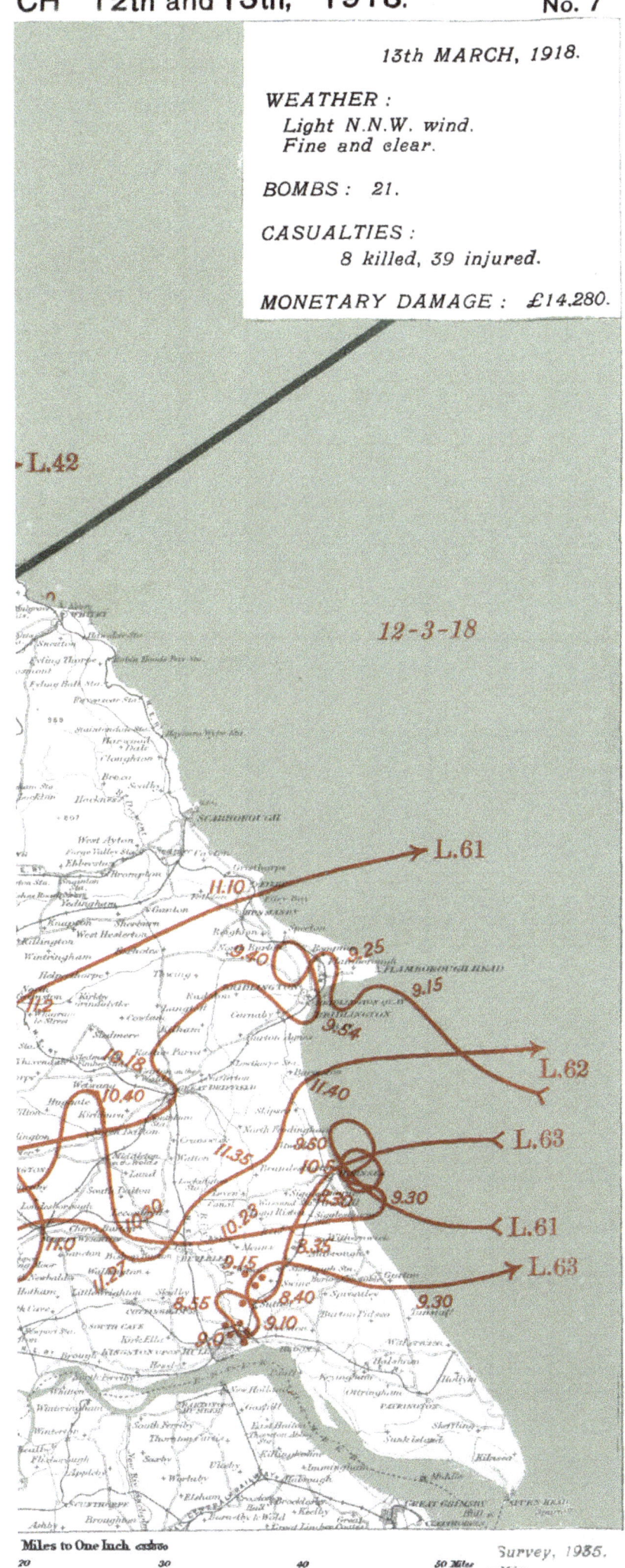

No. 8.
AIRSHIP RAID
12th-18th APRIL, 1918.
Spread 1

No. 8.
AIRSHIP RAID
12th-18th APRIL, 1918.
Spread 2

No. 8.
AIRSHIP RAID
12th-18th APRIL, 1918.
Spread 3

No. 8.
AIRSHIP RAID
12th-18th APRIL, 1918.
Spread 4

Spread 1

Spread 1

AIRSHIP RAID, 12TH-13TH APRIL, 1918.

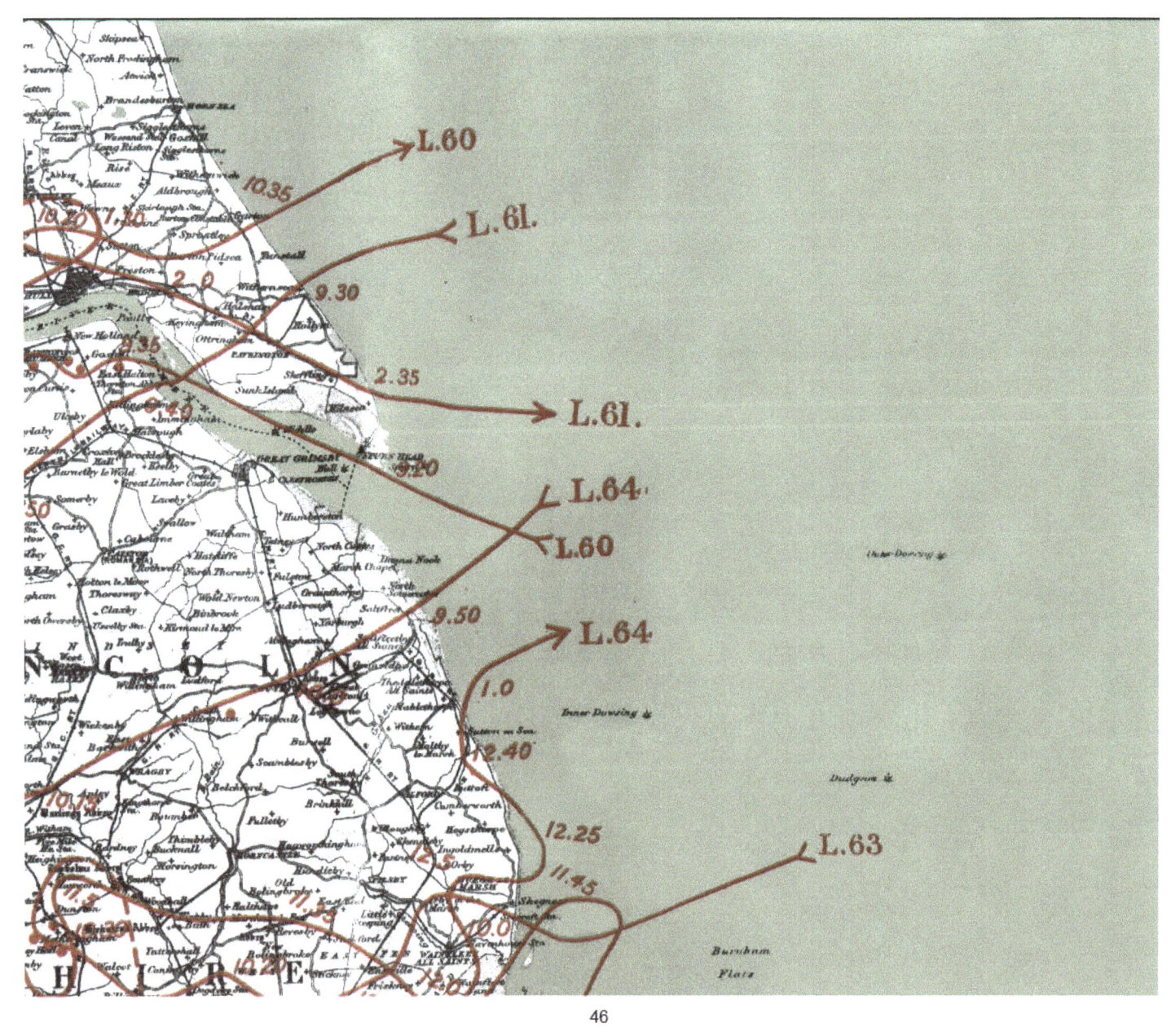

No. 8

Spread 3

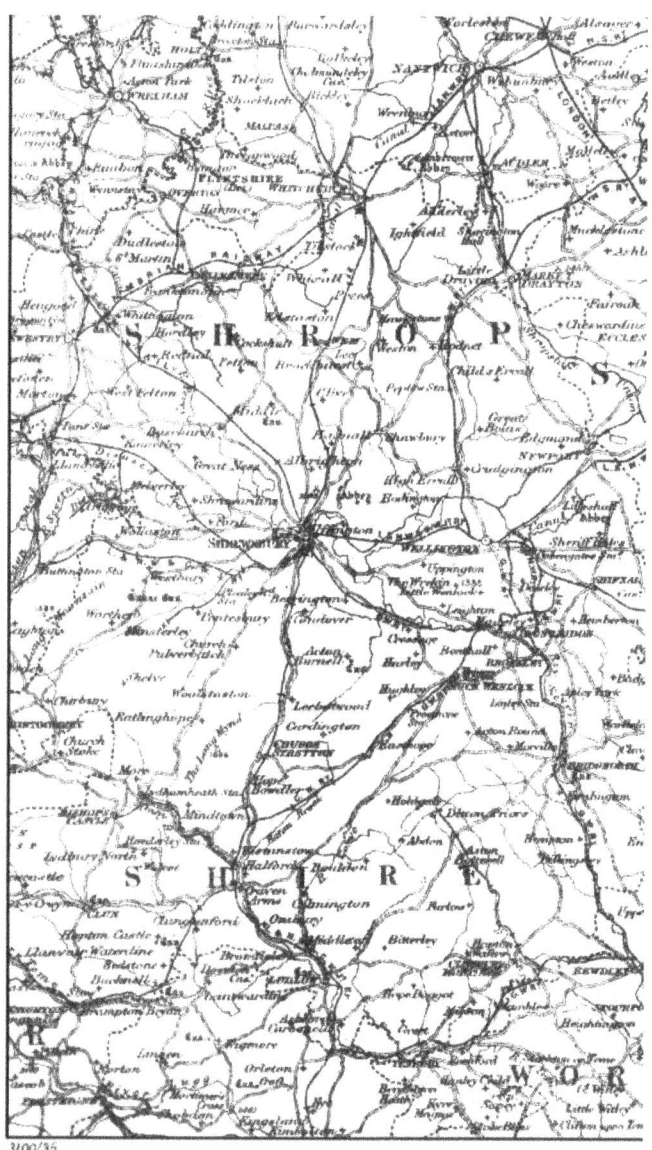

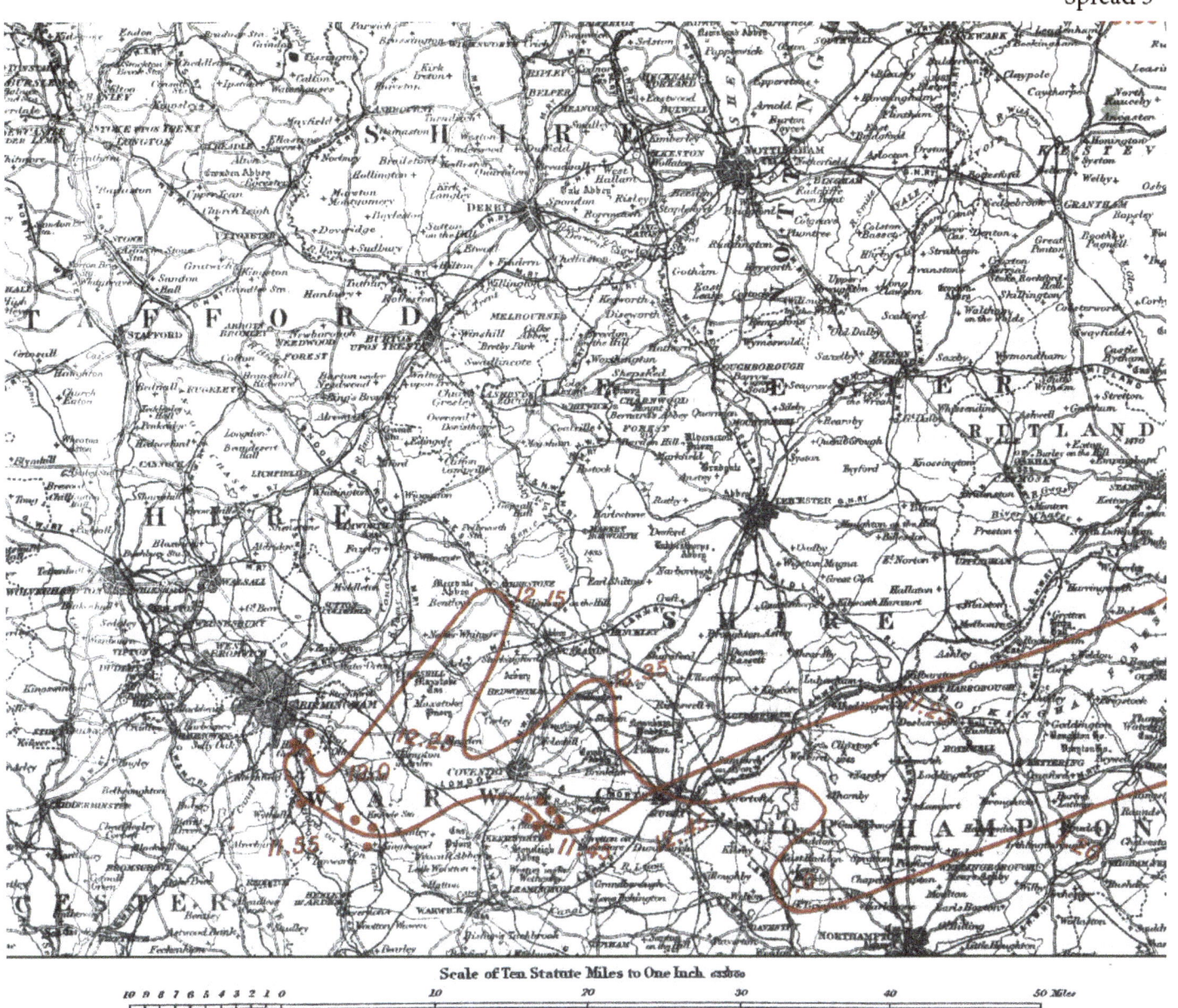

Spread 3

Spread 4

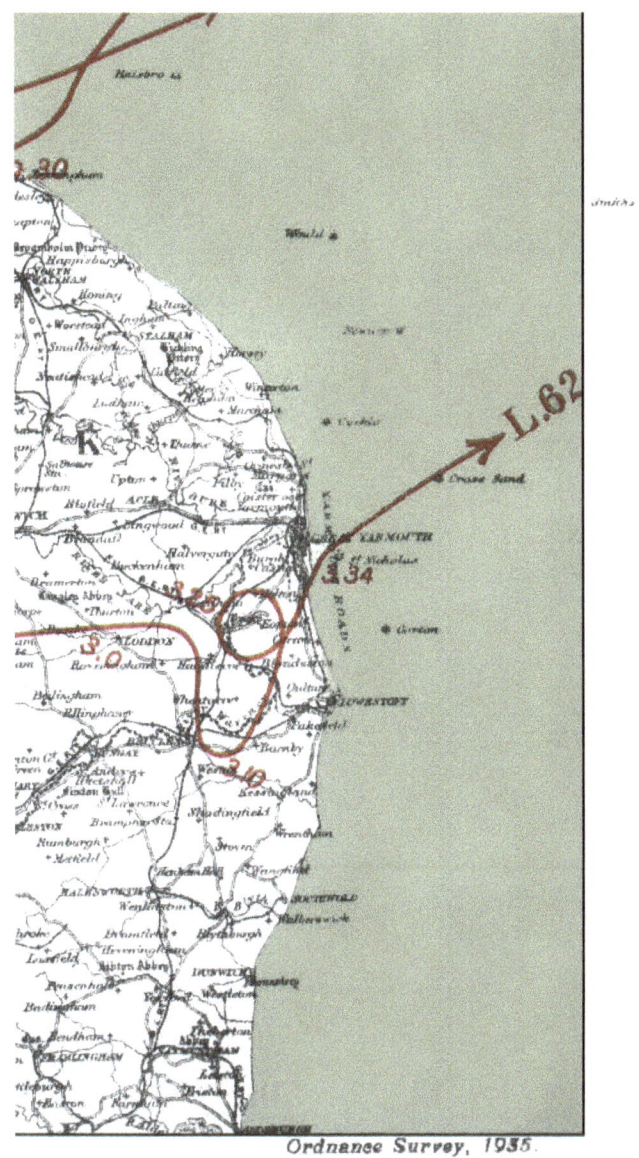

Ordnance Survey, 1935.

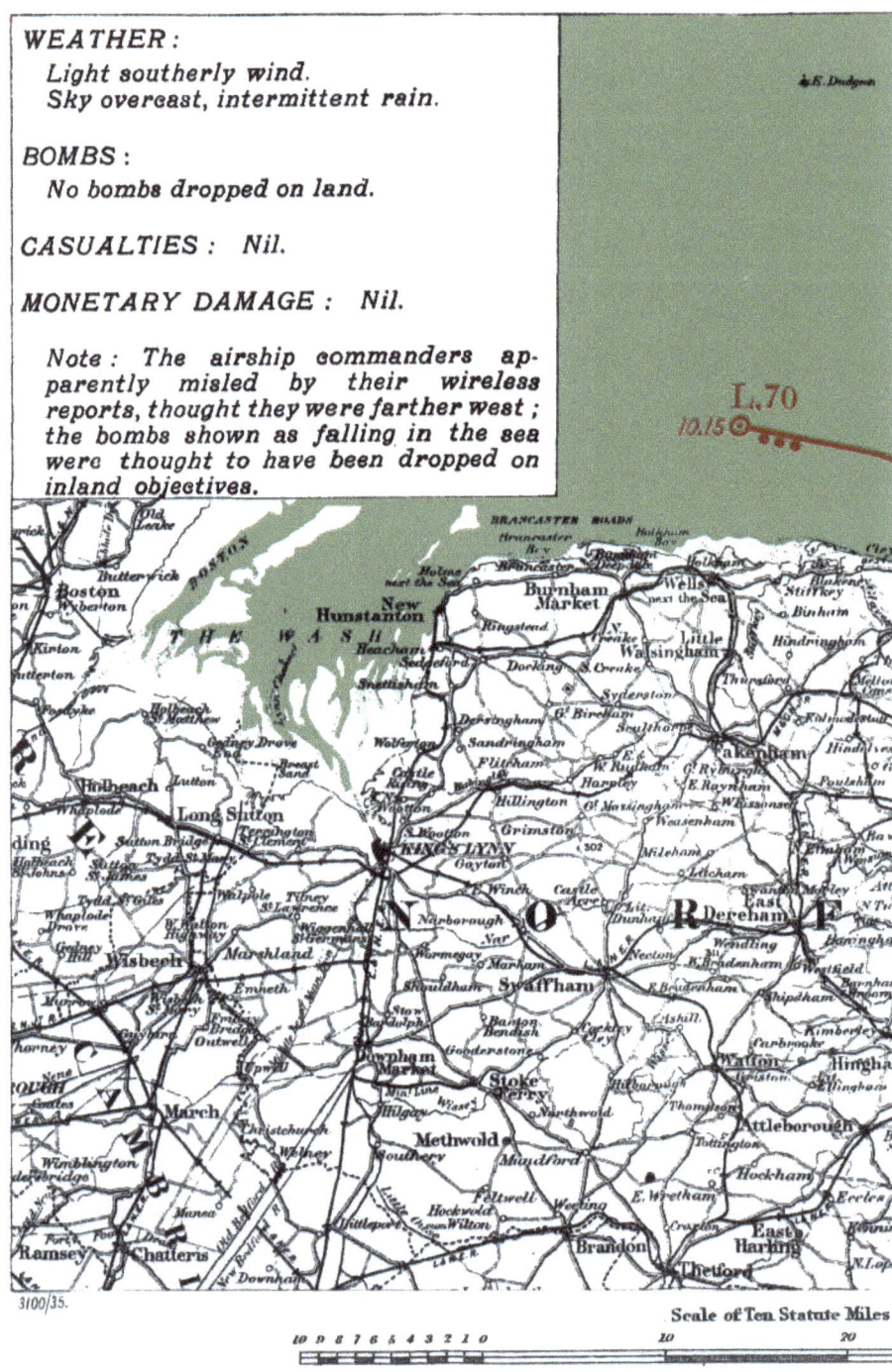

5th-6th AUGUST, 1918.

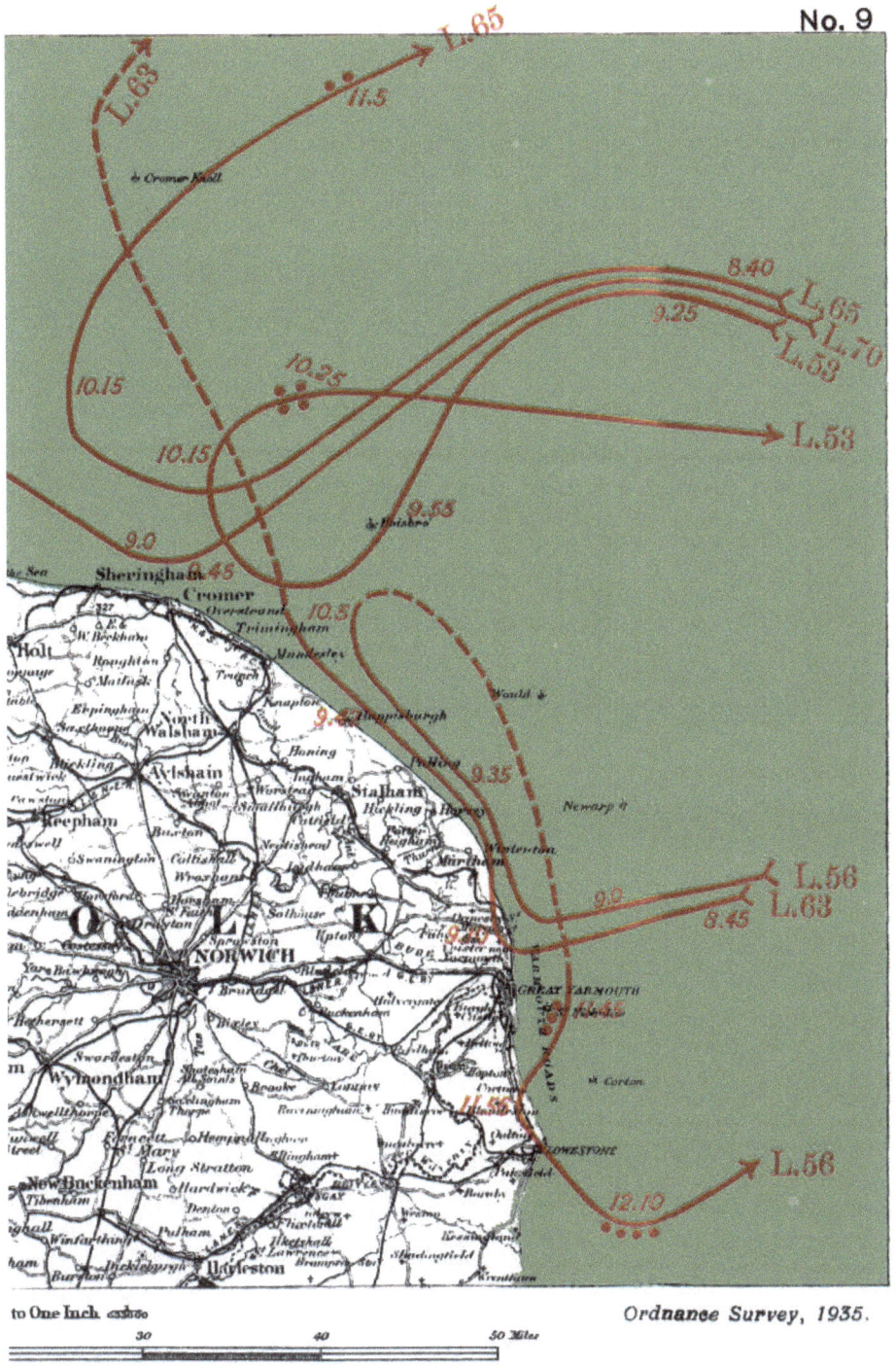

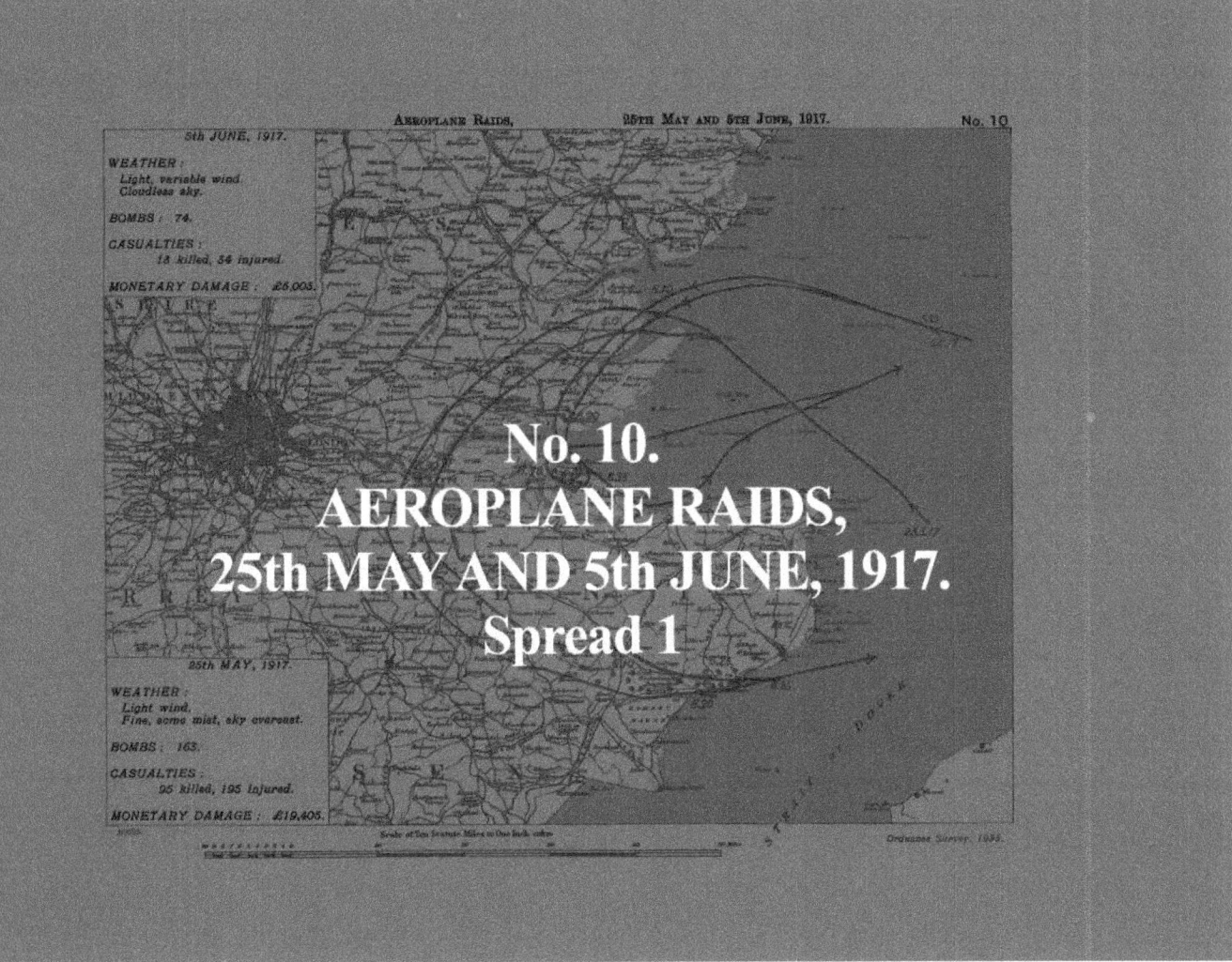

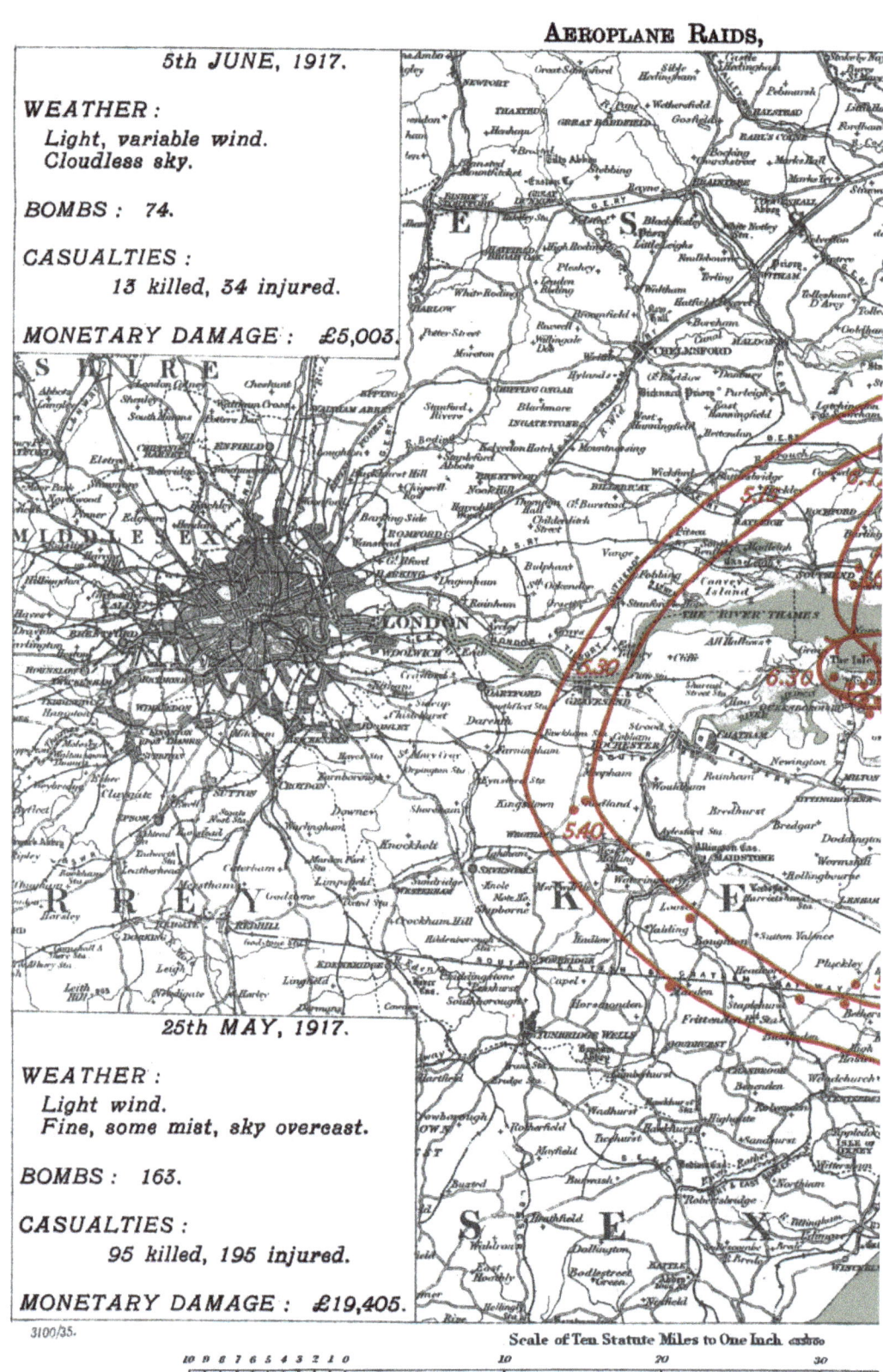

25TH MAY AND 5TH JUNE, 1917.   No. 10

Ordnance Survey, 1935.

DAYLIGHT AEROPLANE ATTACK ON LONDON, 13th JUNE, 1917.

Daylight Aeroplane Attack on London, 7th July, 1917.

No. 12

Approximate position of Exploded bombs ●
       "   "   " Unexploded " ○

WEATHER:
Light easterly wind. Very little cloud.

STRENGTH OF RAIDING SQUADRON:
22 Gotha aeroplanes.

BOMBS: 65.
(In addition, 4 bombs were dropped near Tottenham gasworks, 2 near Ferry Road, Edmonton, one in a field at Chingford, one at Ponders End sewage farm and 3 on Margate).

CASUALTIES:
54 killed and 190 injured.
(In addition, there were 3 killed and 3 injured at Margate).

MONETARY DAMAGE:
London—£205,022. Margate—£600.

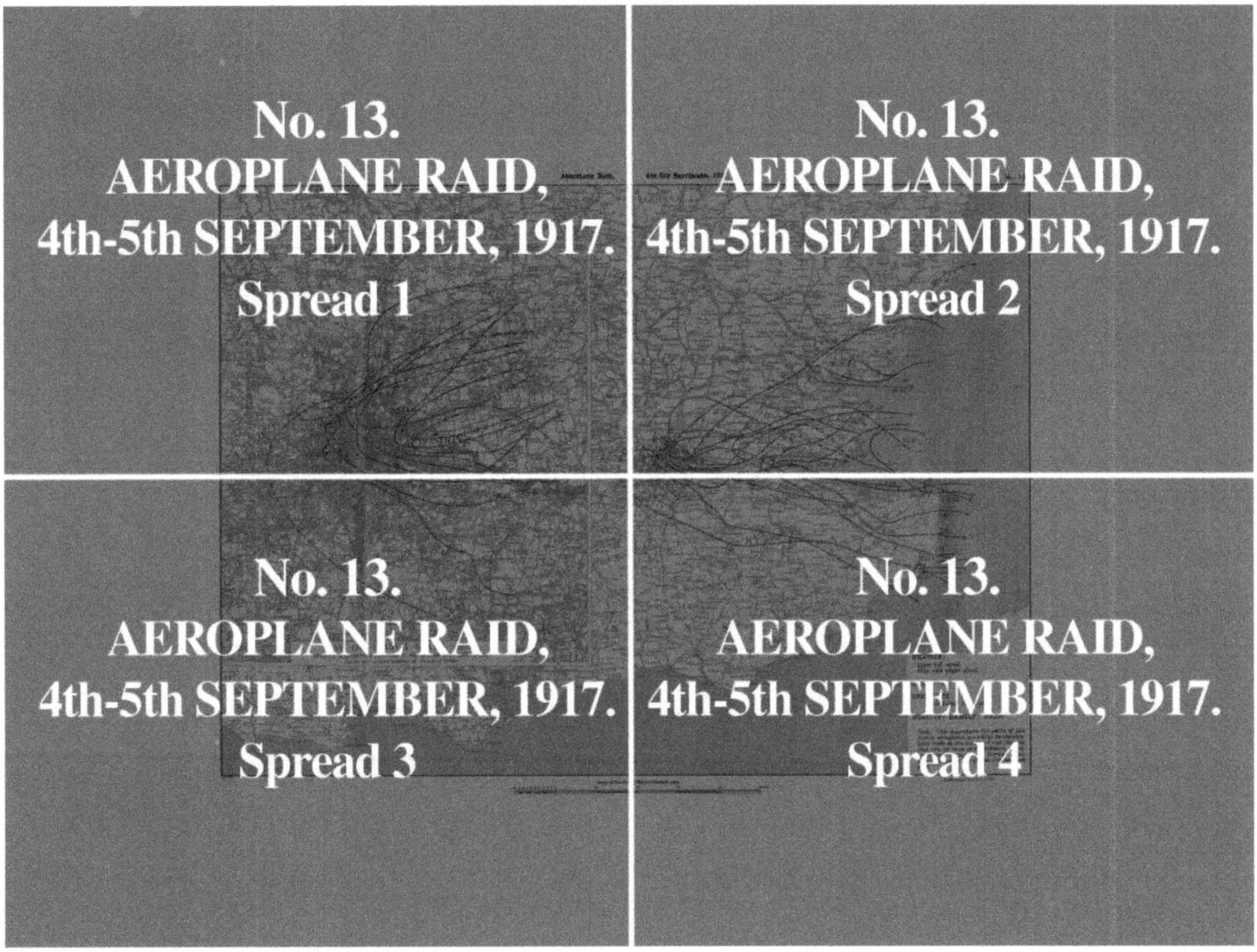

No. 13.
AEROPLANE RAID,
4th-5th SEPTEMBER, 1917.
Spread 1

No. 13.
AEROPLANE RAID,
4th-5th SEPTEMBER, 1917.
Spread 2

No. 13.
AEROPLANE RAID,
4th-5th SEPTEMBER, 1917.
Spread 3

No. 13.
AEROPLANE RAID,
4th-5th SEPTEMBER, 1917.
Spread 4

Spread 1

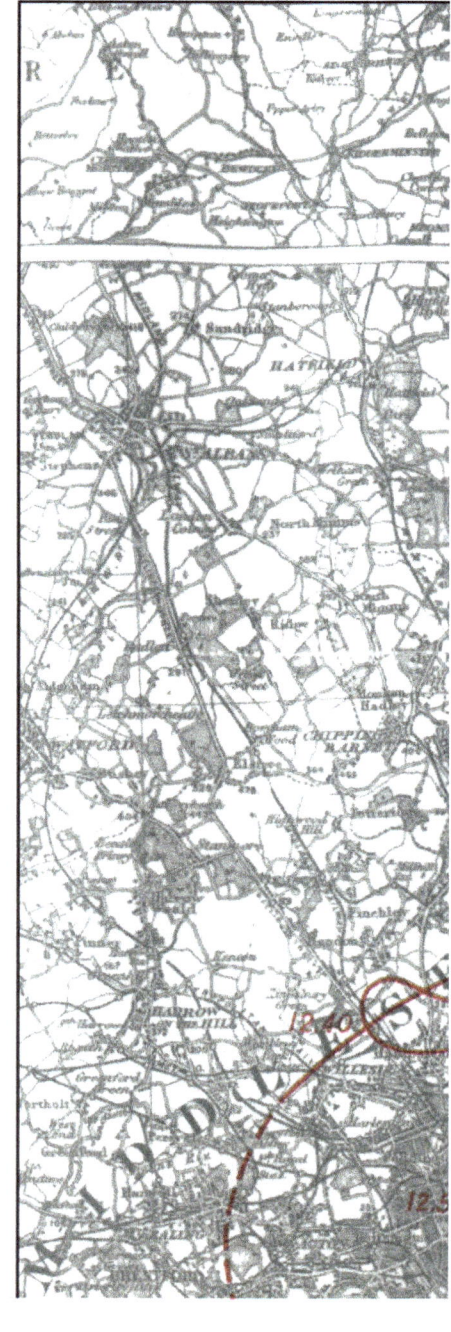

AEROPLANE RAID,

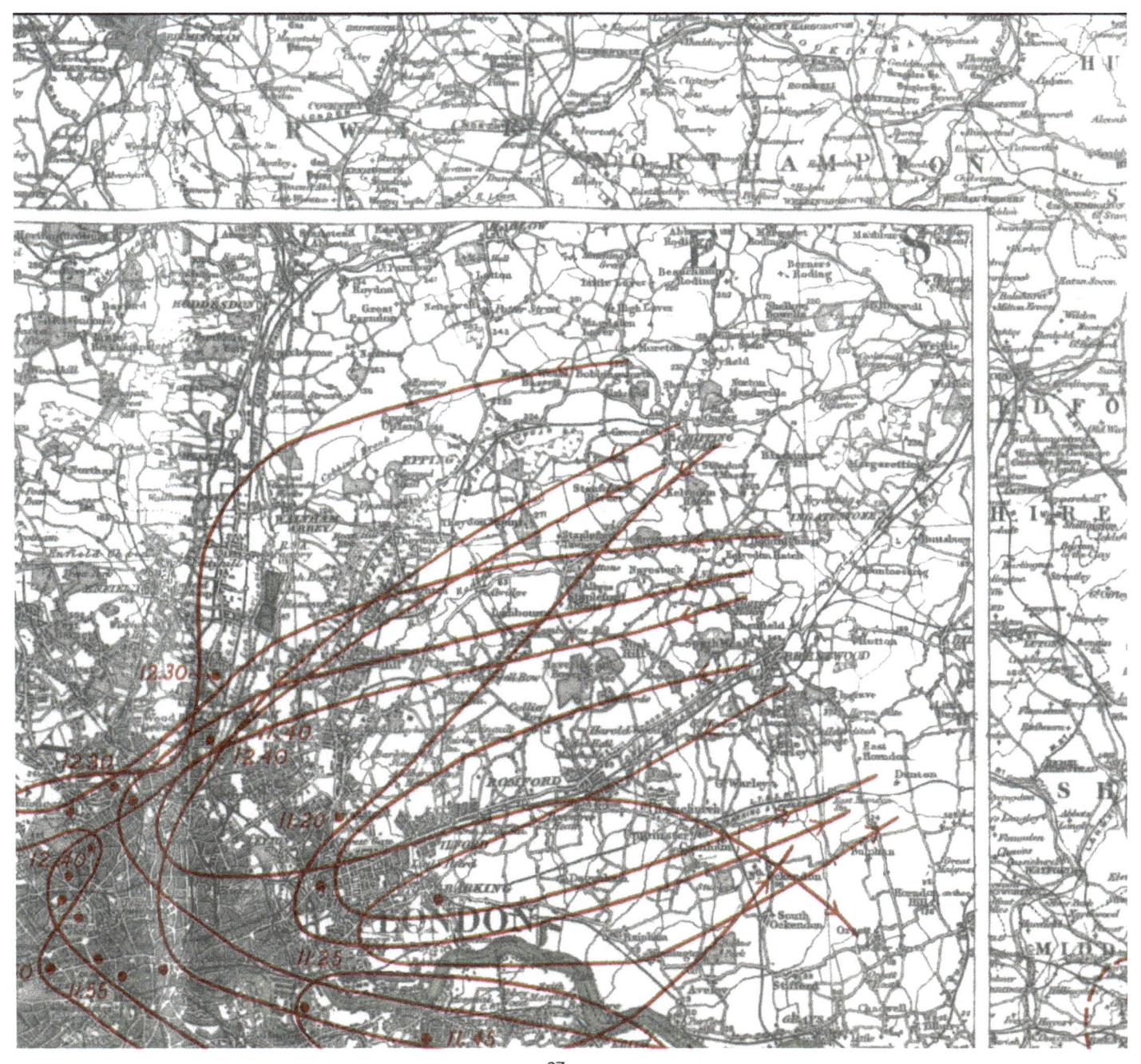

4TH-5TH SEPTEMBER, 1917.

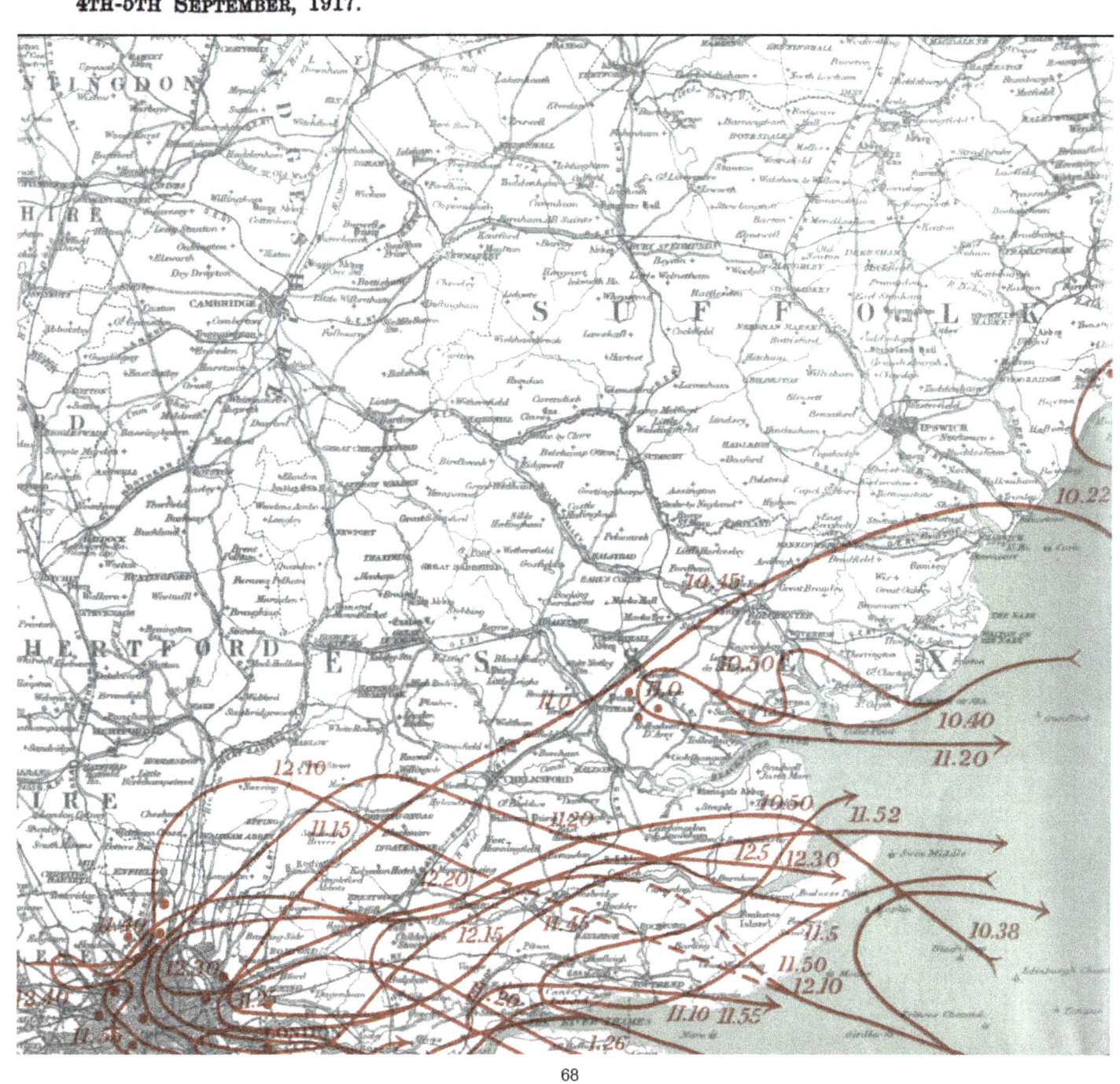

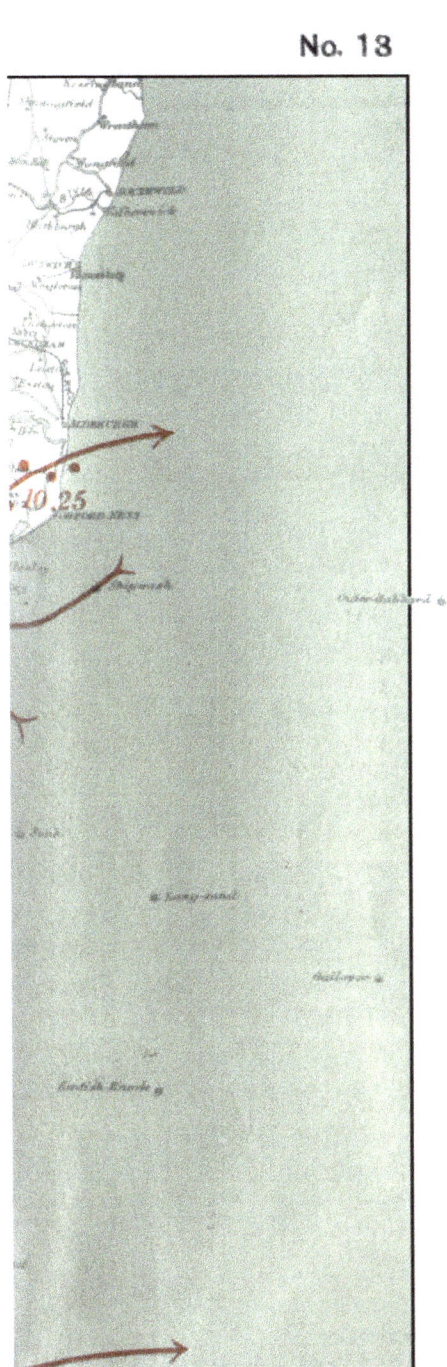

No. 13

Spread 3

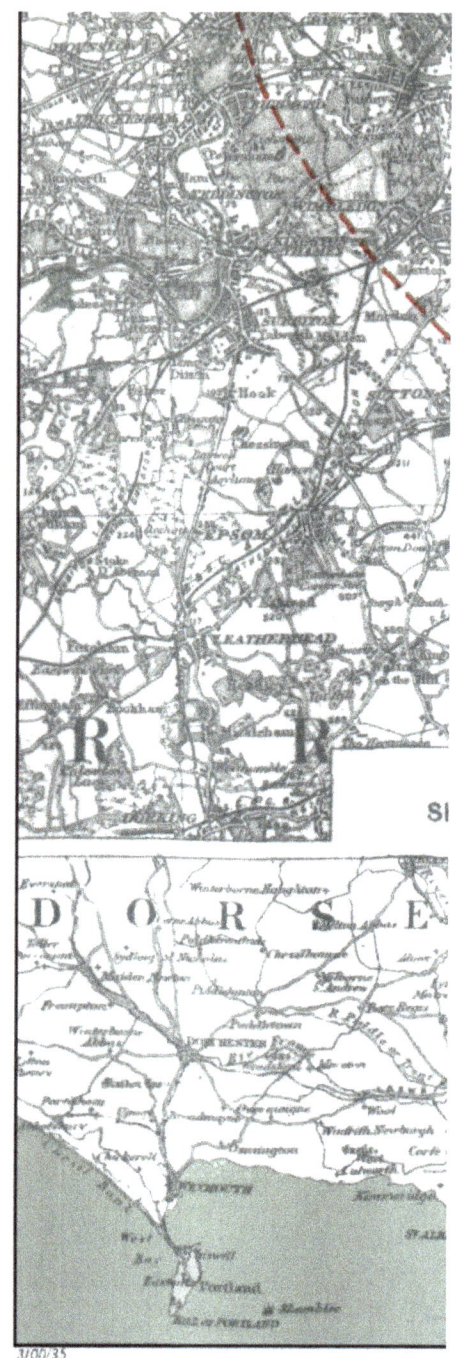

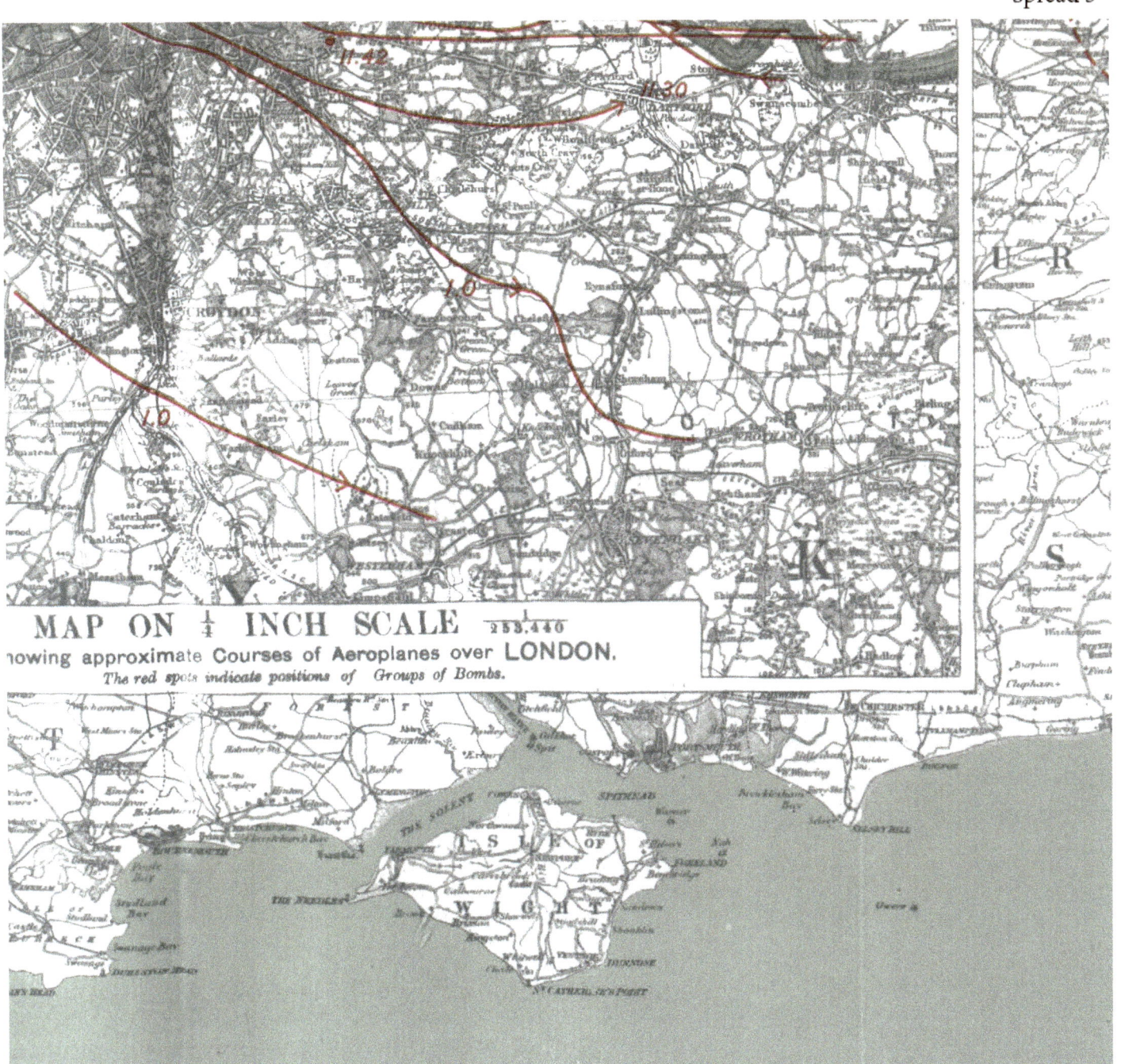

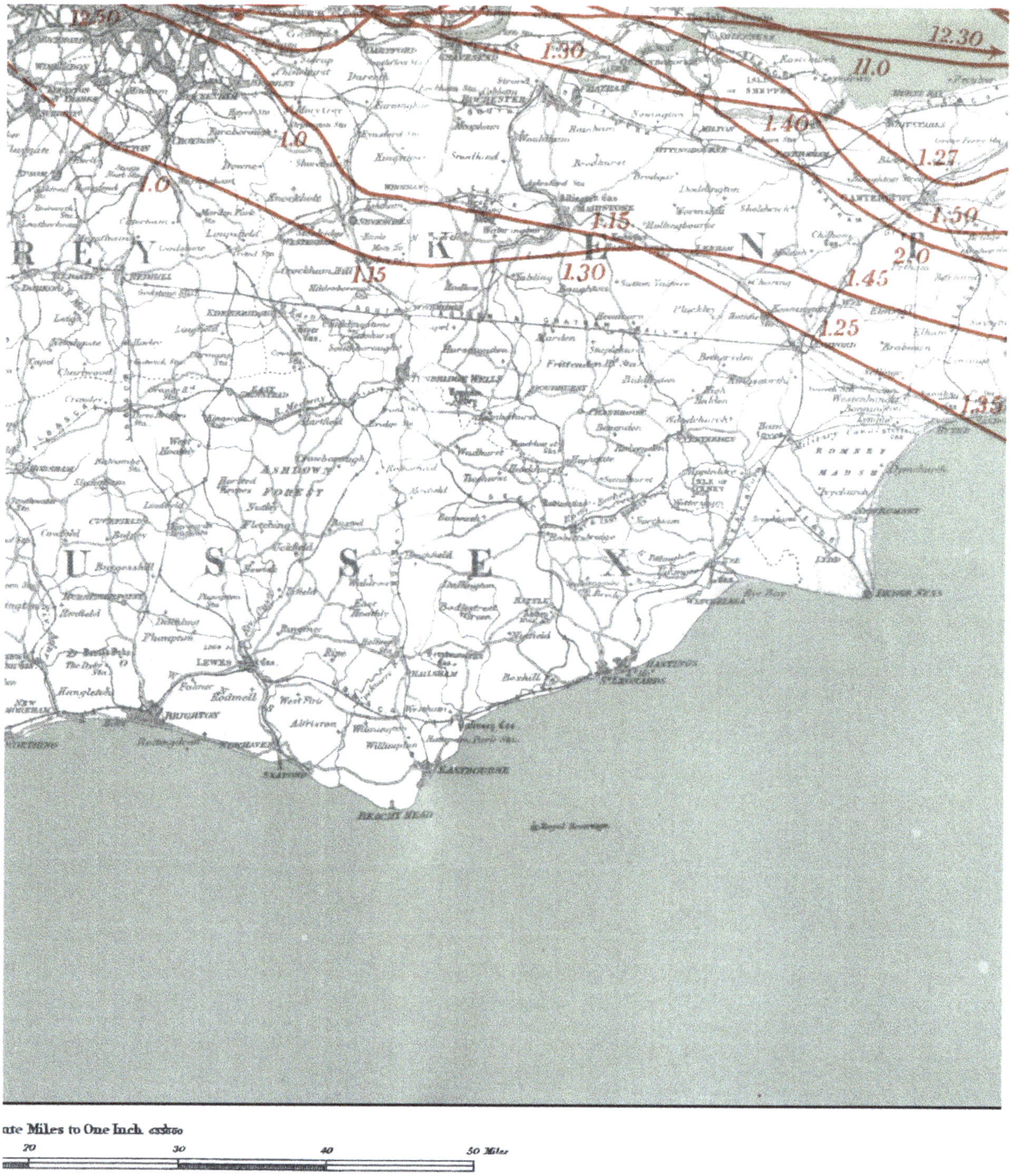
12.50
12.30
11.0
1.30
1.40
1.0
1.27
1.0
1.15
1.50
2.0
1.15
1.30
1.45
1.25
1.35
R E Y
K E N T
S U S S E X
ASHDOWN FOREST
LEWES
BRIGHTON
HASTINGS
EASTBOURNE
BEACHY HEAD
Bexhill
ROMNEY MARSH
Rye Bay
ate Miles to One Inch.
30
40
50 Miles

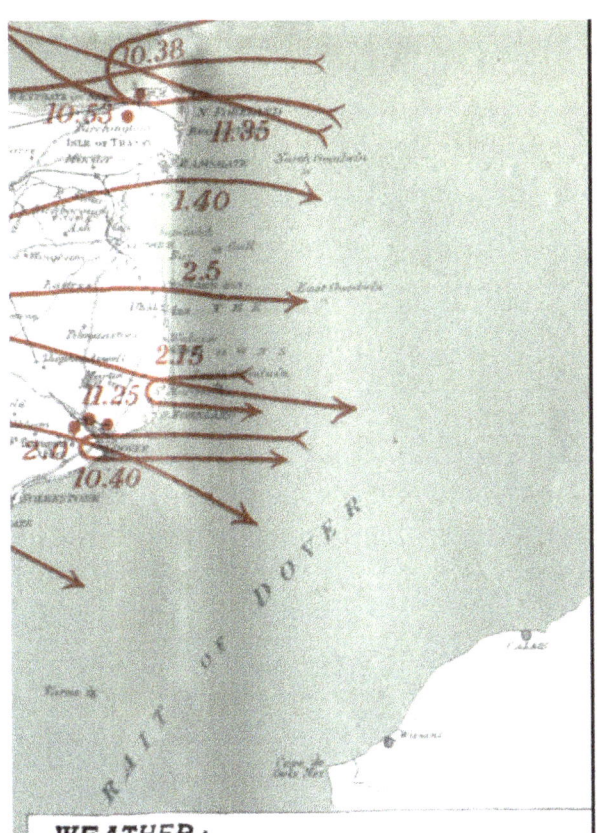

WEATHER:
  Light S.E. wind.
  Fine with slight cloud.

BOMBS: 90.

CASUALTIES:
    19 killed, 71 injured.

MONETARY DAMAGE: £46,047.

Note. This map shows the paths of the hostile aeroplanes according to observations made at the time. It was thought that two, or even more bombers, sometimes came in together. German semi-official accounts say eleven Gothas took part.

Ordnance Survey, 1935.

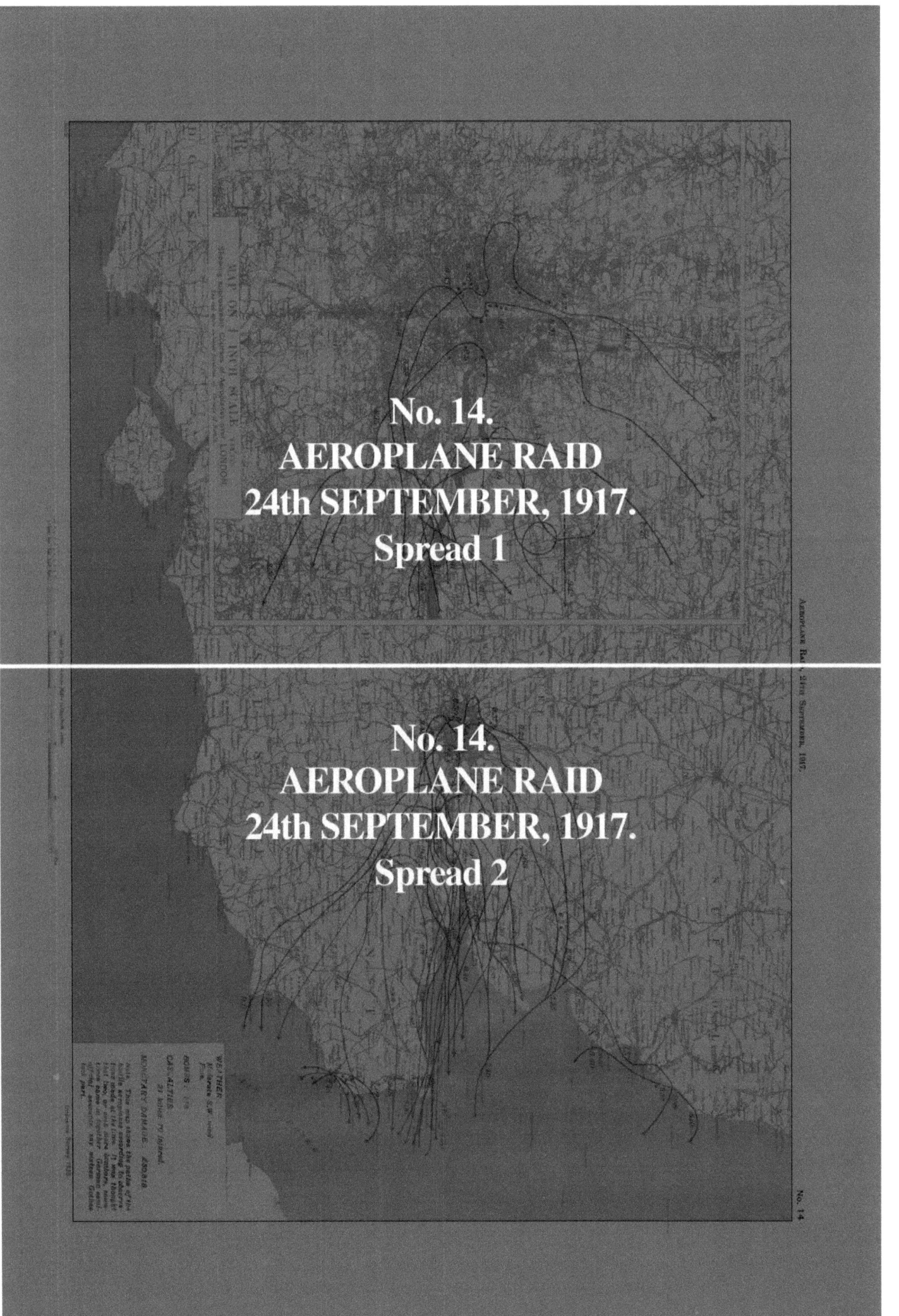

Spread 1

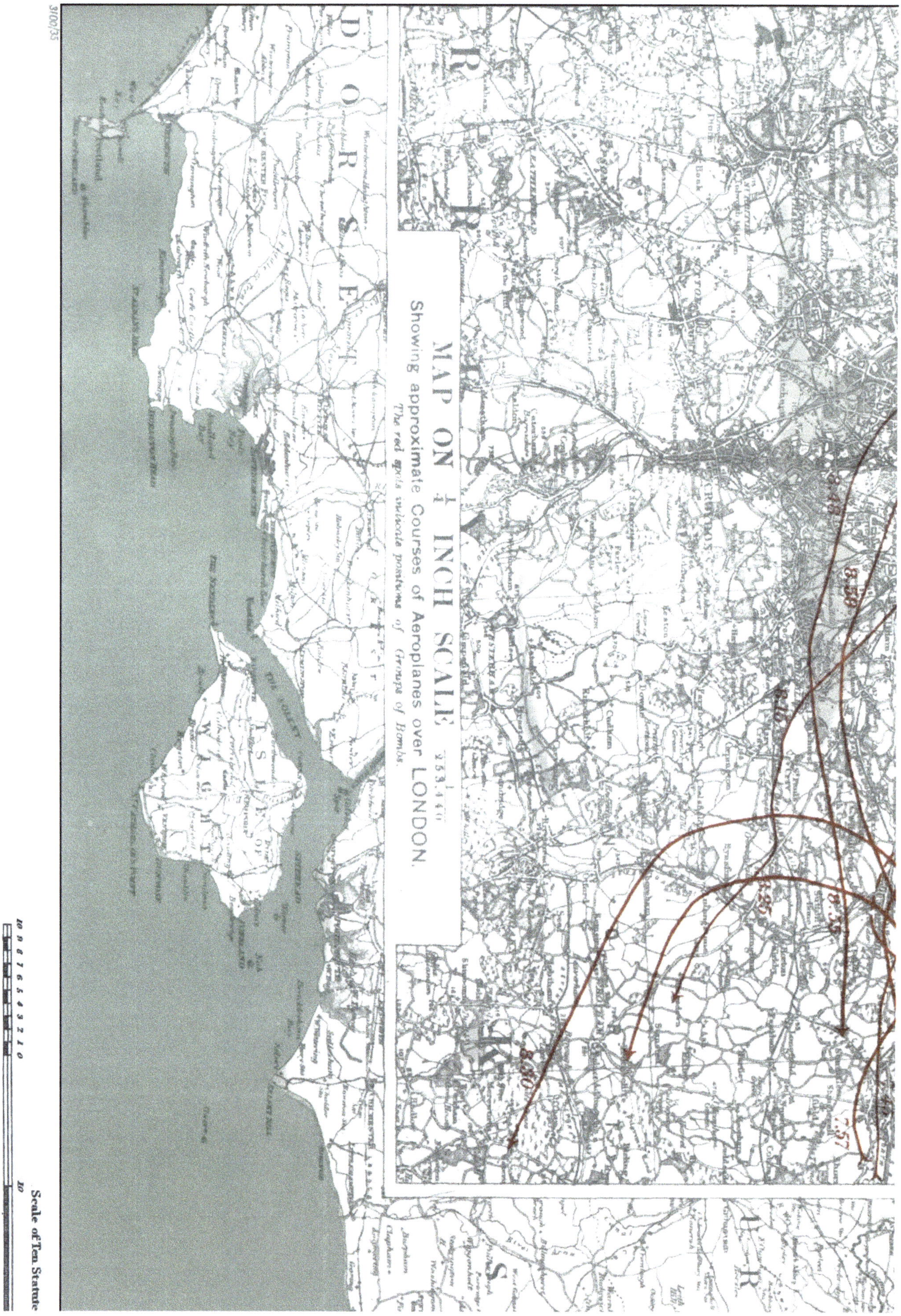
MAP ON 1/4 INCH SCALE 1/253,440
Showing approximate Courses of Aeroplanes over LONDON.
The red spots indicate positions of Groups of Bombs.
Scale of Ten Statute
DORSET
ISLE OF WIGHT
THE SOLENT

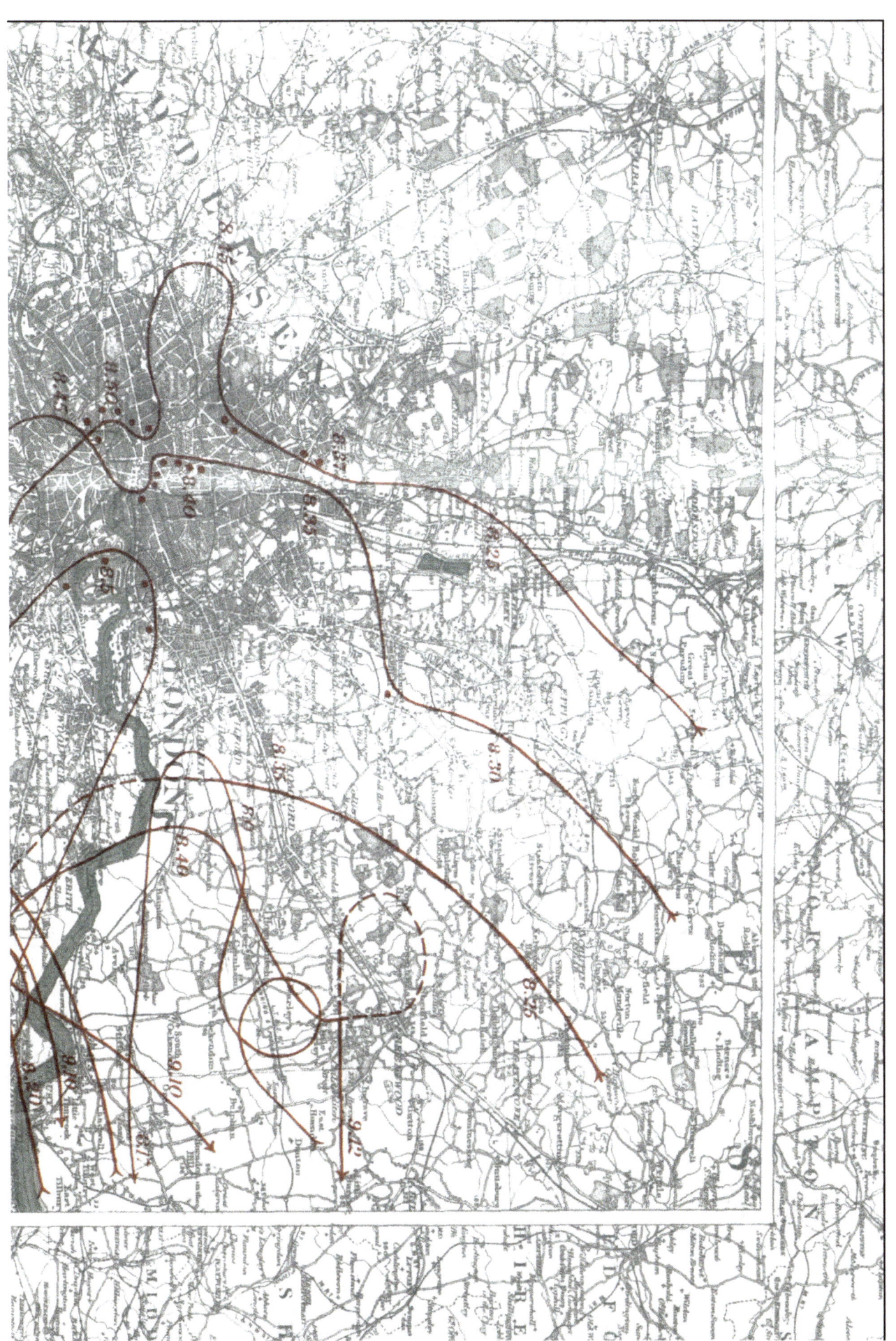

Aeroplane Raid, Spread 1

Spread 2

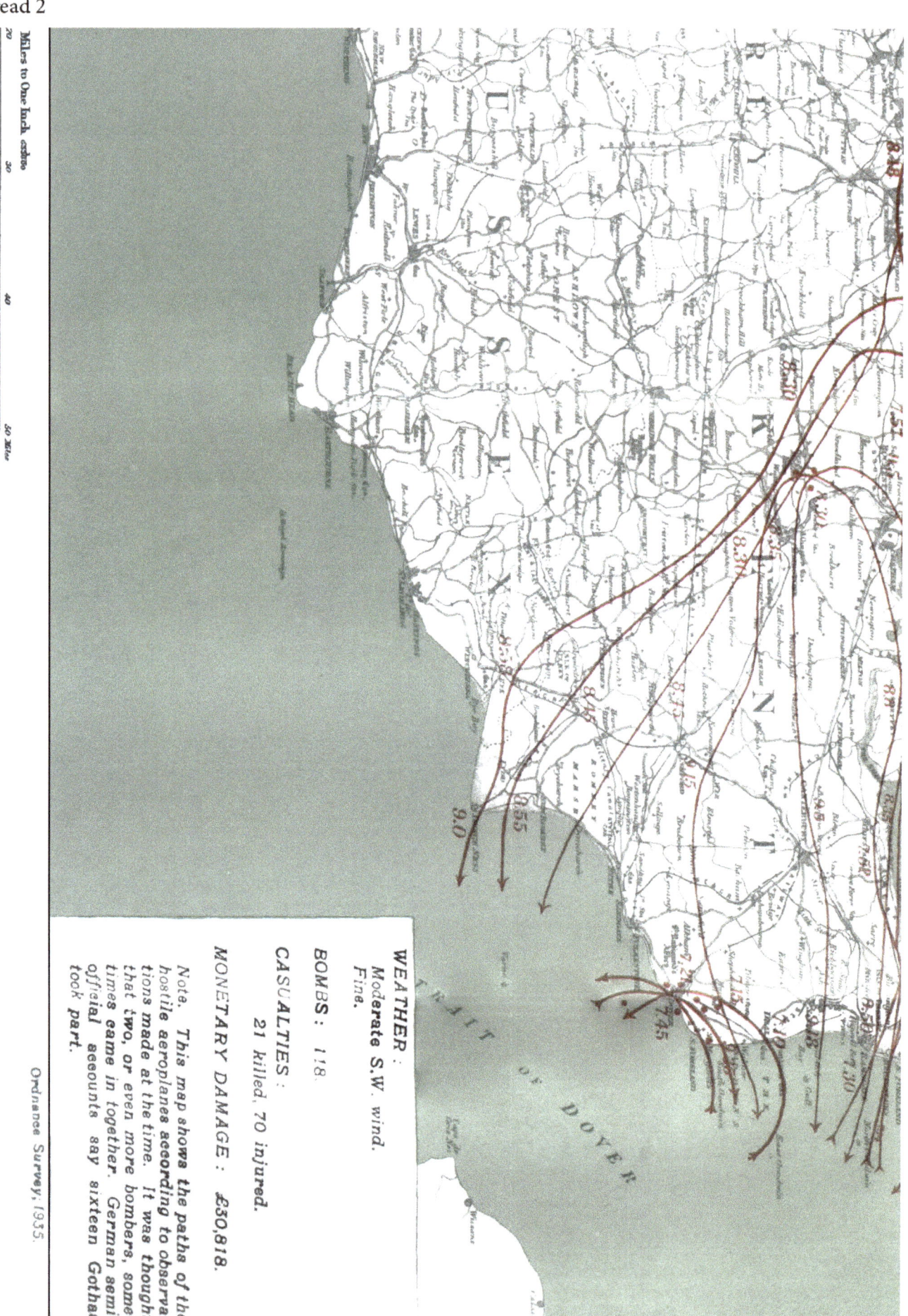

WEATHER:
Moderate S.W. wind.
Fine.

BOMBS: 118.

CASUALTIES:
21 killed, 70 injured.

MONETARY DAMAGE: £30,818.

Note. This map shows the paths of the hostile aeroplanes according to observations made at the time. It was thought that two, or even more bombers, sometimes came in together. German semi-official accounts say sixteen Gothas took part.

Ordnance Survey, 1935.

24TH SEPTEMBER, 1917.   No. 14

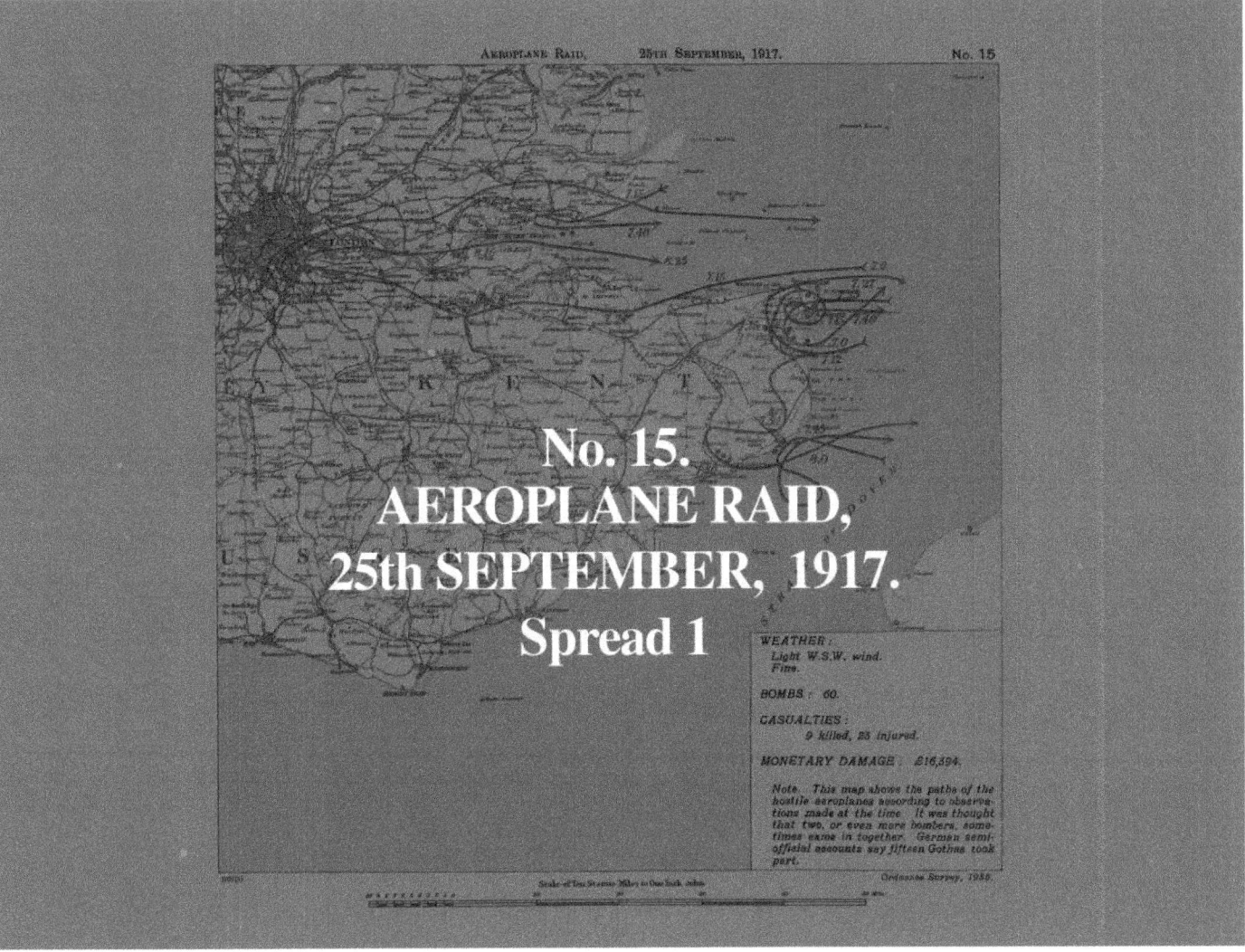

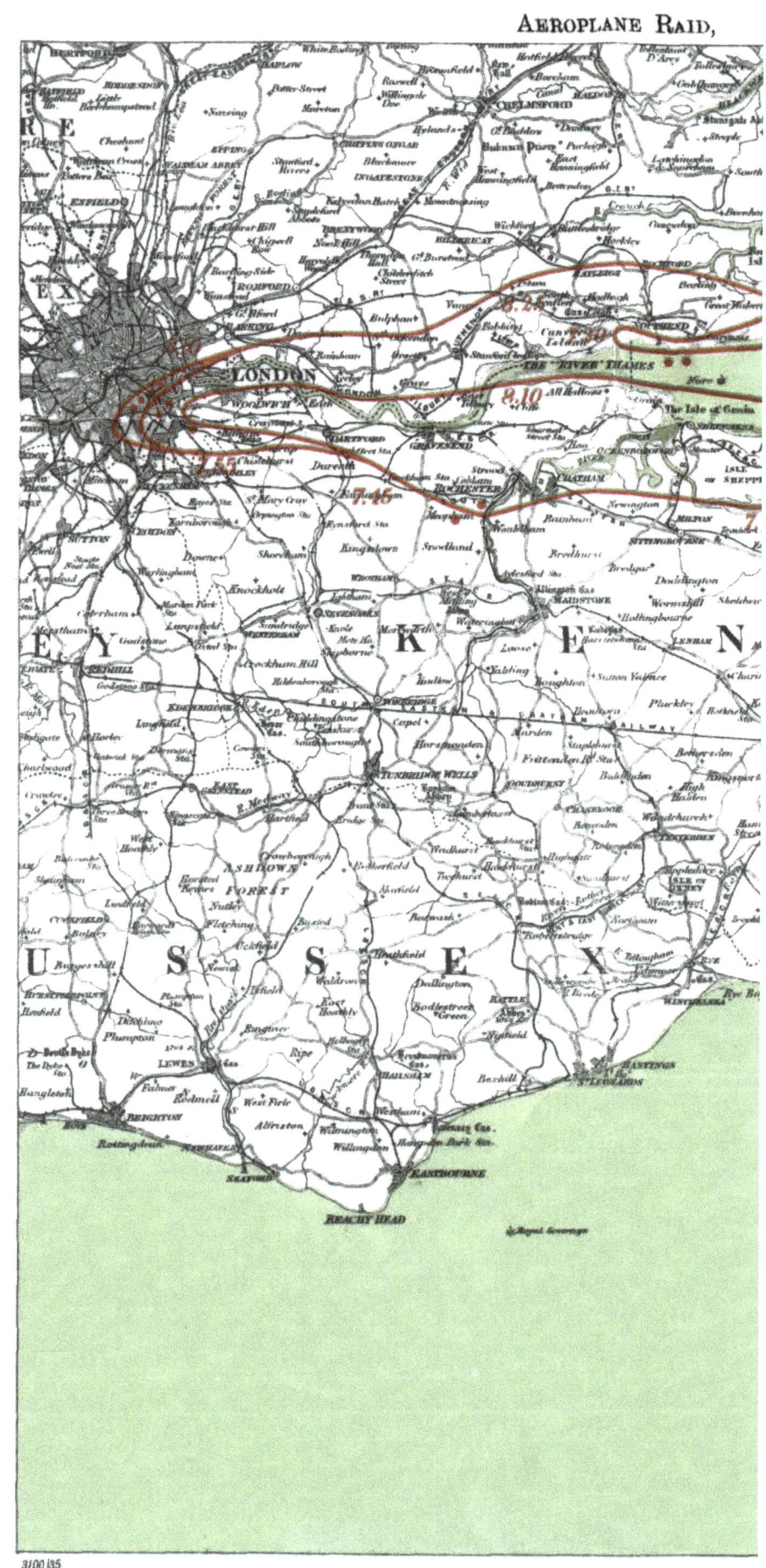

25TH SEPTEMBER, 1917.   No. 15

WEATHER:
Light W.S.W. wind.
Fine.

BOMBS: 60.

CASUALTIES:
9 killed, 23 injured.

MONETARY DAMAGE: £16,394.

Note. This map shows the paths of the hostile aeroplanes according to observations made at the time. It was thought that two, or even more bombers, sometimes came in together. German semi-official accounts say fifteen Gothas took part.

Ordnance Survey, 1935.

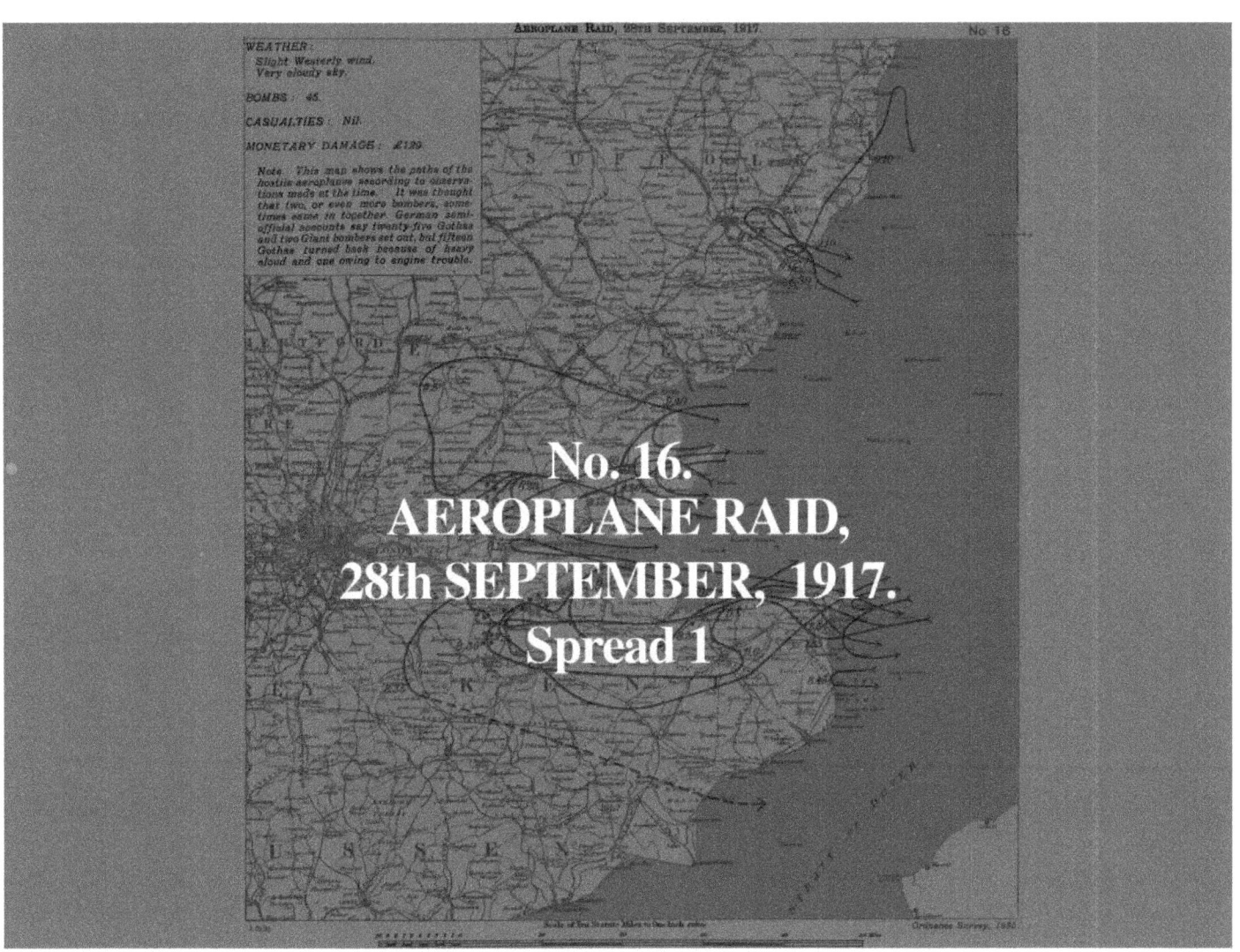

Spread 1

WEATHER:
Slight Westerly wind.
Very cloudy sky.

BOMBS: 45.

CASUALTIES: Nil.

MONETARY DAMAGE: £129.

Note. This map shows the paths of the hostile aeroplanes according to observations made at the time. It was thought that two, or even more bombers, sometimes came in together. German semi-official accounts say twenty-five Gothas and two Giant bombers set out, but fifteen Gothas turned back because of heavy cloud and one owing to engine trouble.

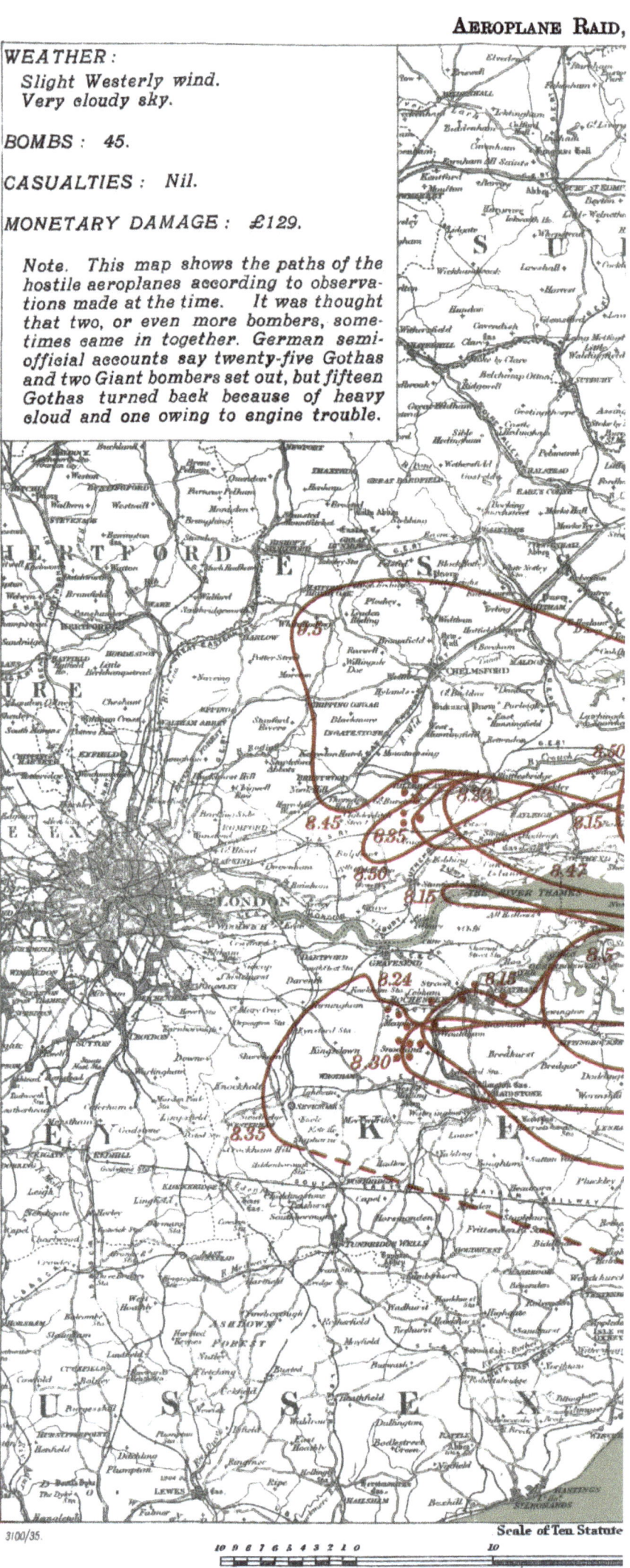

86

28TH SEPTEMBER, 1917.   No. 16

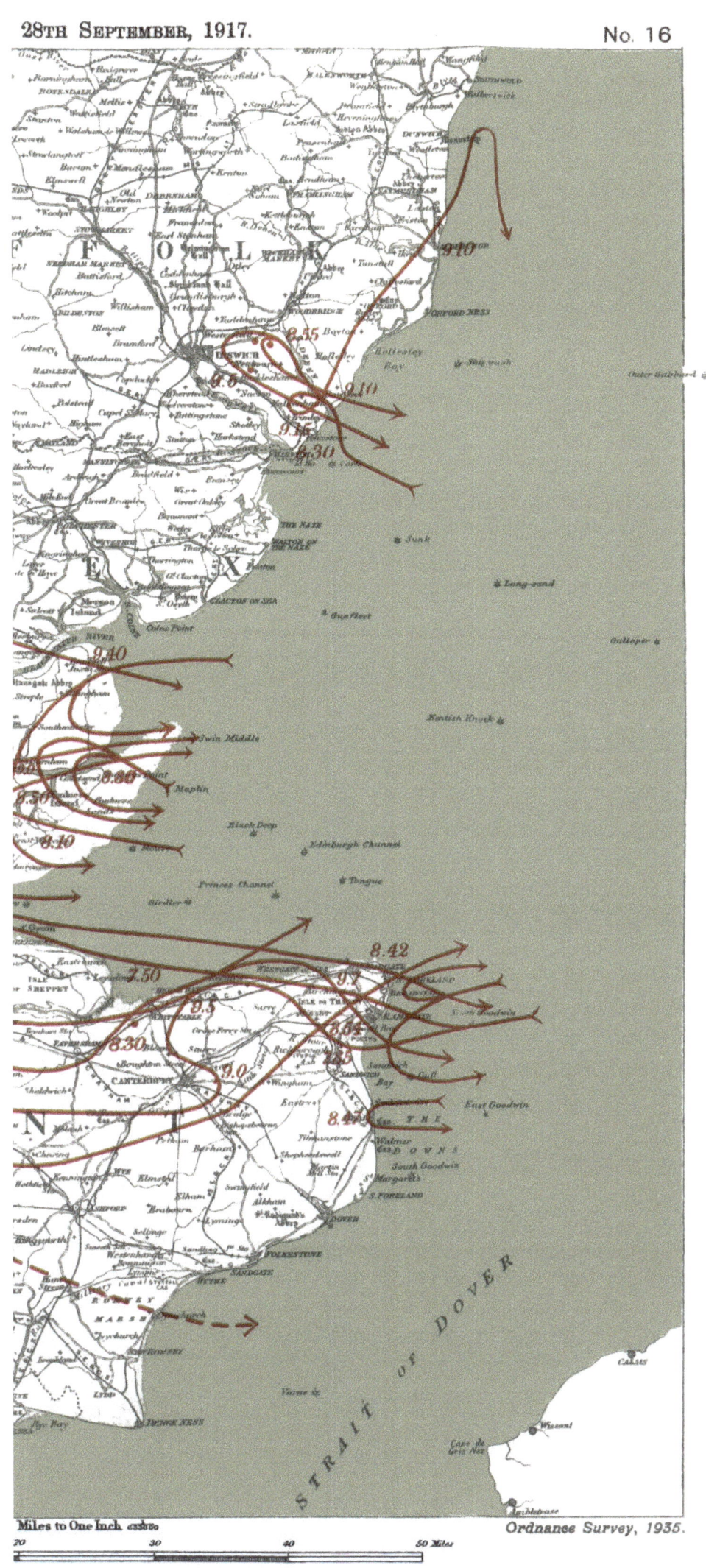

No. 17.
AEROPLANE RAID,
29th SEPTEMBER, 1917.
Spread 1

No. 17.
AEROPLANE RAID,
29th SEPTEMBER, 1917.
Spread 2

No. 17.
AEROPLANE RAID,
29th SEPTEMBER, 1917.
Spread 3

No. 17.
AEROPLANE RAID,
29th SEPTEMBER, 1917.
Spread 4

Spread 1

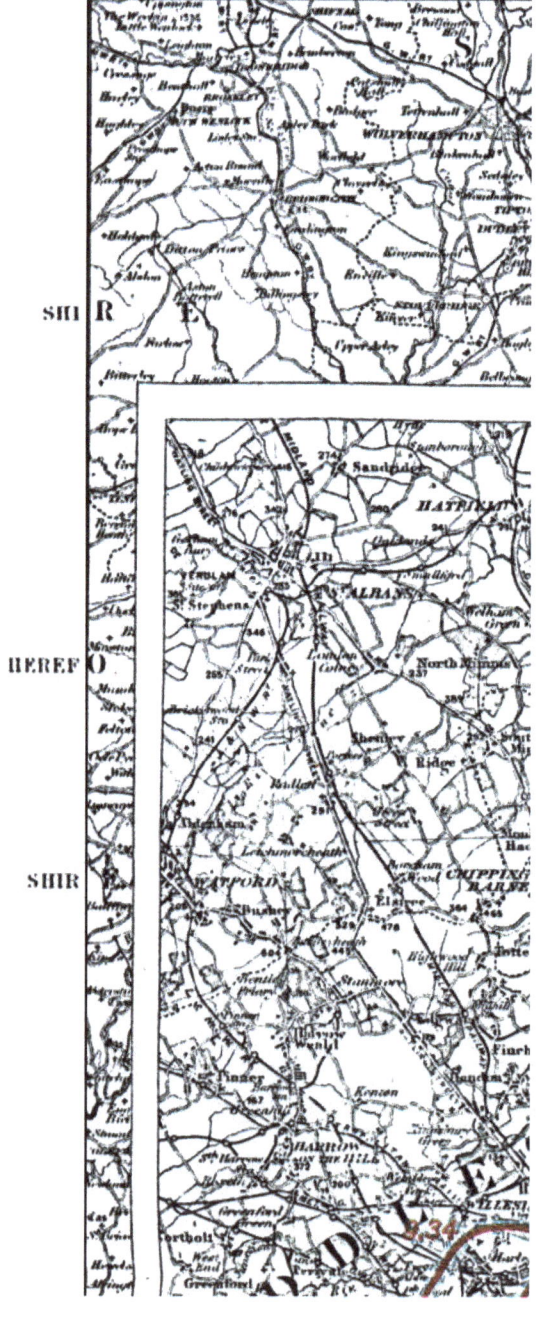

AEROPLANE RAID,

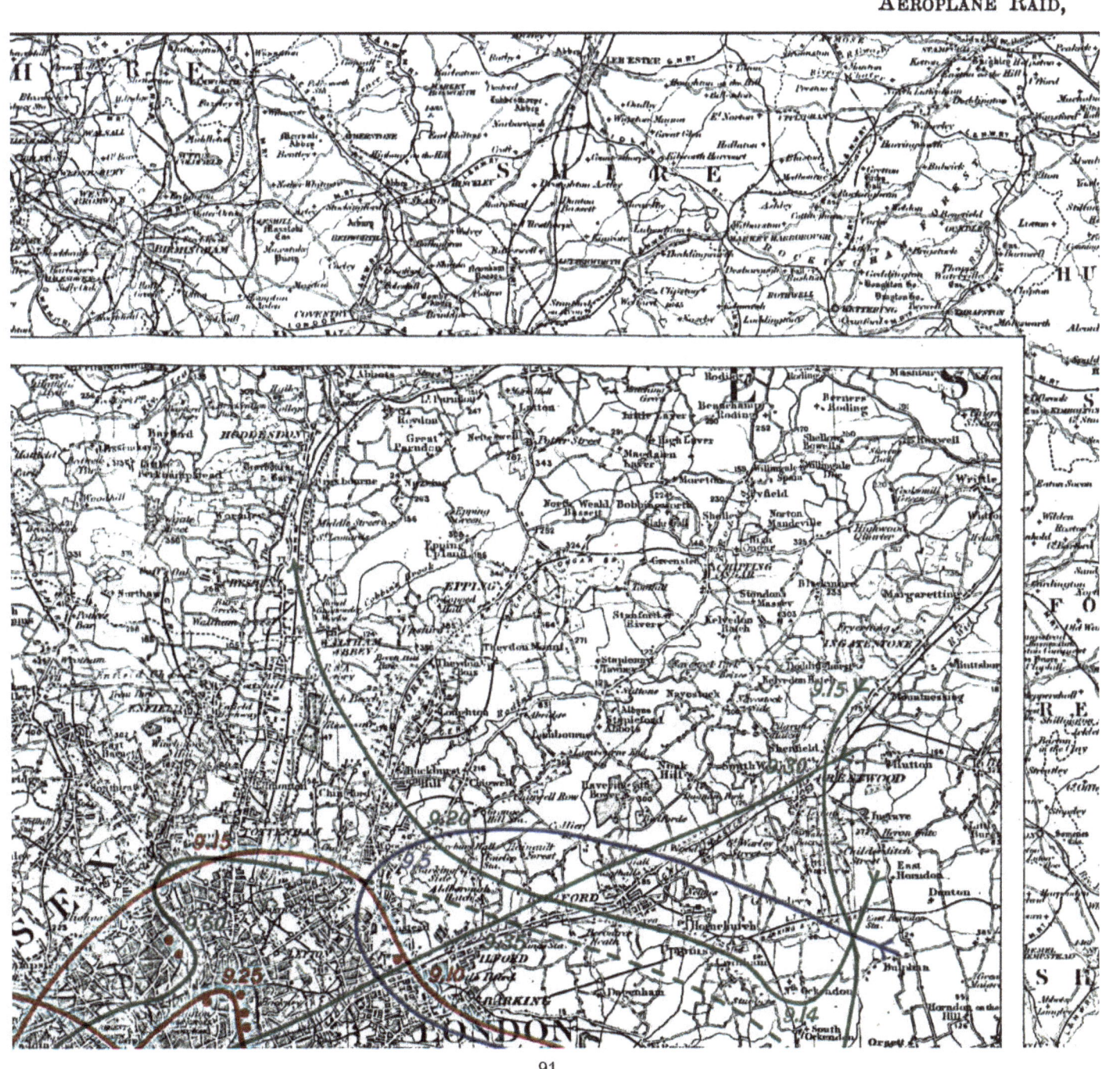

29th September, 1917.

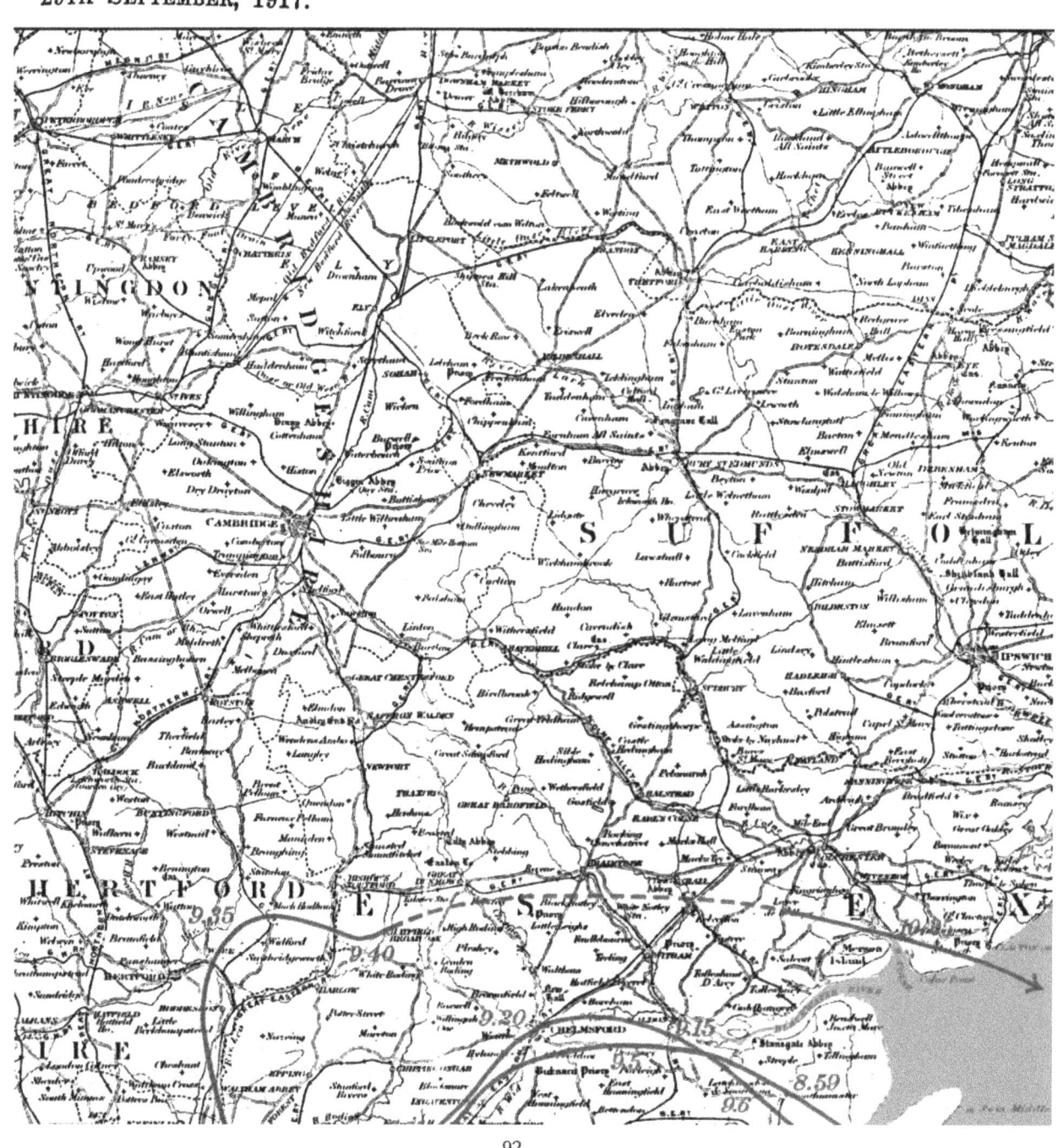

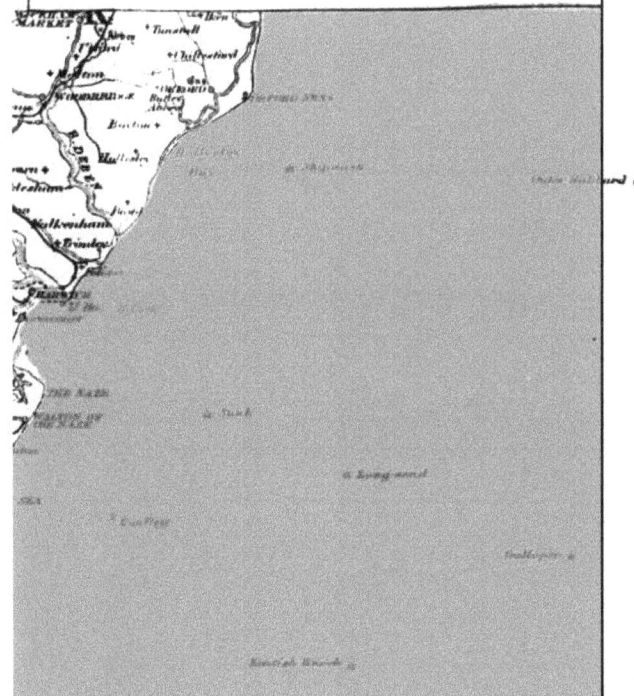

No. 17

WEATHER:
  Light, variable westerly wind.
  Fine.

BOMBS: 55.

CASUALTIES:
  14 killed, 87 injured.

MONETARY DAMAGE: £23,154.

Note. This map shows the paths of the hostile aeroplanes according to observations made at the time. It was thought that two, or even more bombers, sometimes came in together. German semi-official accounts say seven Gothas and three Giant bombers took part in the raid.

Spread 3

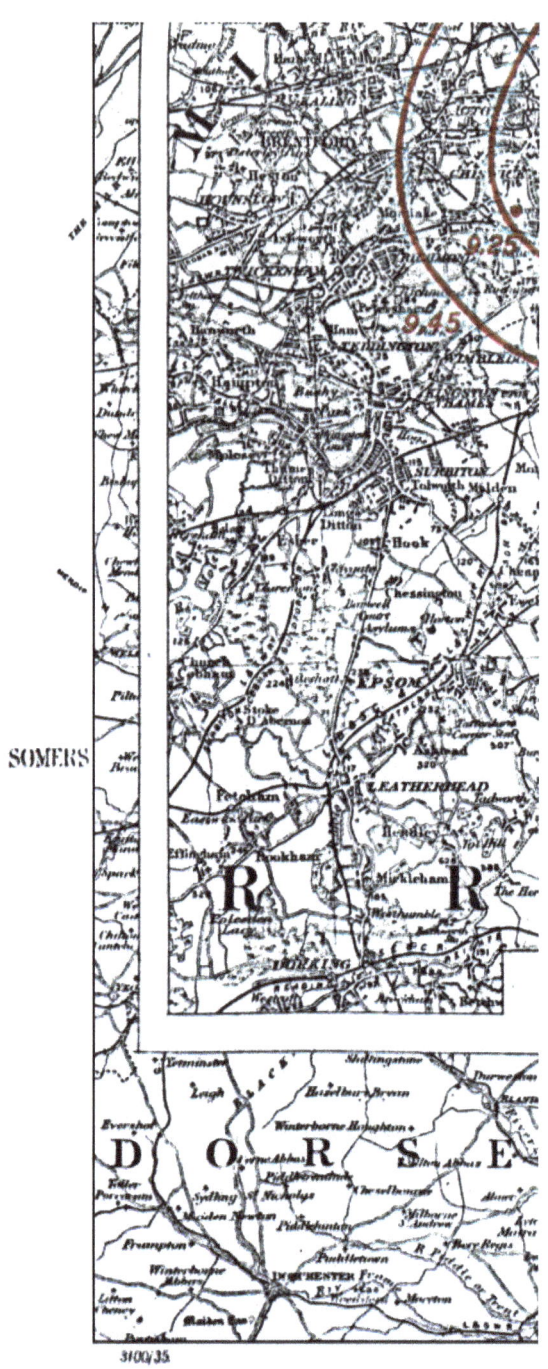

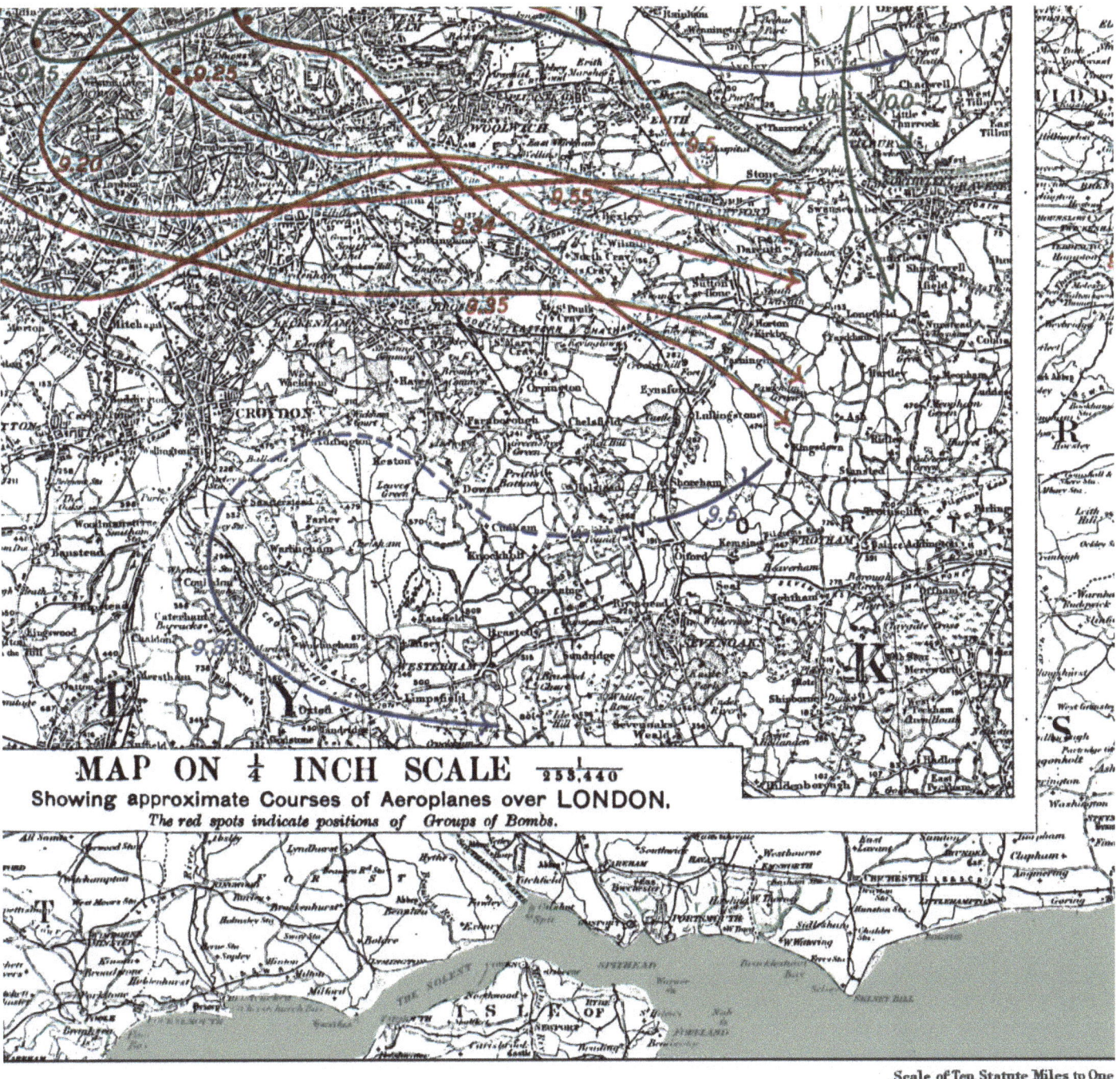

MAP ON ¼ INCH SCALE 1/253,440
Showing approximate Courses of Aeroplanes over LONDON.
The red spots indicate positions of Groups of Bombs.

Scale of Ten Statute Miles to One

Spread 4

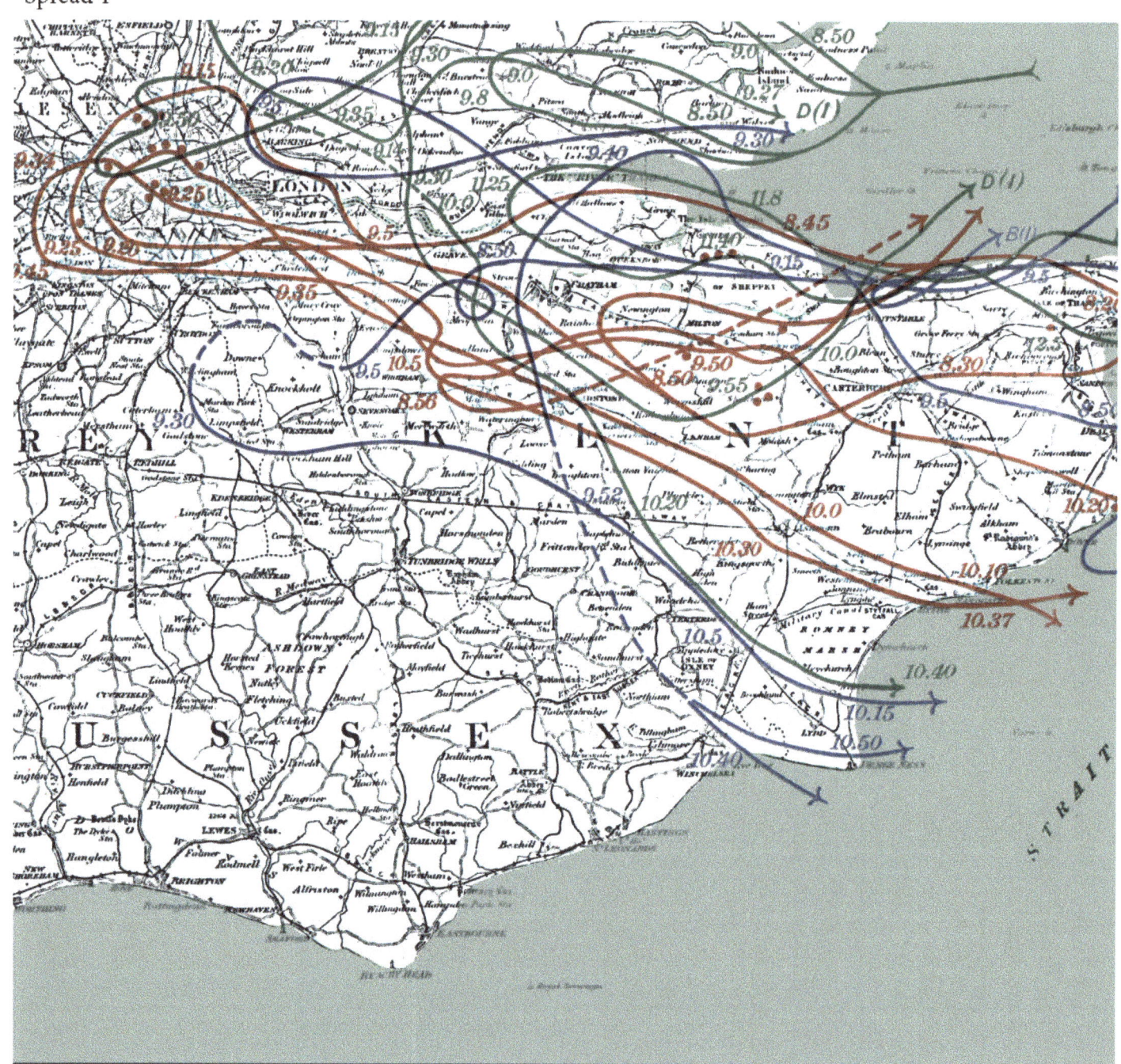

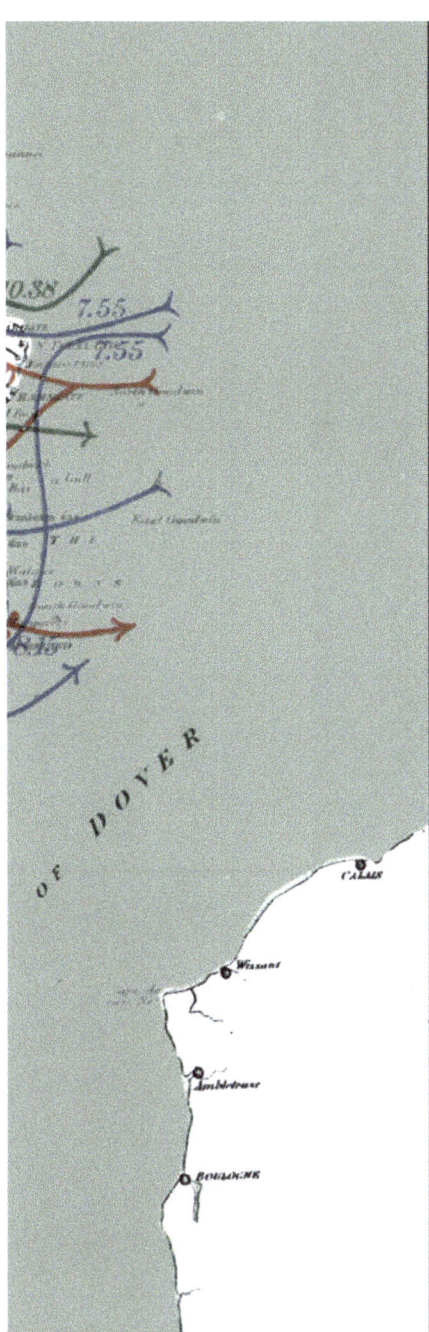

nance Survey, 1935.

No. 18. AEROPLANE RAID, 30th SEPTEMBER, 1917.
Spread 1

No. 18. AEROPLANE RAID, 30th SEPTEMBER, 1917.
Spread 2

No. 18. AEROPLANE RAID, 30th SEPTEMBER, 1917.
Spread 3

No. 18. AEROPLANE RAID, 30th SEPTEMBER, 1917.
Spread 4

Spread 1

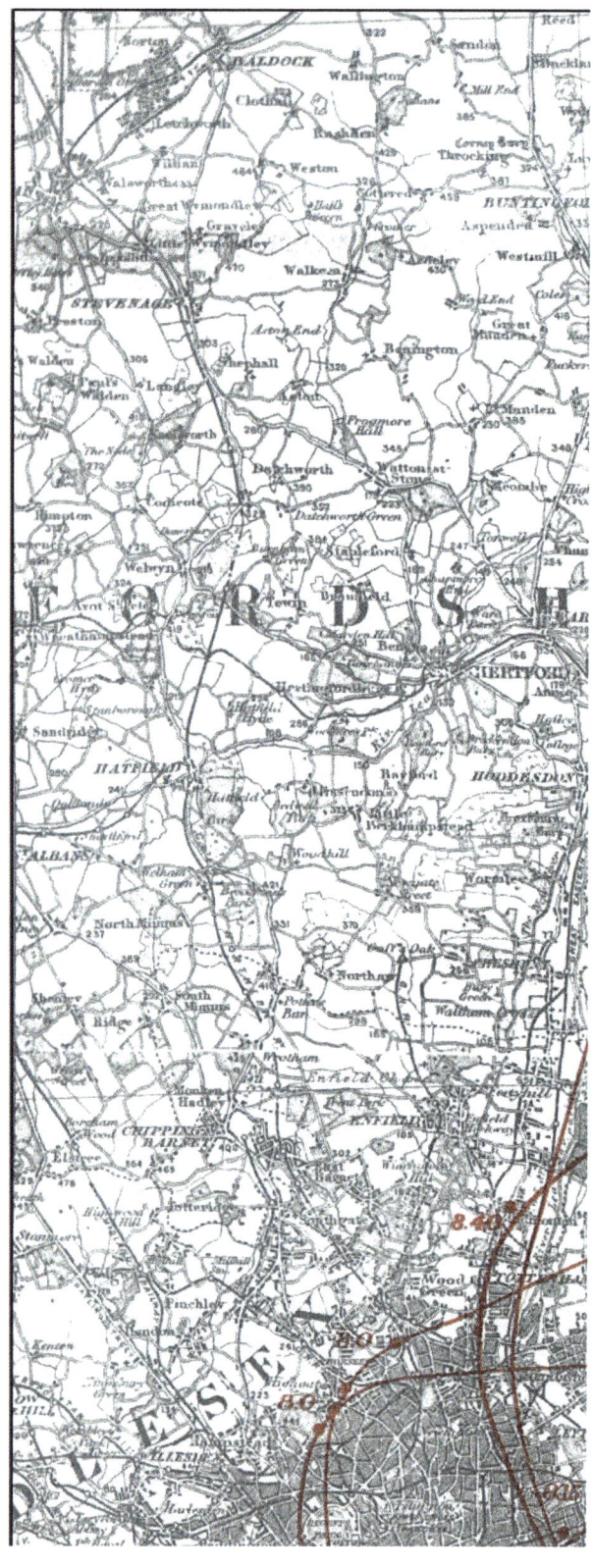

Spread 1

Aeroplane Raid,

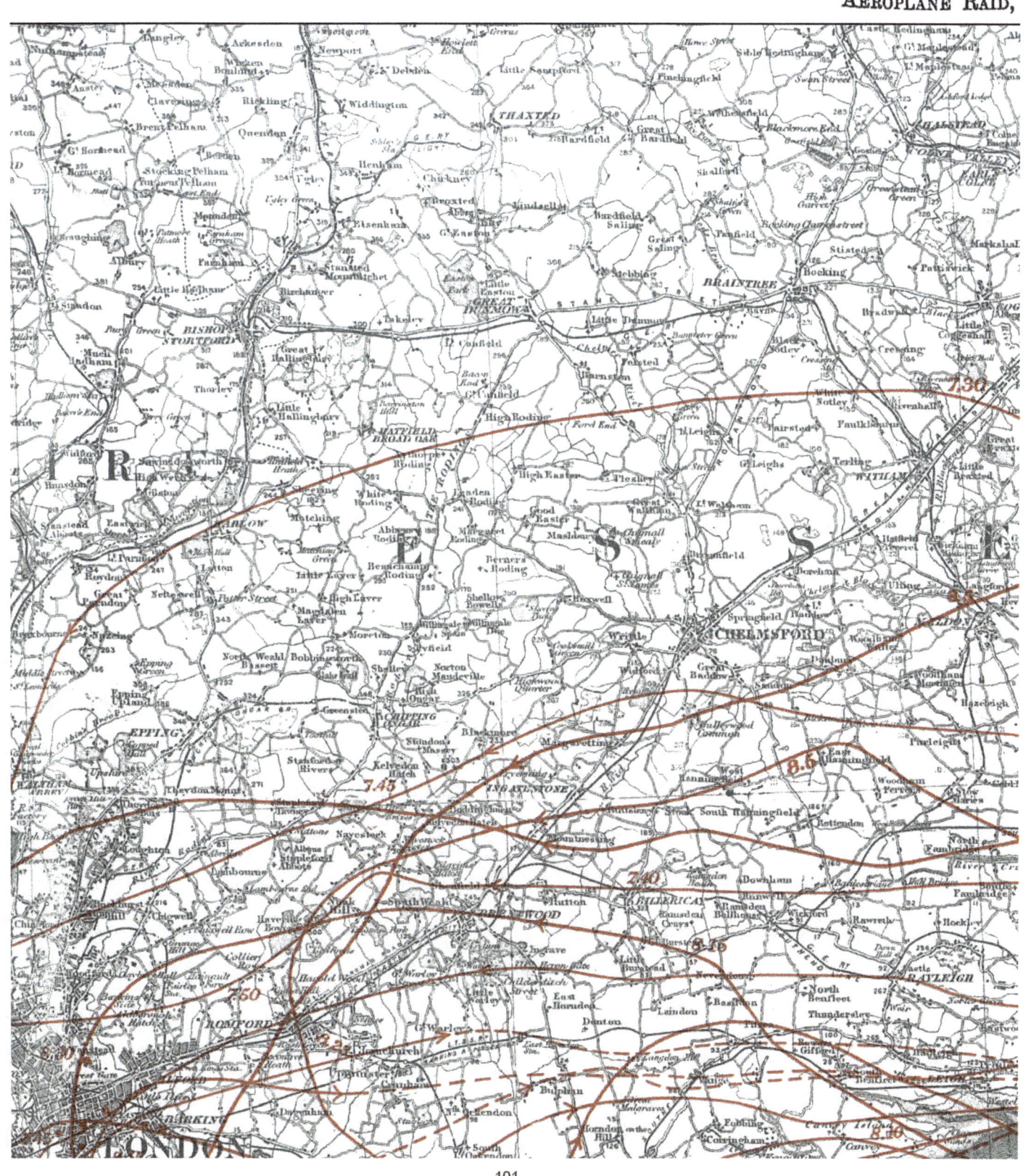

30TH SEPTEMBER, 1917.

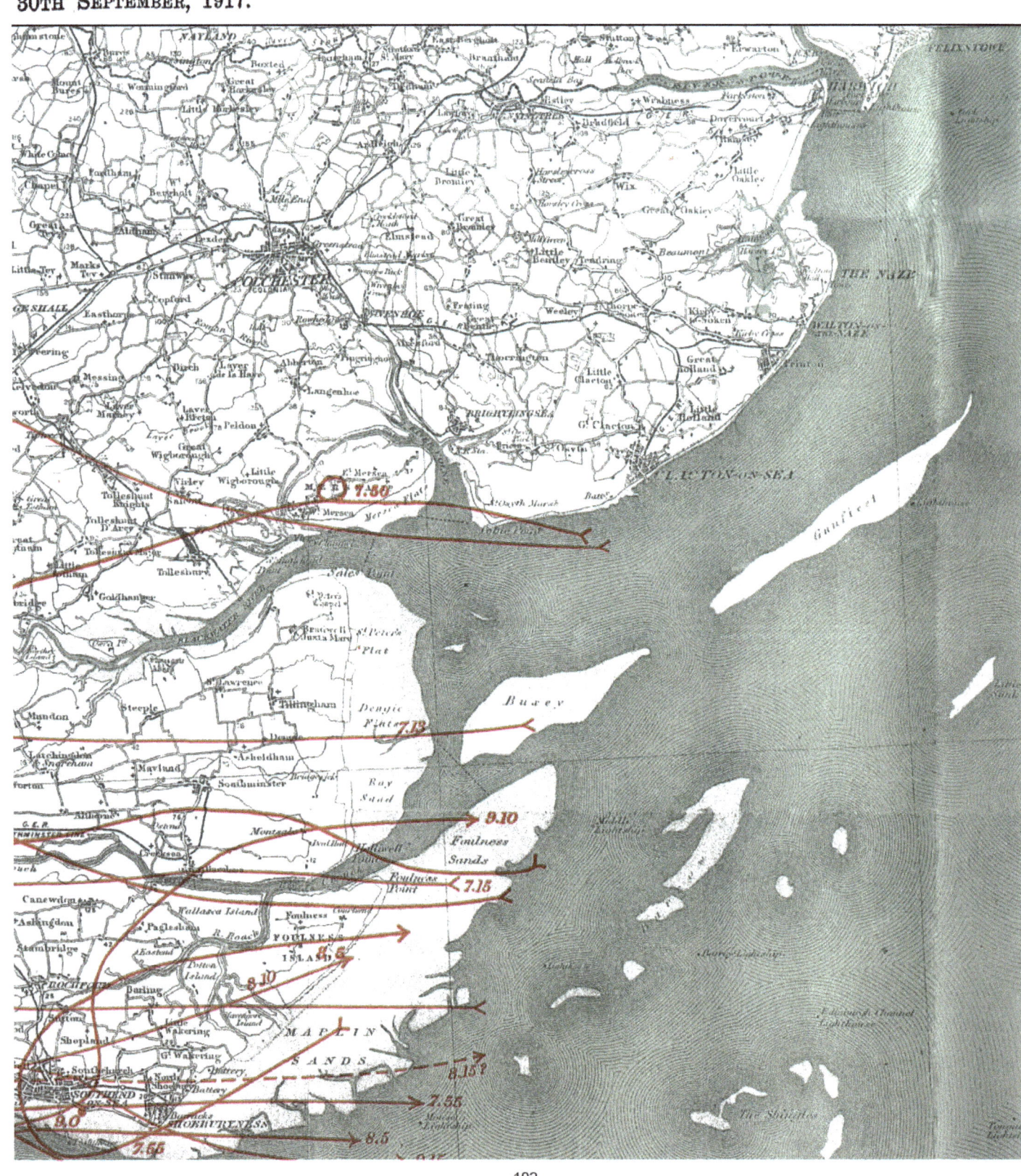

No. 18

WEATHER:
  Light S.W. wind.
  Fine, some cloud.

BOMBS: 92.

CASUALTIES:
  14 killed, 38 injured.

MONETARY DAMAGE: £21,482.

Note. This map shows the paths of the hostile aeroplanes according to observations made at the time. It was thought that two, or even more bombers, sometimes came in together. German semi-official accounts say only ten Gothas and one smaller type bomber took part in the raid.

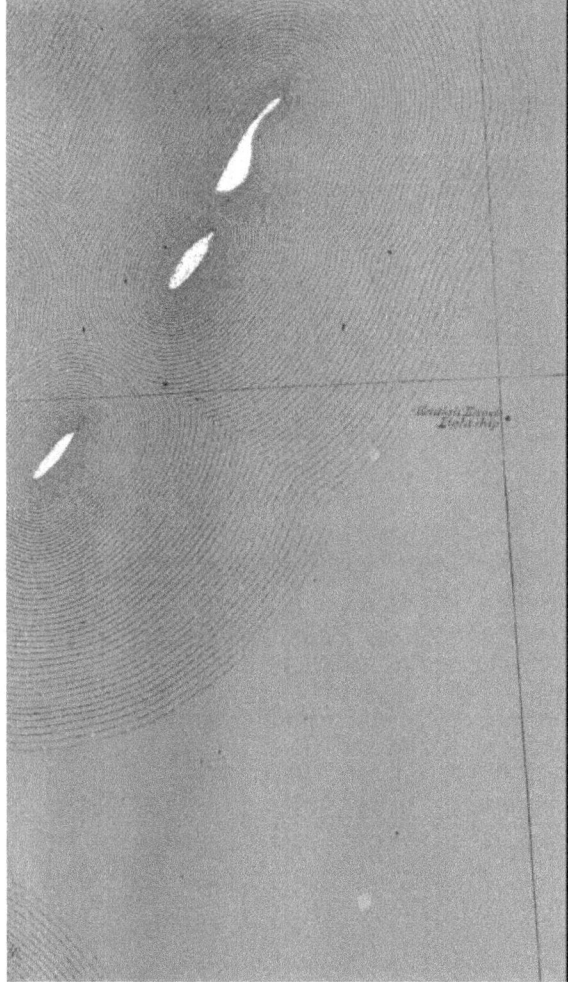

Spread 3

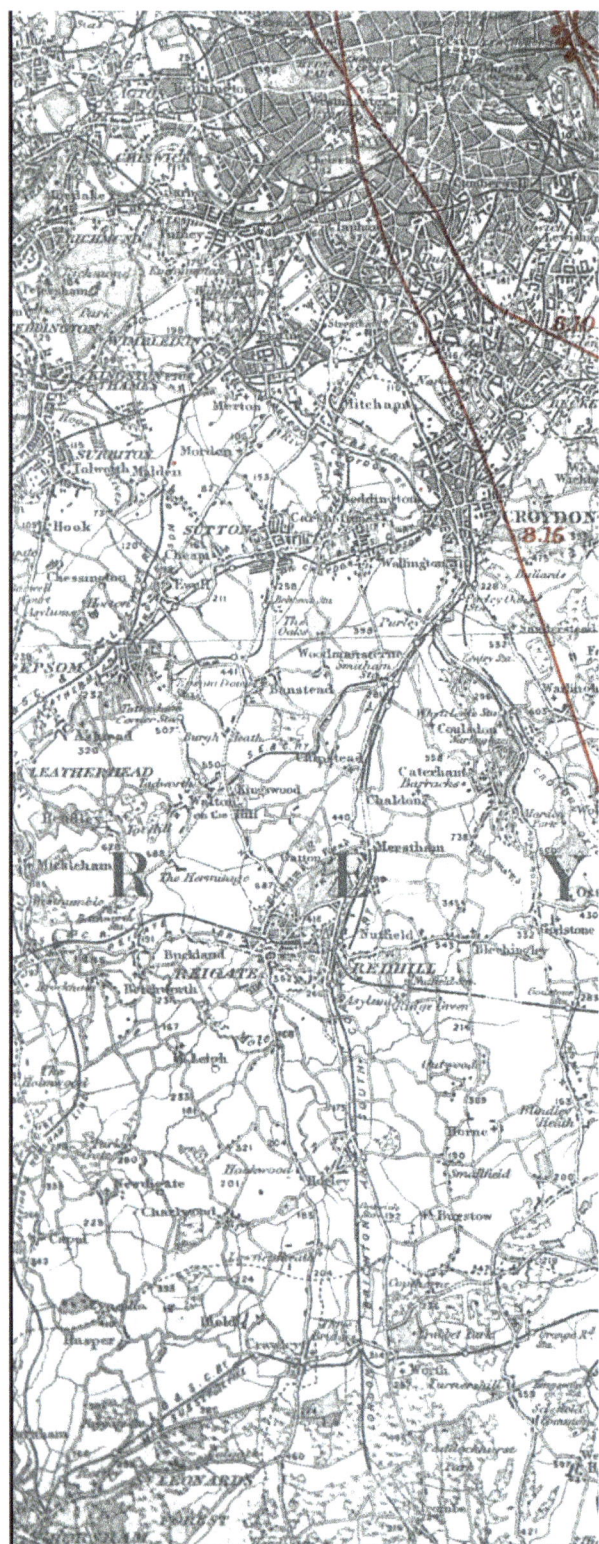

Ordnance Survey, 1935.

Spread 4

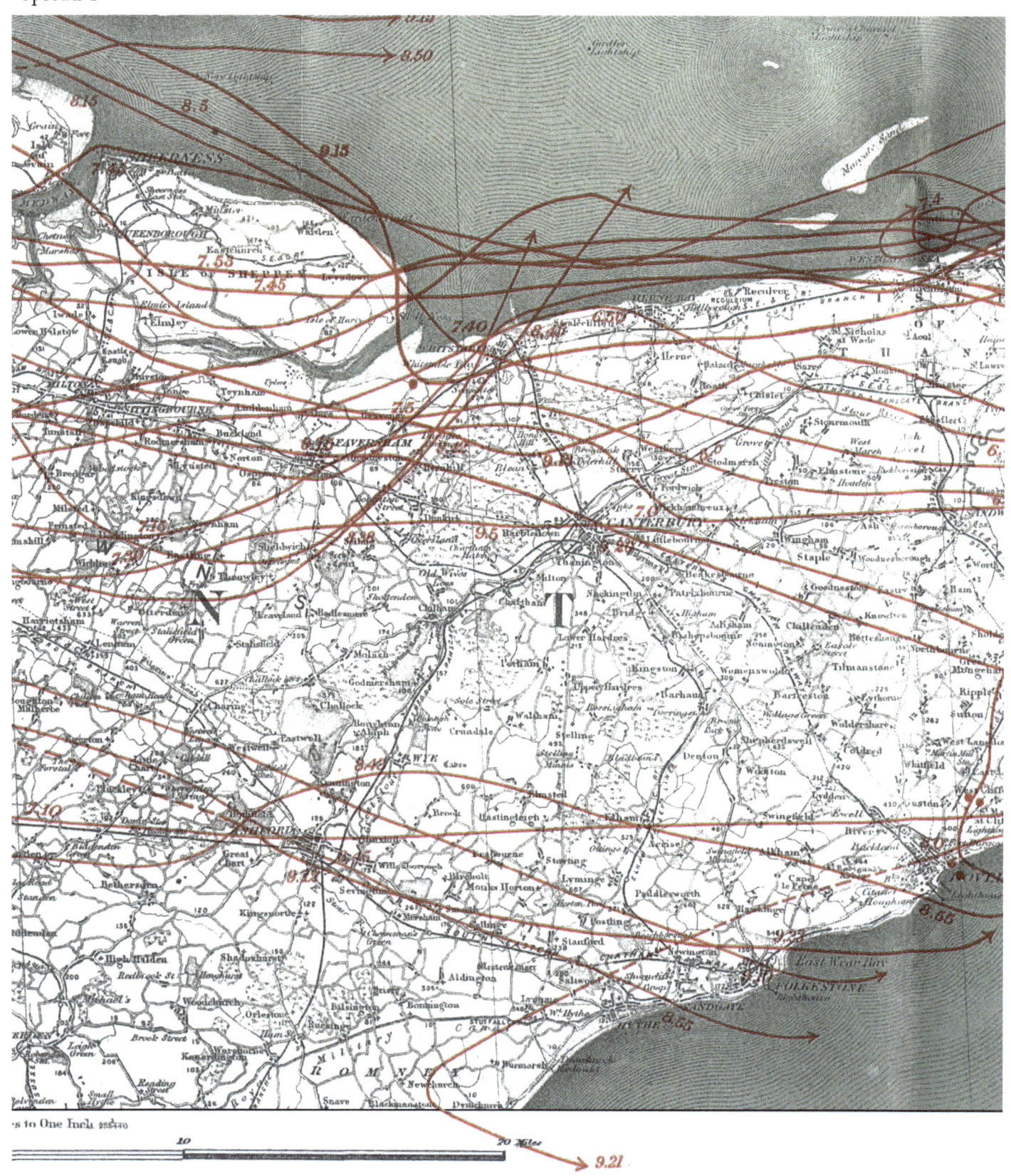

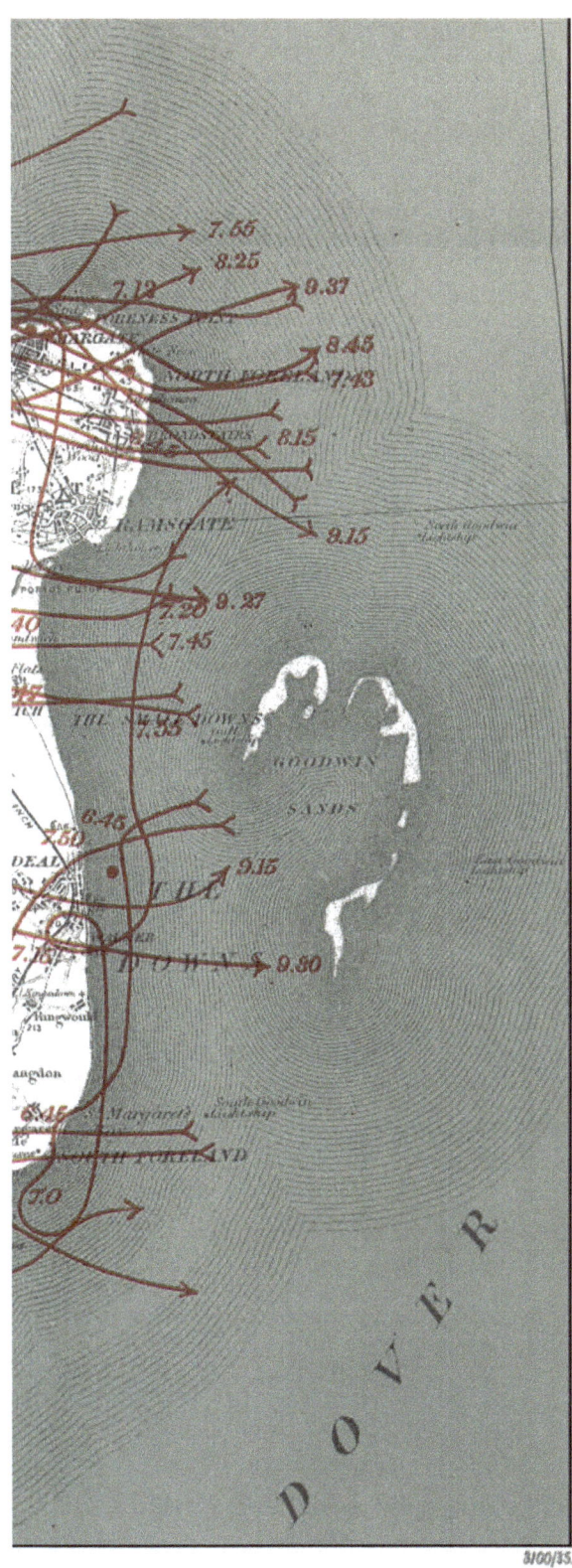

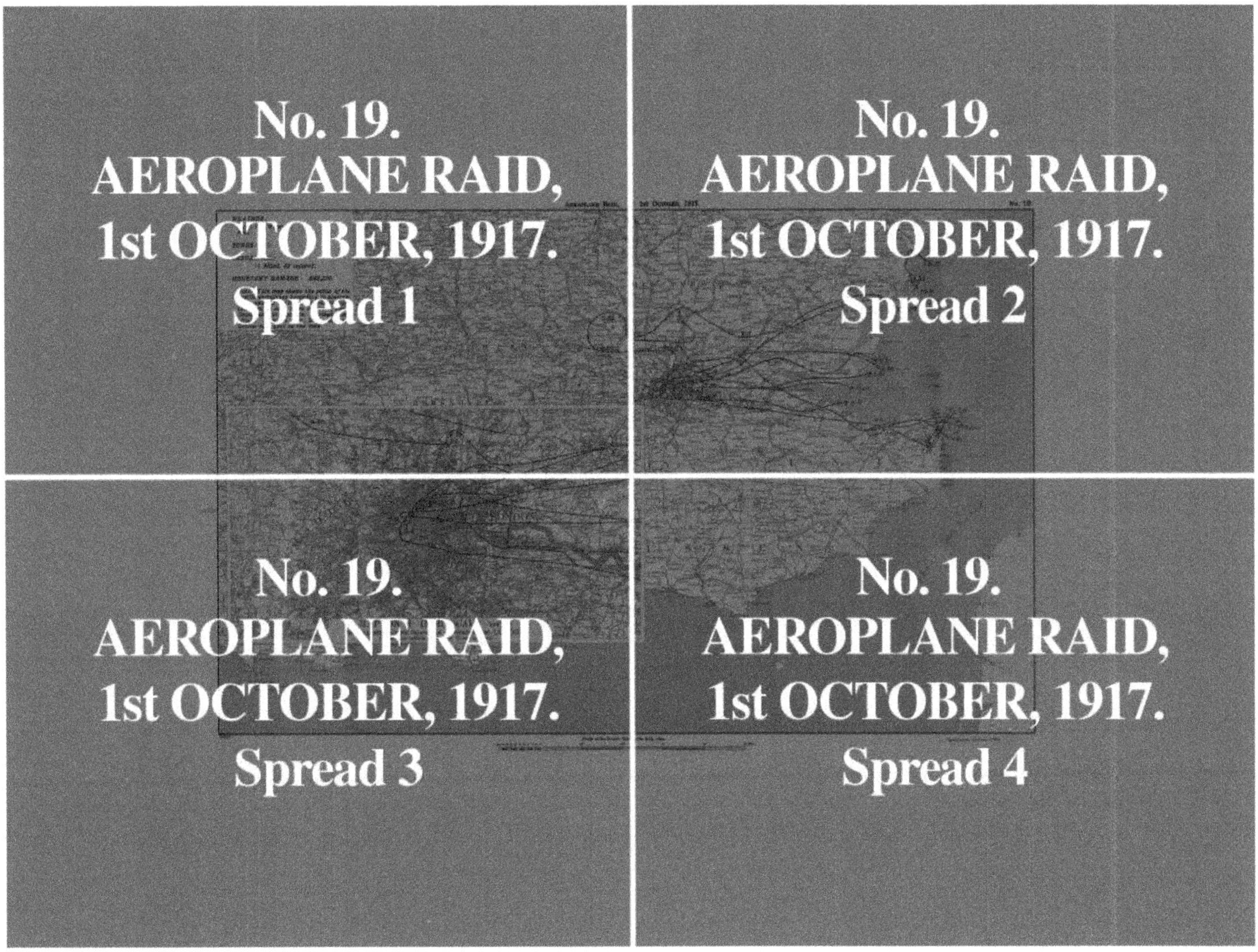

No. 19.
AEROPLANE RAID,
1st OCTOBER, 1917.
Spread 1

No. 19.
AEROPLANE RAID,
1st OCTOBER, 1917.
Spread 2

No. 19.
AEROPLANE RAID,
1st OCTOBER, 1917.
Spread 3

No. 19.
AEROPLANE RAID,
1st OCTOBER, 1917.
Spread 4

Spread 1

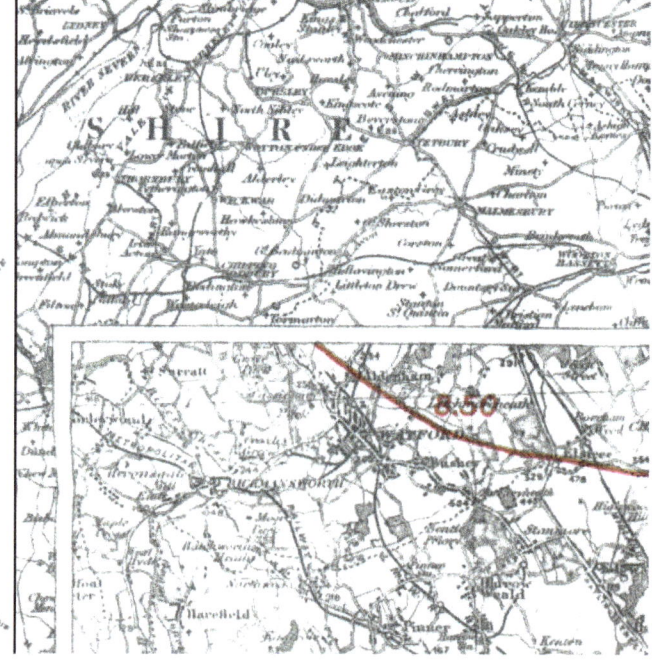

WEATHER:
  Light W.S.W. wind.
  Fine.

BOMBS: 81.

CASUALTIES:
    11 killed, 42 injured.

MONETARY DAMAGE: £45,570.

Note. This map shows the paths of the hostile aeroplanes according to observations made at the time. It was thought that two, or even more bombers, sometimes came in together. German semi-official accounts say that eighteen Gothas took part in the raid.

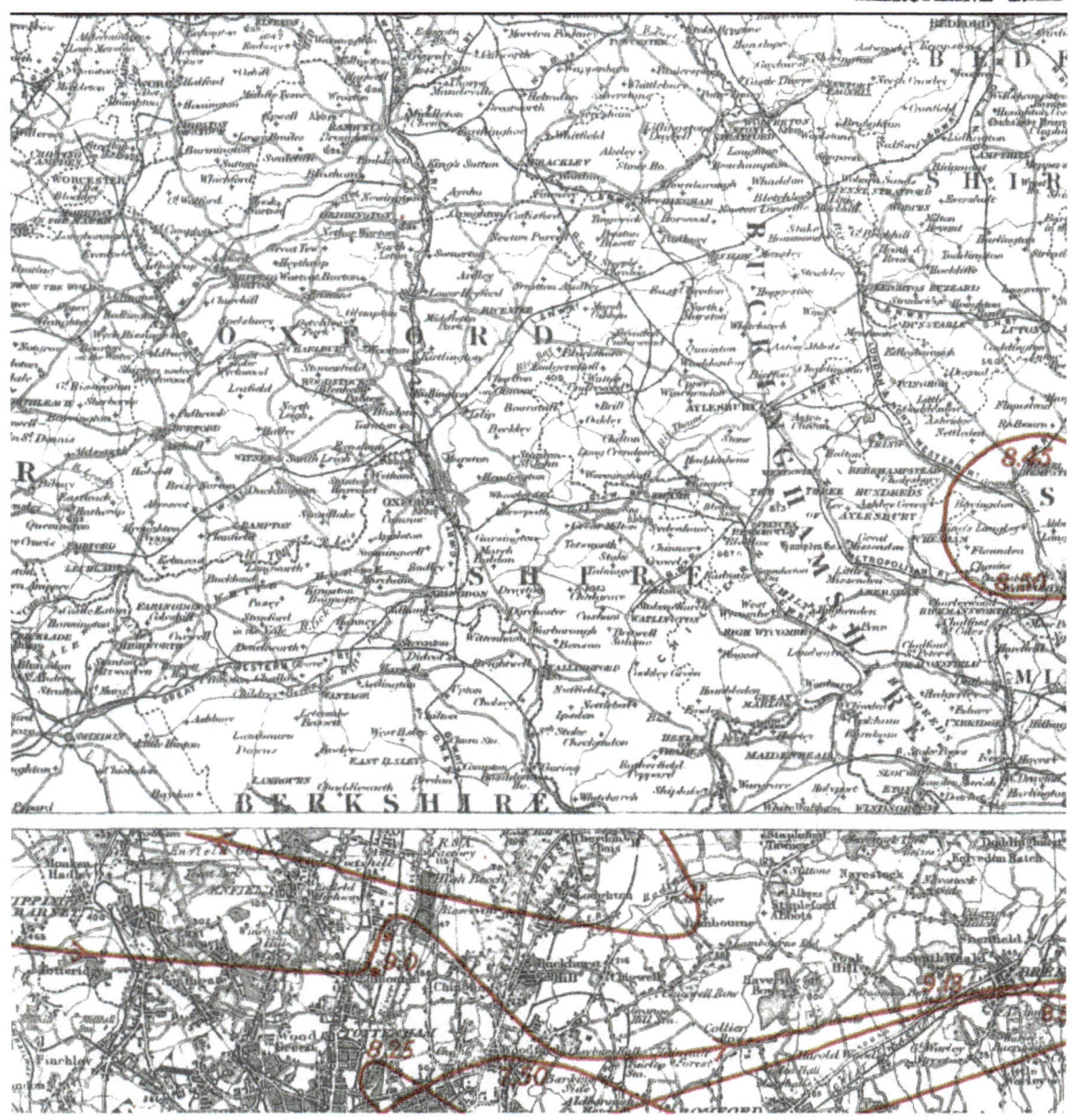

Aeroplane Raid

Spread 2

1st October, 1917.

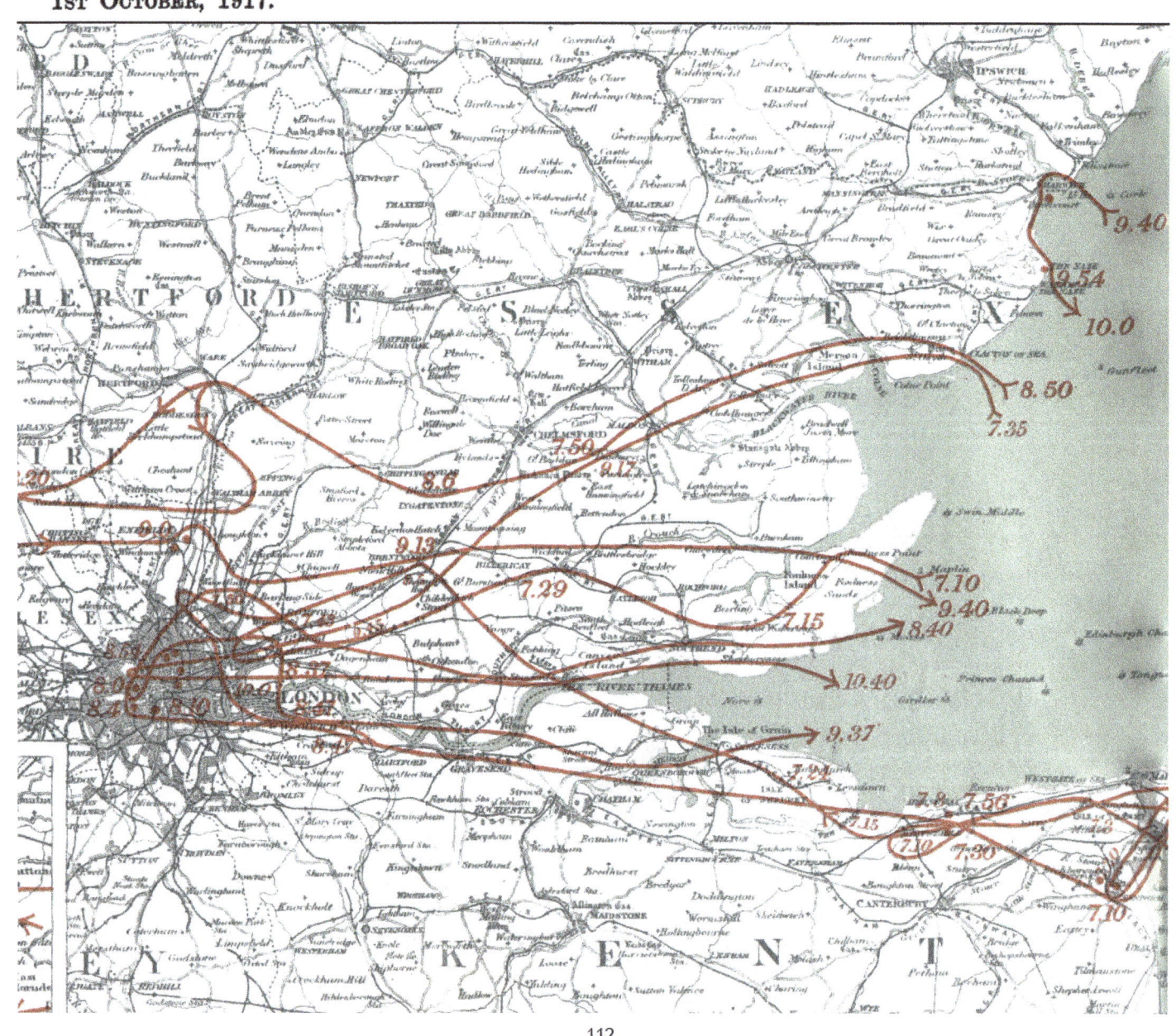

No. 19

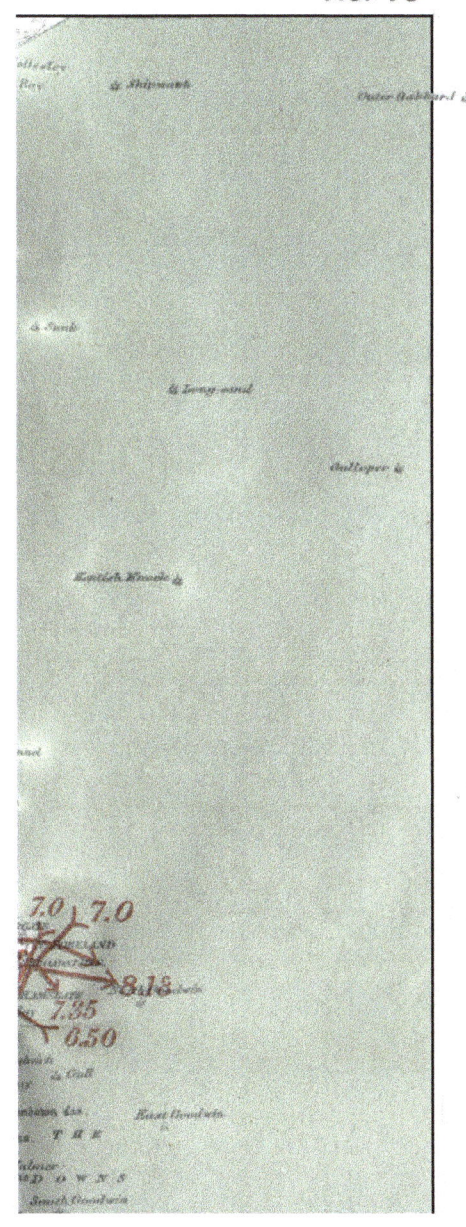

Spread 3

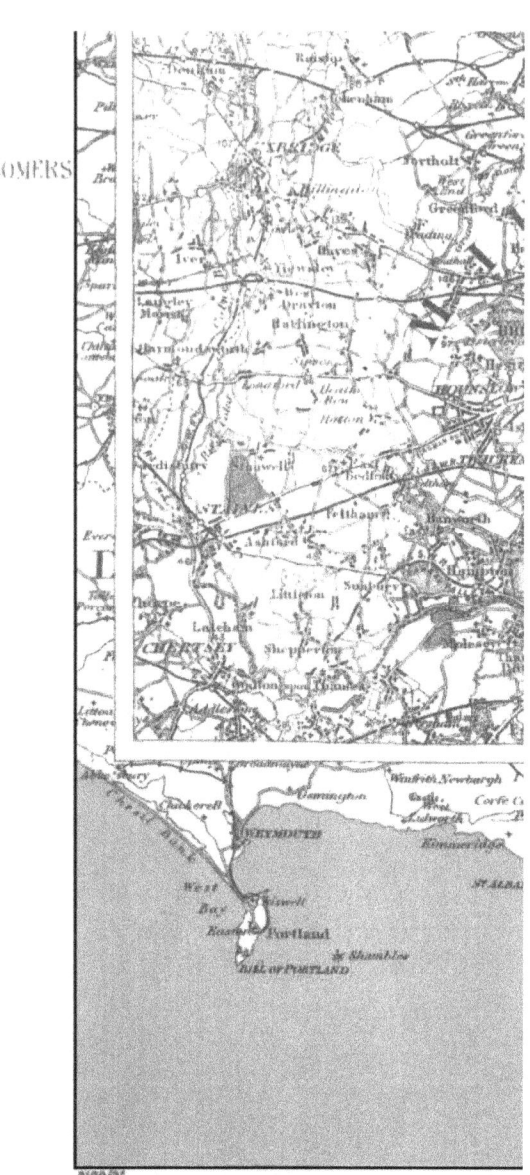

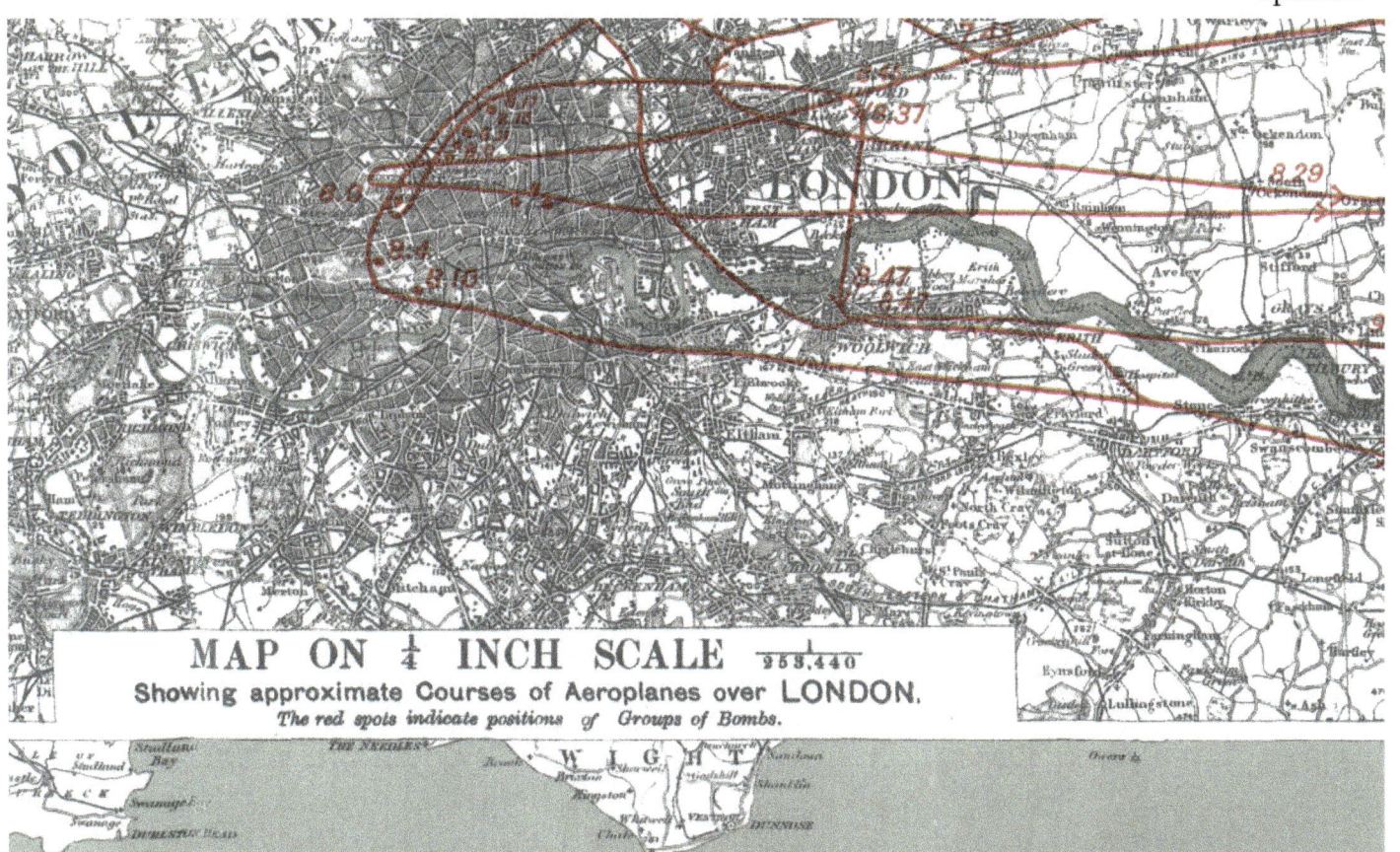

Spread 4

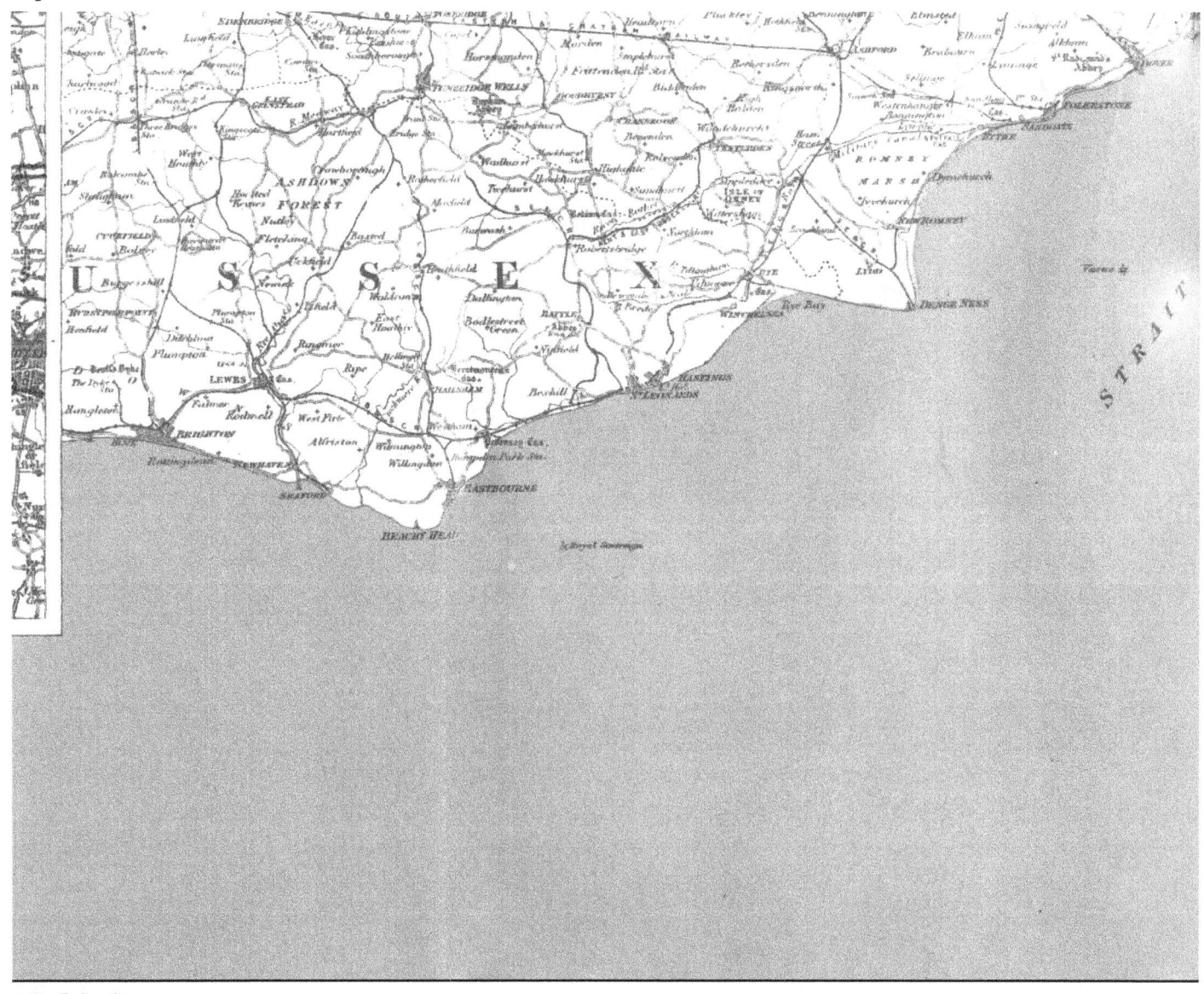

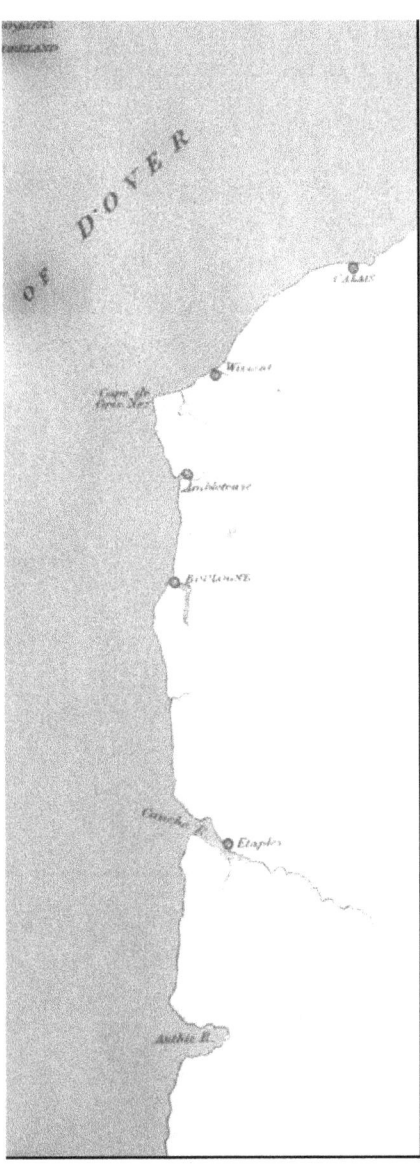

Ordnance Survey, 1935

No. 20.
AEROPLANE RAID, 31st OCTOBER, 1917.
Spread 1

No. 20.
AEROPLANE RAID, 31st OCTOBER, 1917.
Spread 2

No. 20.
AEROPLANE RAID, 31st OCTOBER, 1917.
Spread 3

No. 20.
AEROPLANE RAID, 31st OCTOBER, 1917.
Spread 4

Spread 1

AEROPLANE RAID,

Spread 2

31st October, 1917.

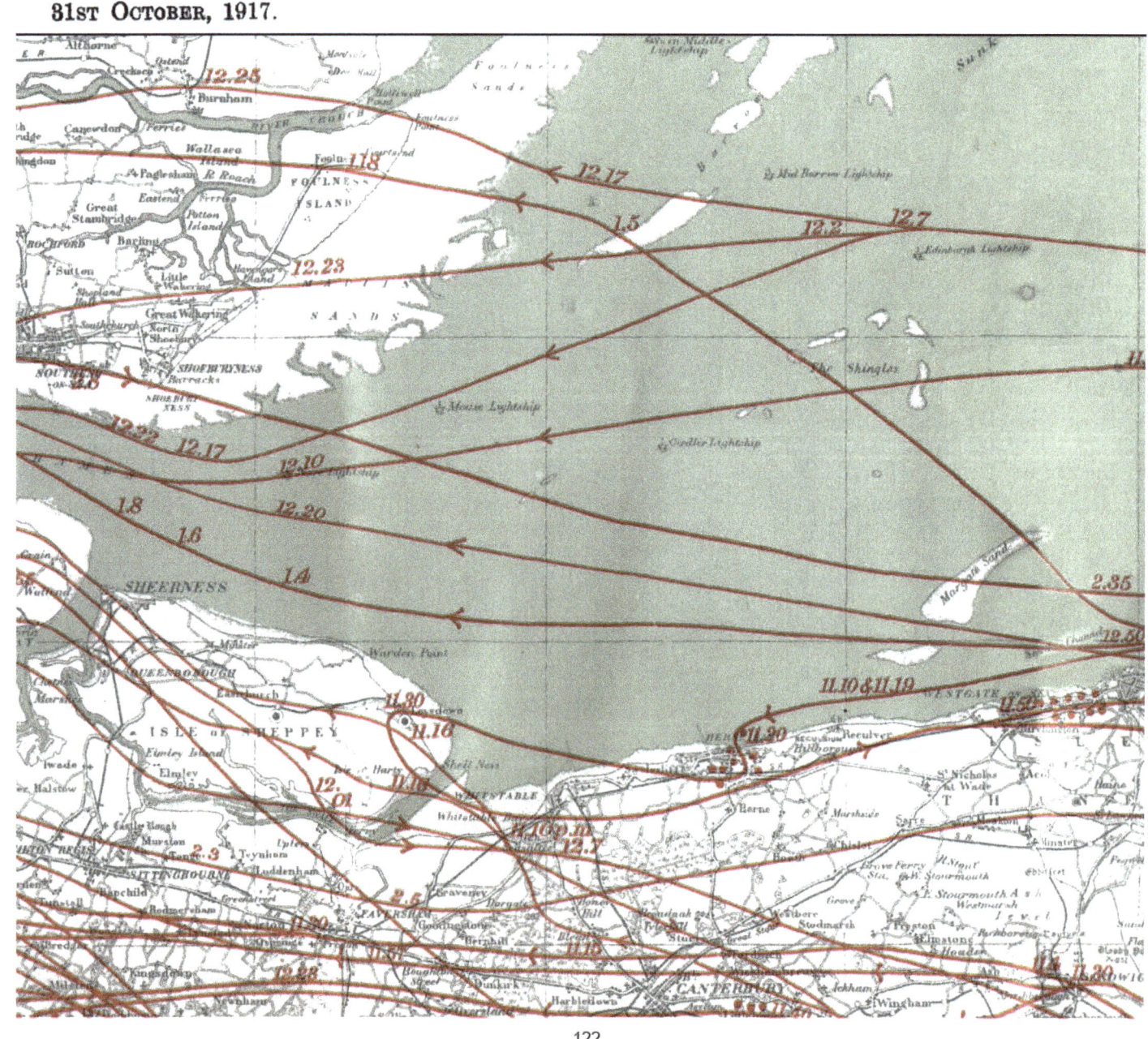

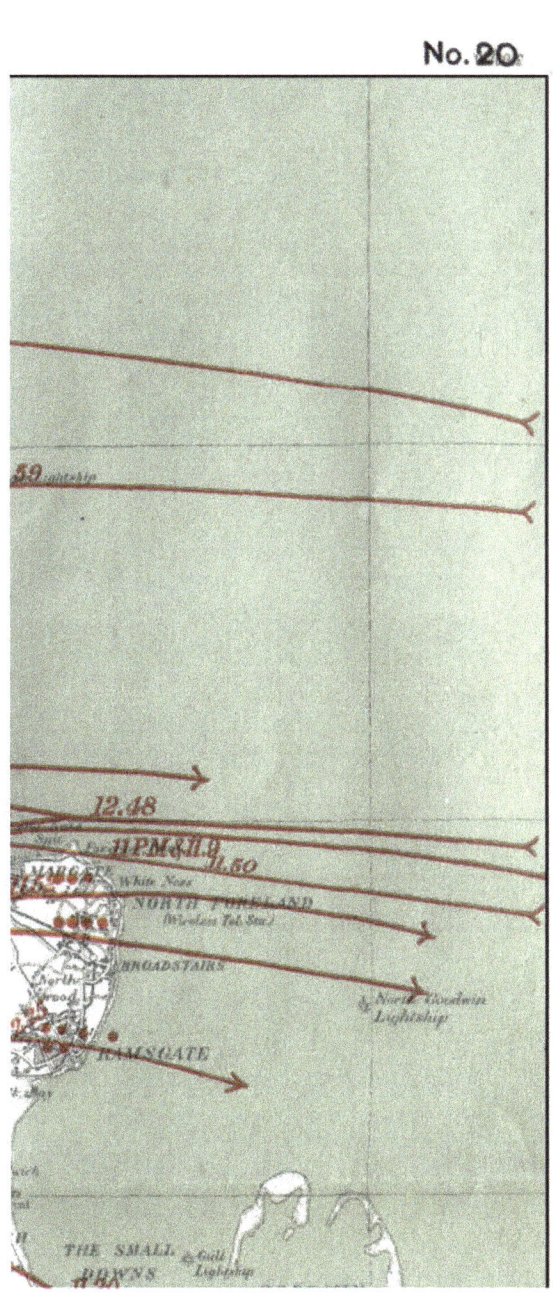

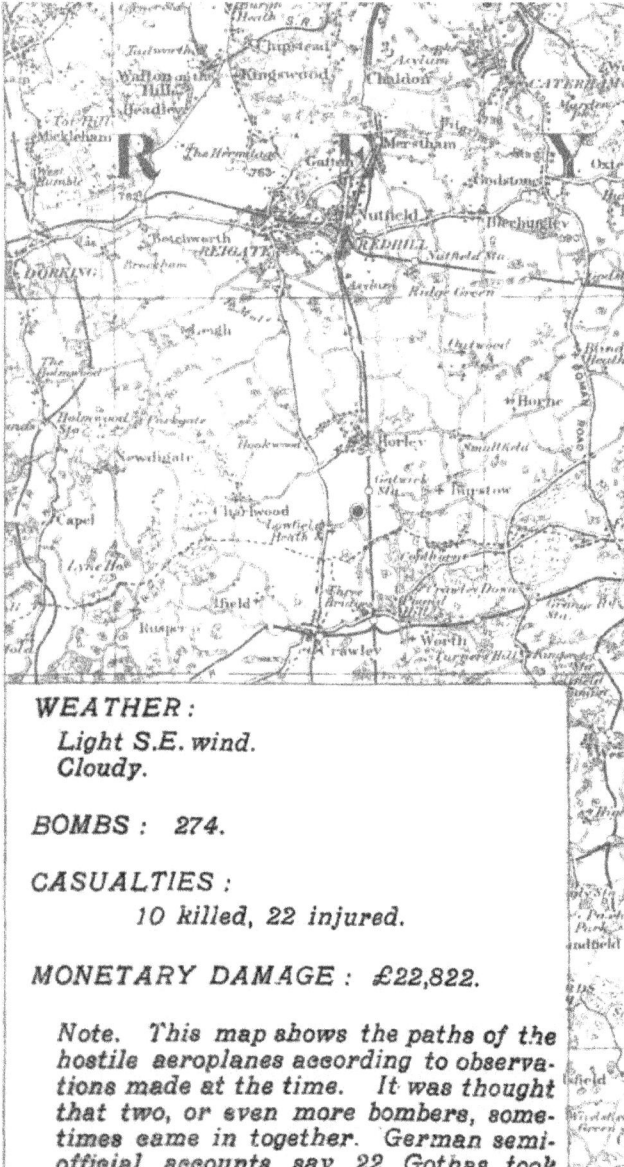

WEATHER:
Light S.E. wind.
Cloudy.

BOMBS: 274.

CASUALTIES:
10 killed, 22 injured.

MONETARY DAMAGE: £22,822.

Note. This map shows the paths of the hostile aeroplanes according to observations made at the time. It was thought that two, or even more bombers, sometimes came in together. German semi-official accounts say 22 Gothas took part in the raid.

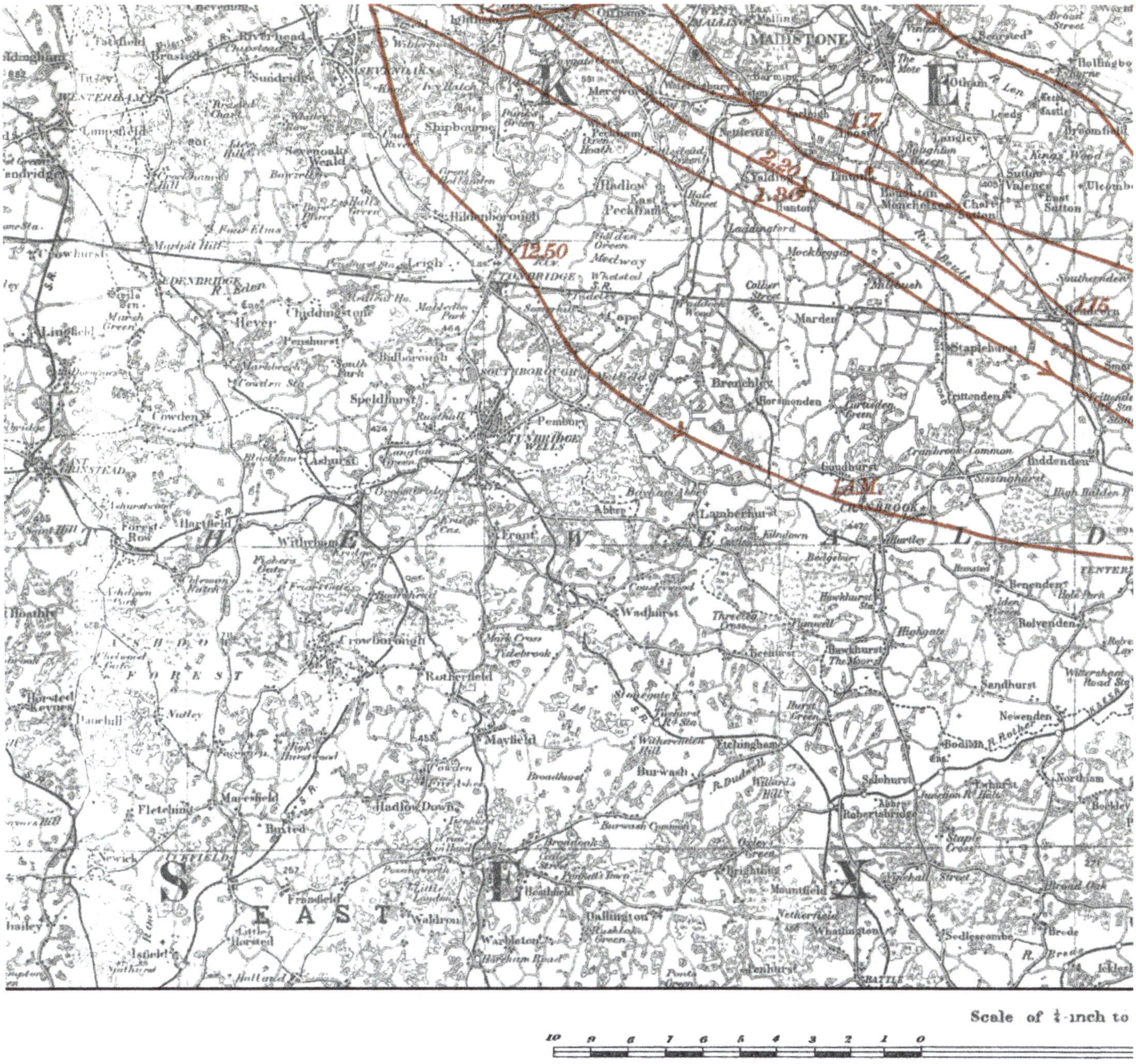
MAIDSTONE
K
E
Shipbourne
Sevenoaks Weald
Hildenborough
Hadlow
East Peckham
Yalding
Marden
Staplehurst
Leigh
TONBRIDGE
Penshurst
Chiddingstone
Hever
EDENBRIDGE
Speldhurst
Pembury
TUNBRIDGE WELLS
Brenchley
Horsmonden
Goudhurst
CRANBROOK
Lamberhurst
Frant
Wadhurst
Crowborough
Rotherfield
Mayfield
Burwash
Etchingham
Robertsbridge
Hartfield
Forest Row
Withyham
Fletching
Maresfield
Buxted
Hadlow Down
Heathfield
Dallington
Mountfield
Brightling
Waldron
Framfield
Sandhurst
Newenden
Northiam
Rolvenden
Benenden
Biddenden
Sissinghurst
Frittenden
Hawkhurst
W
E
A
L
D
S
E
X
EAST
12.50
1.7
2.20
1.30
1.15
1 A.M.
Scale of ¼-inch to
10 9 8 7 6 5 4 3 2 1 0

Spread 4

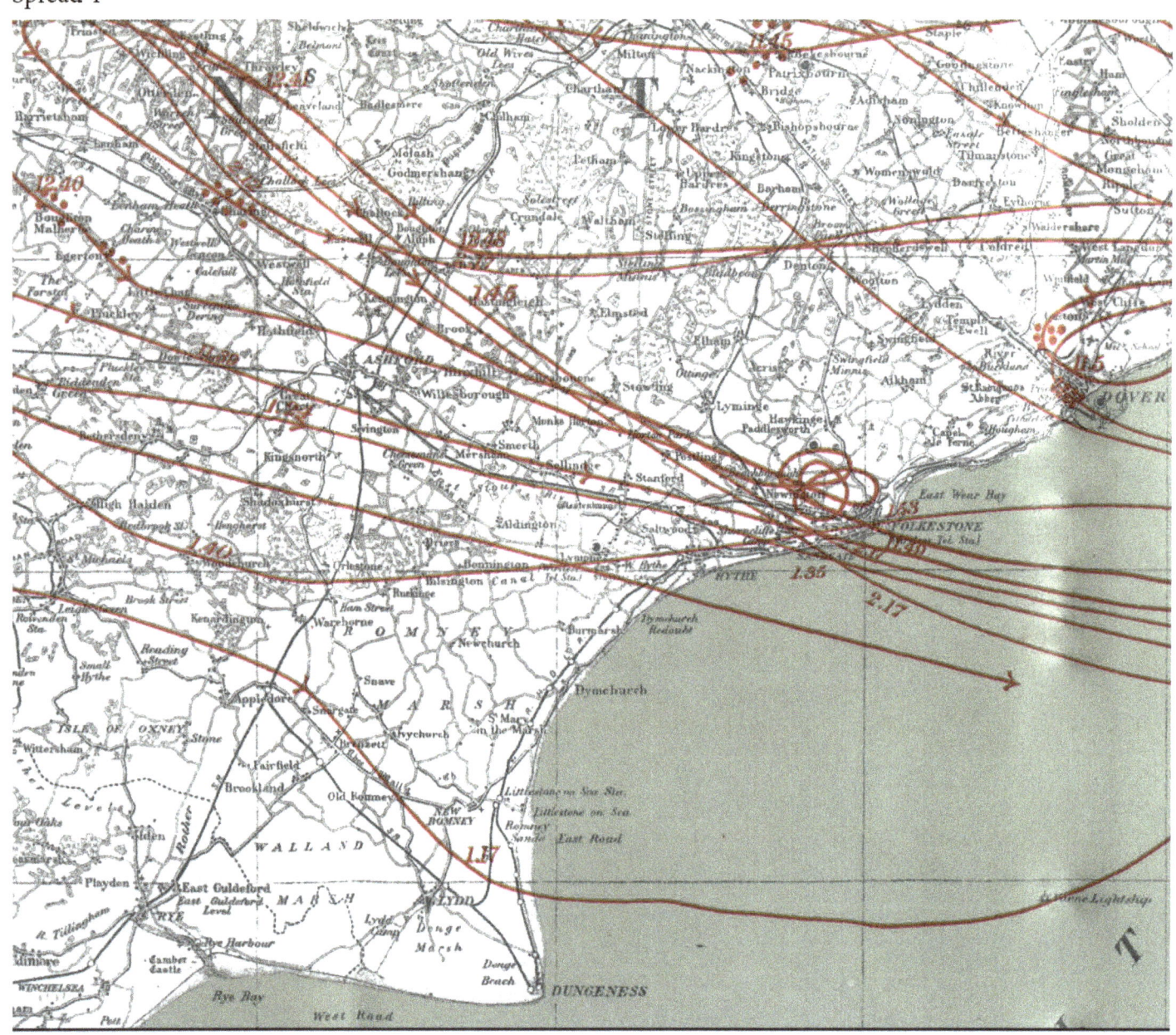

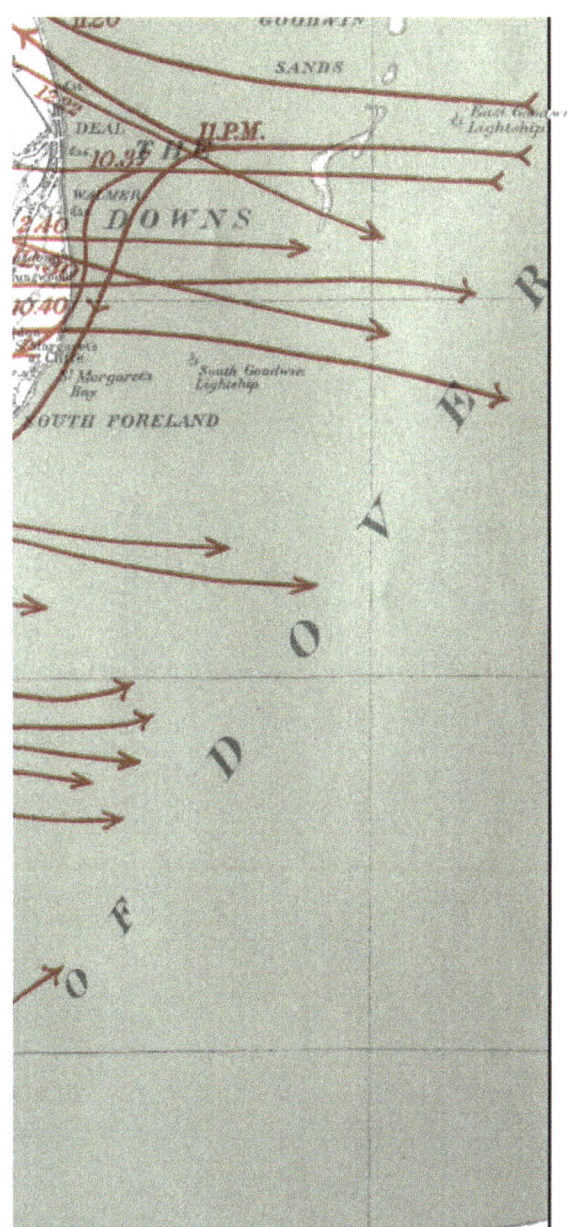

Ordnance Survey, 1935.

No. 21.
AEROPLANE RAID,
6st DECEMBER, 1917.
Spread 1

No. 21.
AEROPLANE RAID,
6st DECEMBER, 1917.
Spread 2

No. 21.
AEROPLANE RAID,
6st DECEMBER, 1917.
Spread 3

No. 21.
AEROPLANE RAID,
6st DECEMBER, 1917.
Spread 4

Spread 1

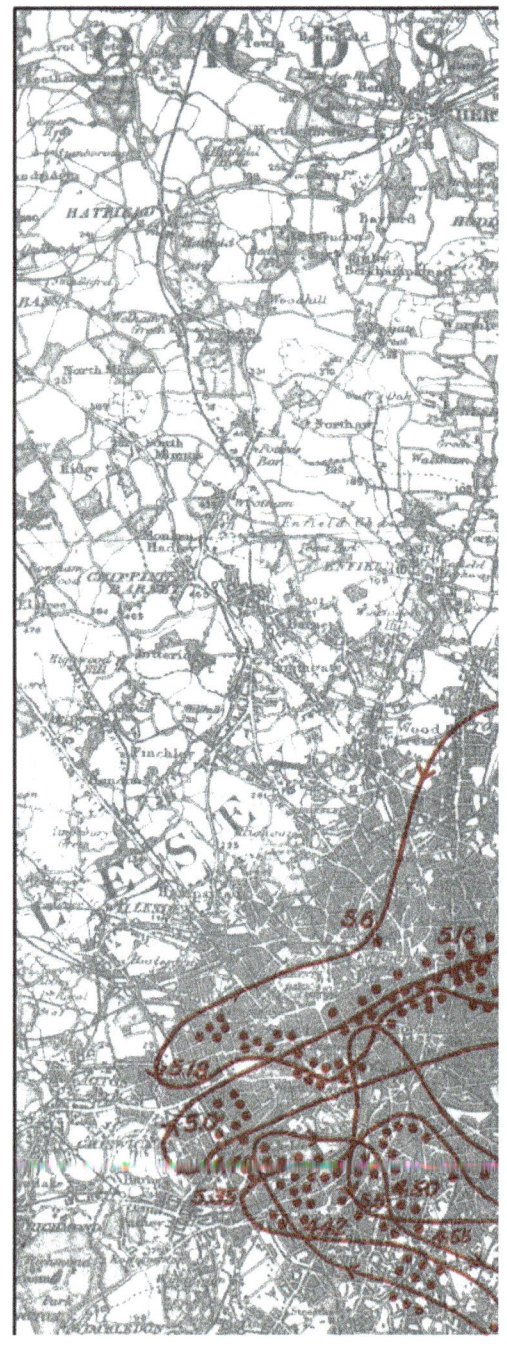

Aeroplane Raid,

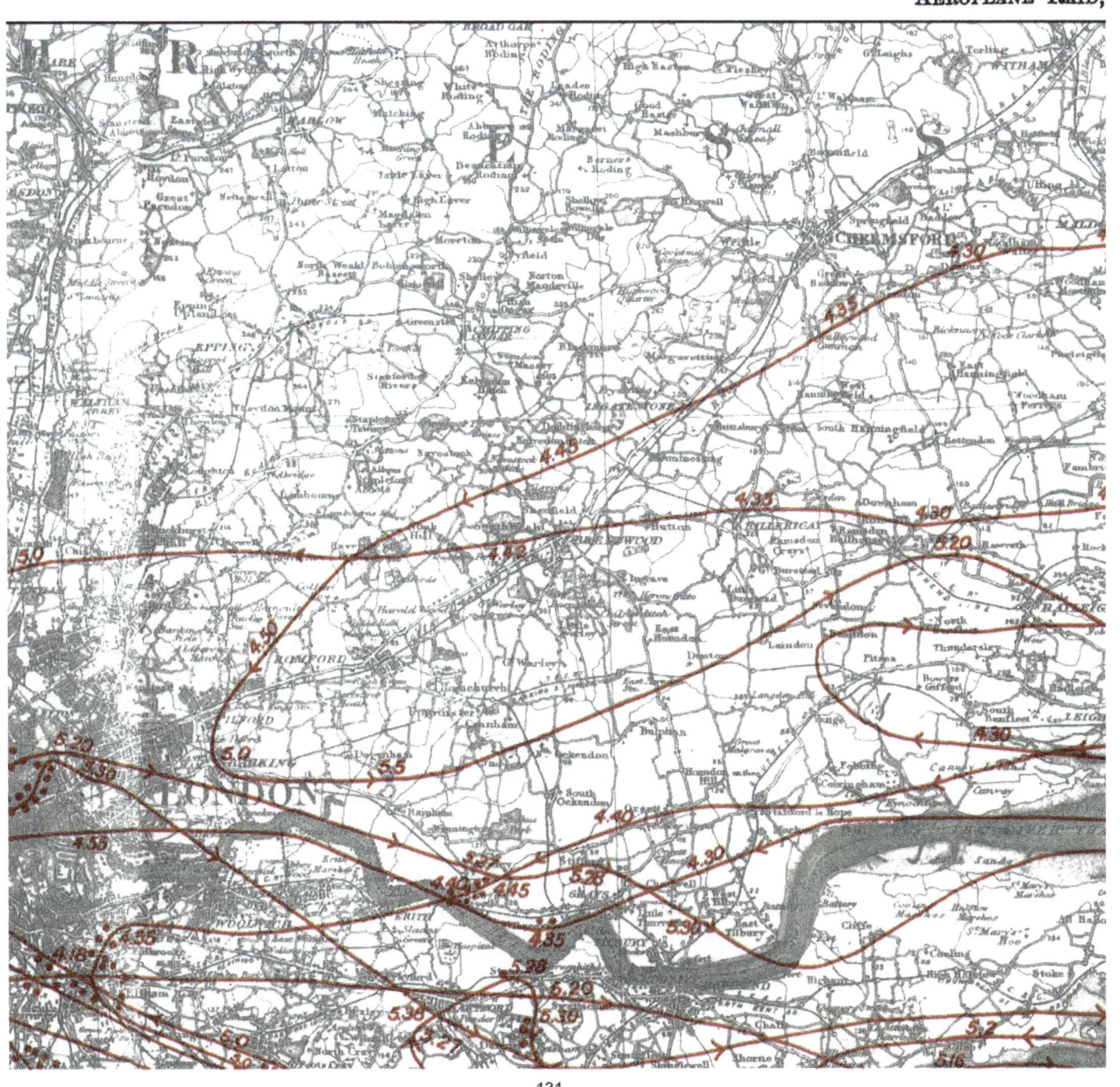

Spread 2

6TH DECEMBER, 1917.

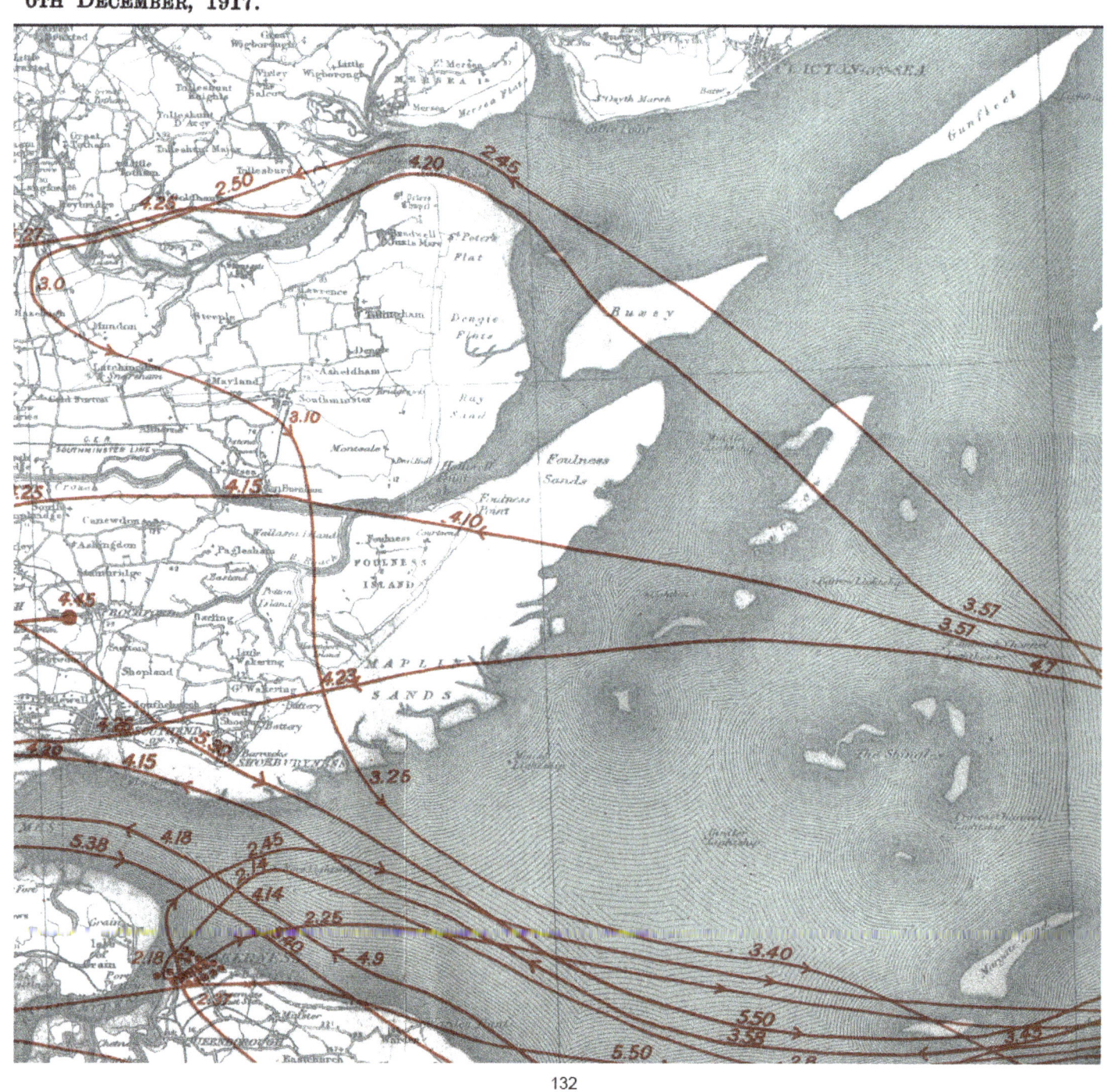

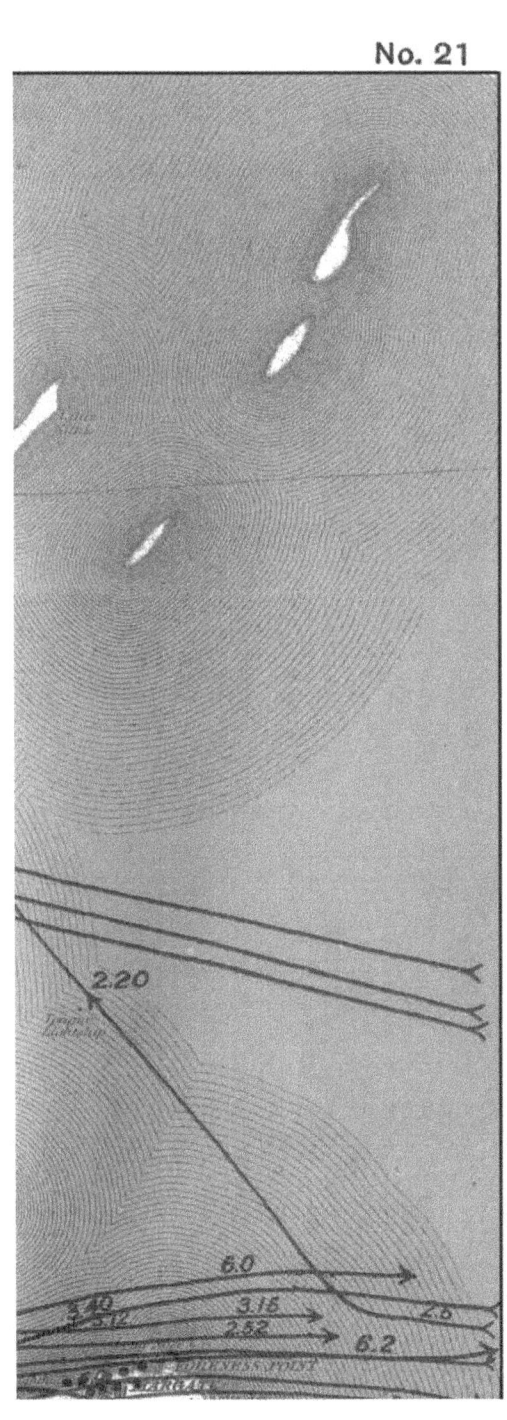

Spread 3

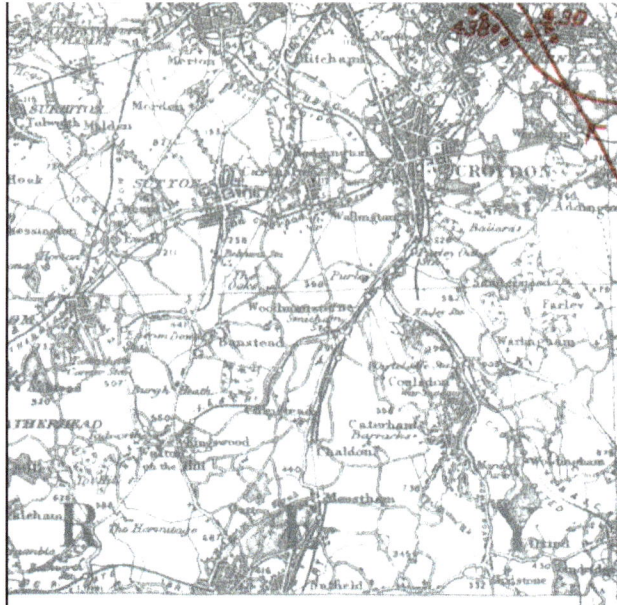

WEATHER:
Light S.W. wind.
Cloudless sky.

BOMBS: 423.

CASUALTIES:
    8 killed, 28 injured.

MONETARY DAMAGE: £103,408.

Note. This map shows the paths of the hostile aeroplanes according to observations made at the time. It was thought that two, or even more bombers, sometimes came in together. German semi-official records say two Giant bombers and nineteen Gothas, of which three turned back with engine trouble, took part in the raid.

Spread 3

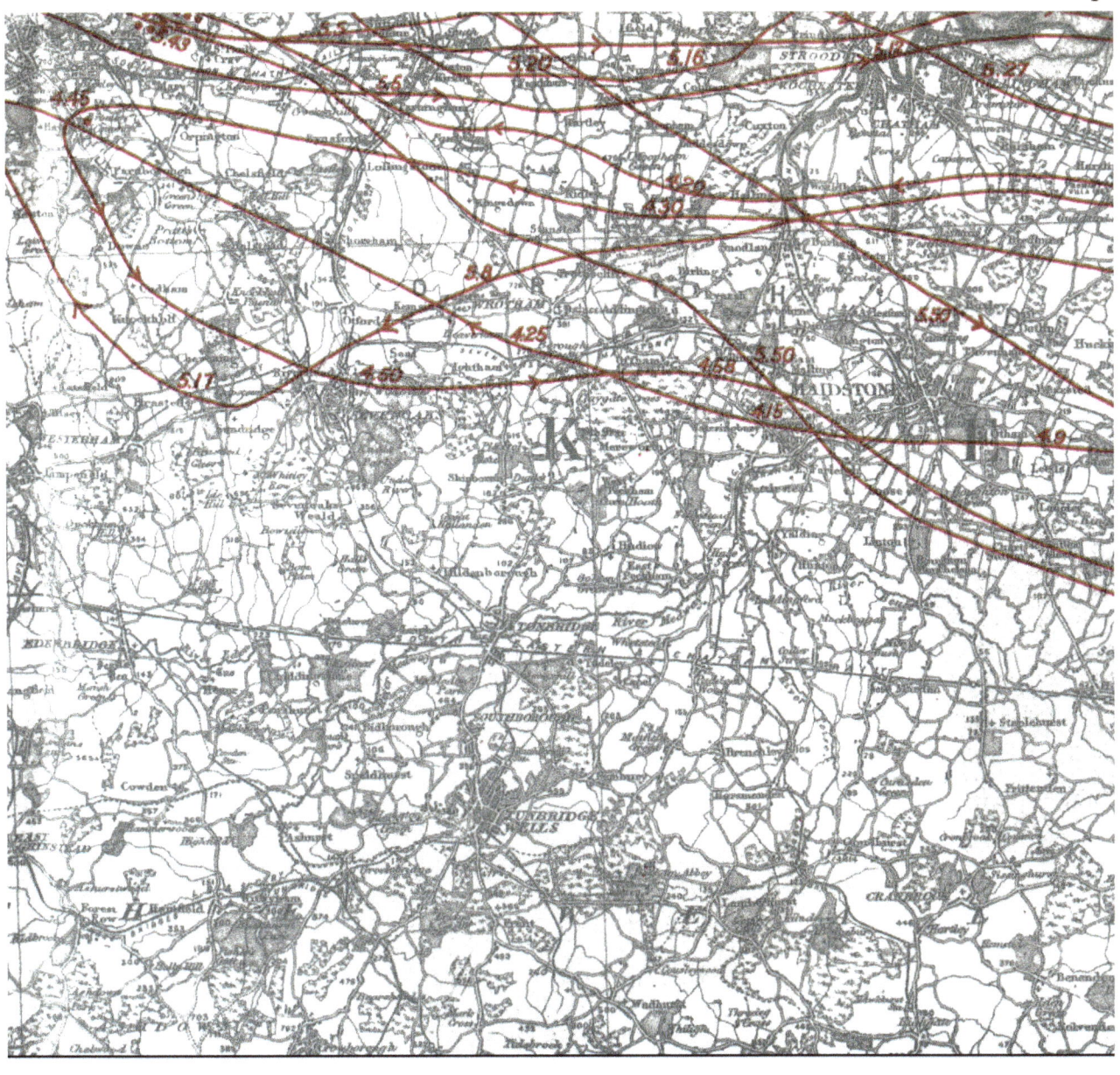

Spread 4

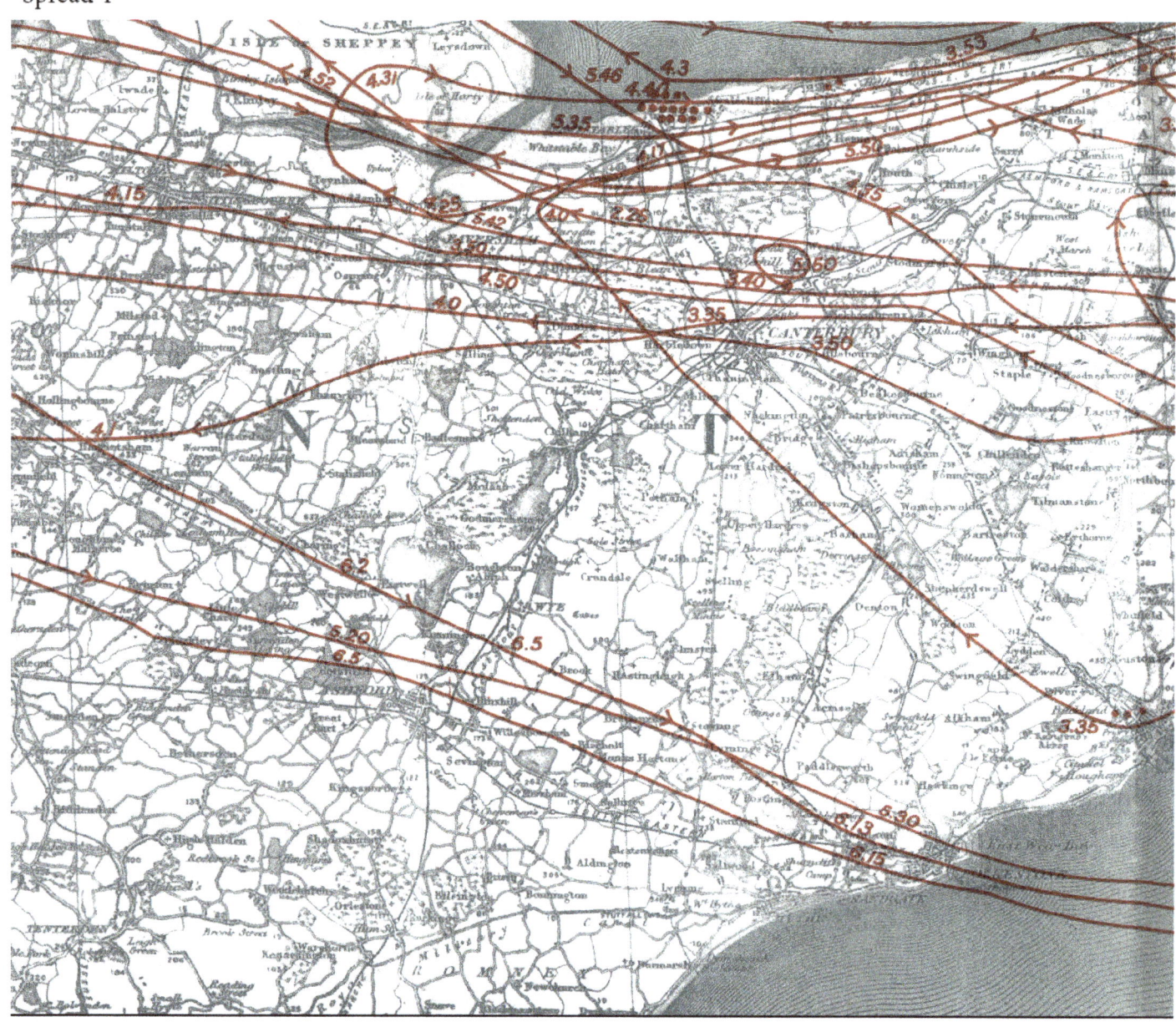

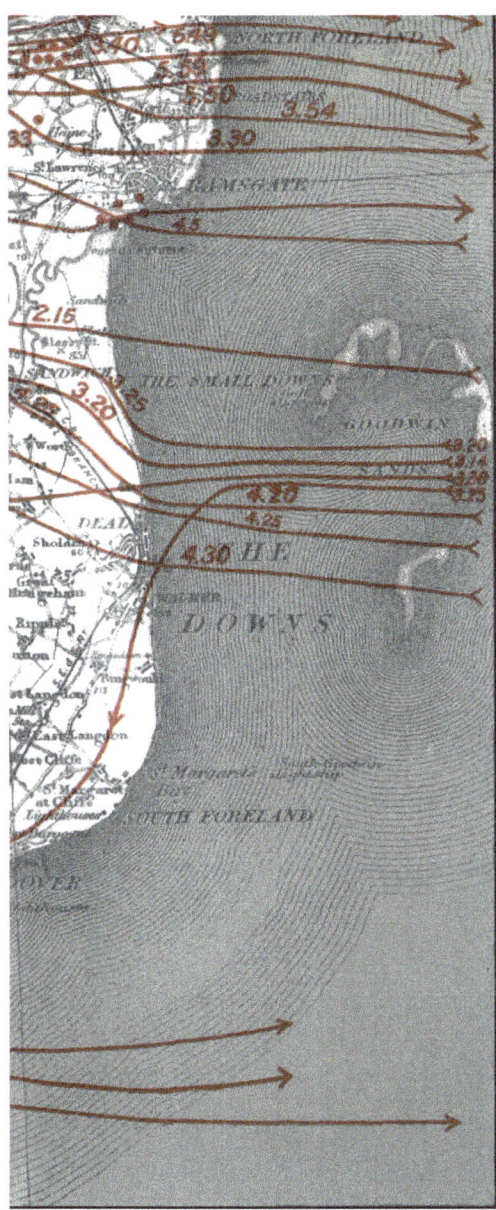

Ordnance Survey, 1935.

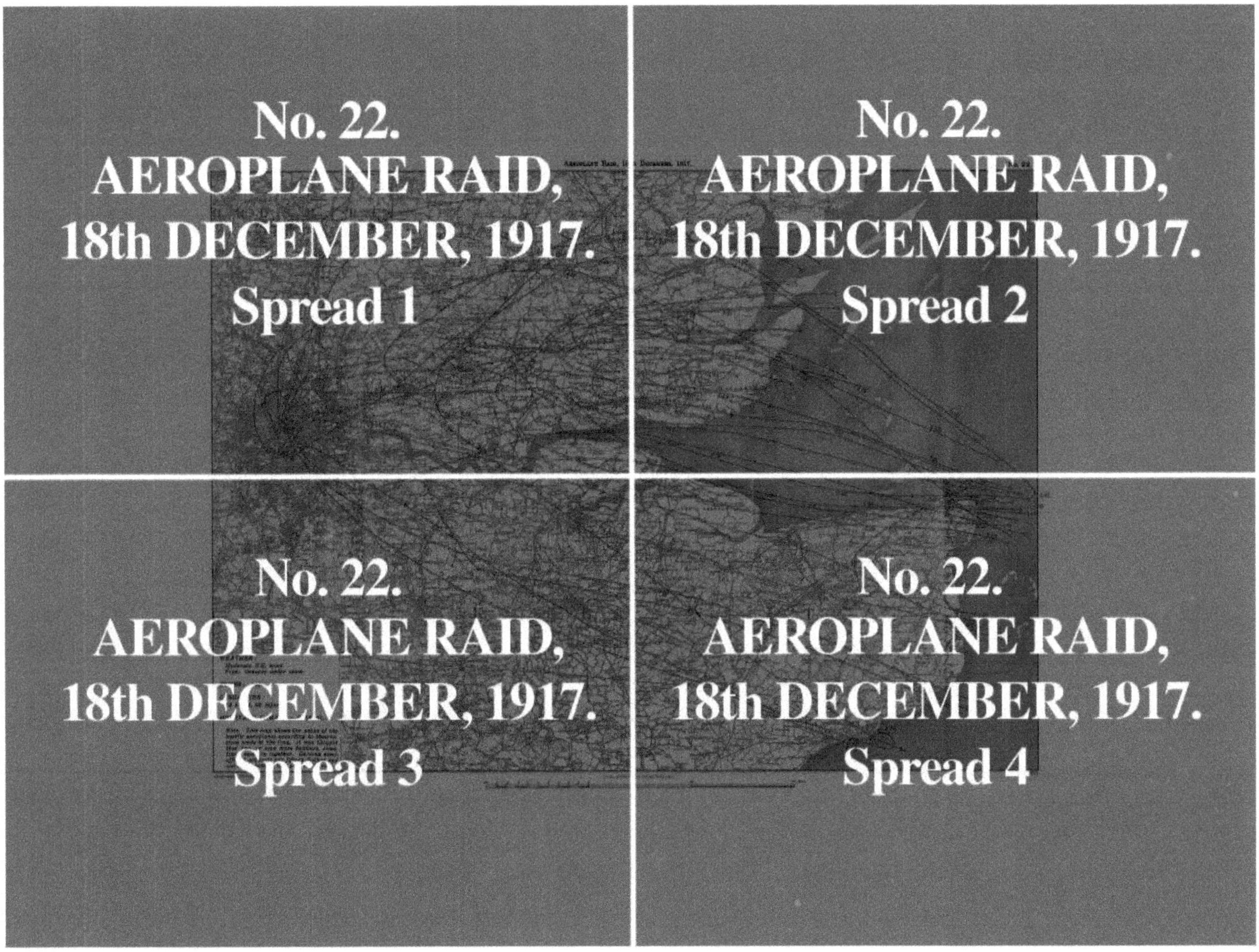

No. 22. AEROPLANE RAID, 18th DECEMBER, 1917.

Spread 1

No. 22. AEROPLANE RAID, 18th DECEMBER, 1917.

Spread 2

No. 22. AEROPLANE RAID, 18th DECEMBER, 1917.

Spread 3

No. 22. AEROPLANE RAID, 18th DECEMBER, 1917.

Spread 4

Spread 1

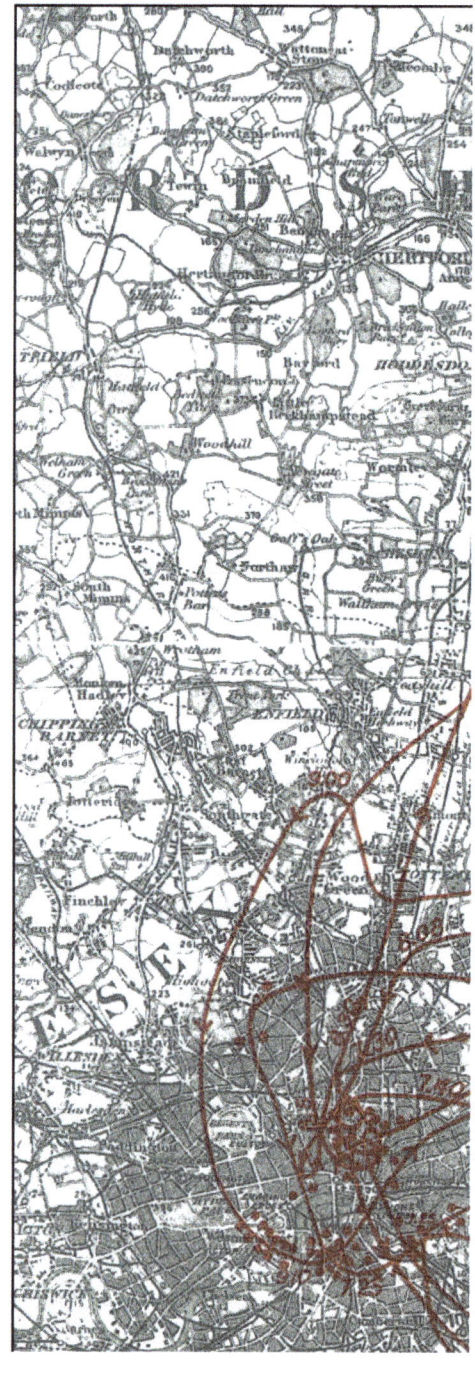

Aeroplane Raid, 18

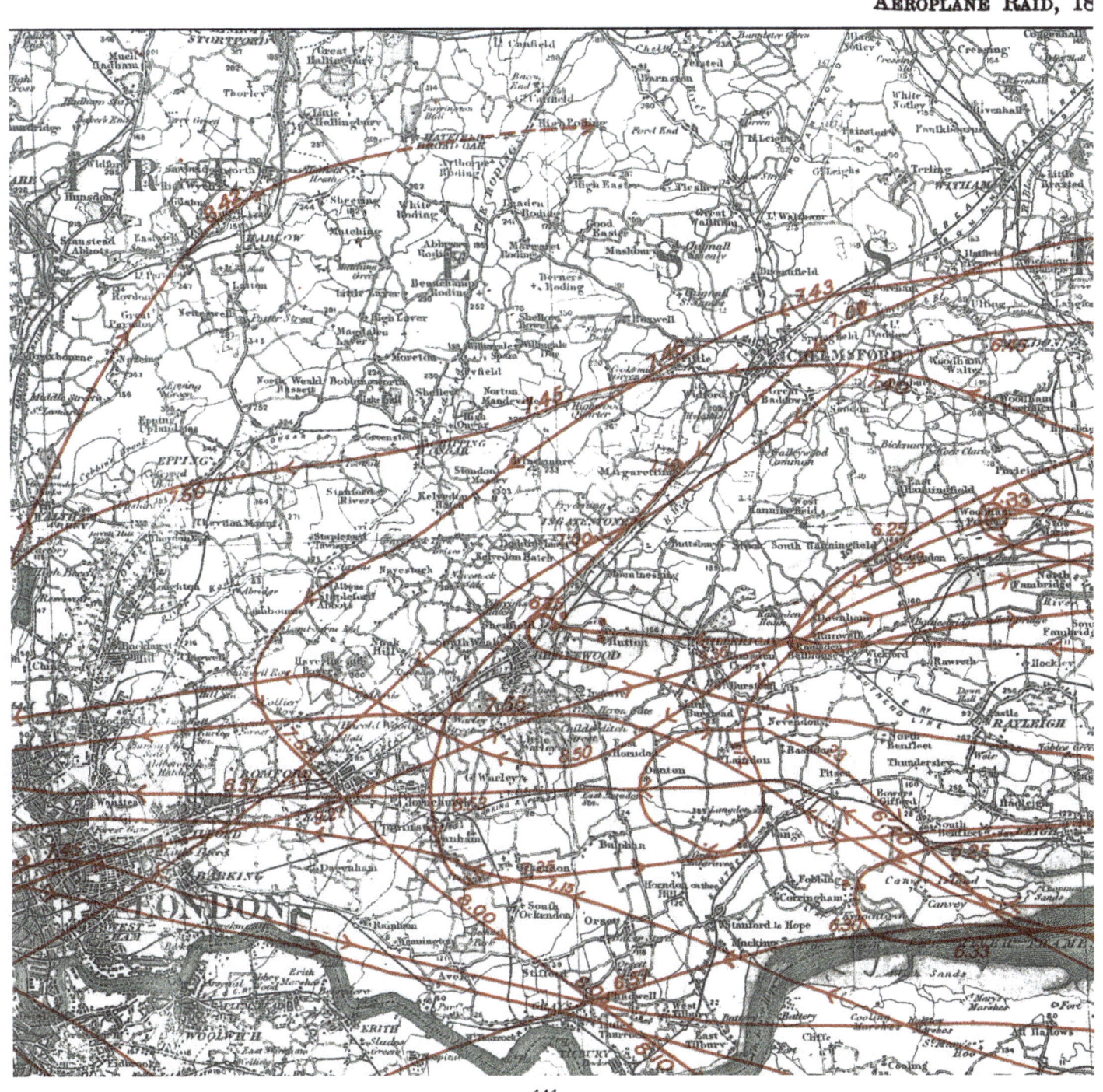

Spread 2

TH DECEMBER, 1917.

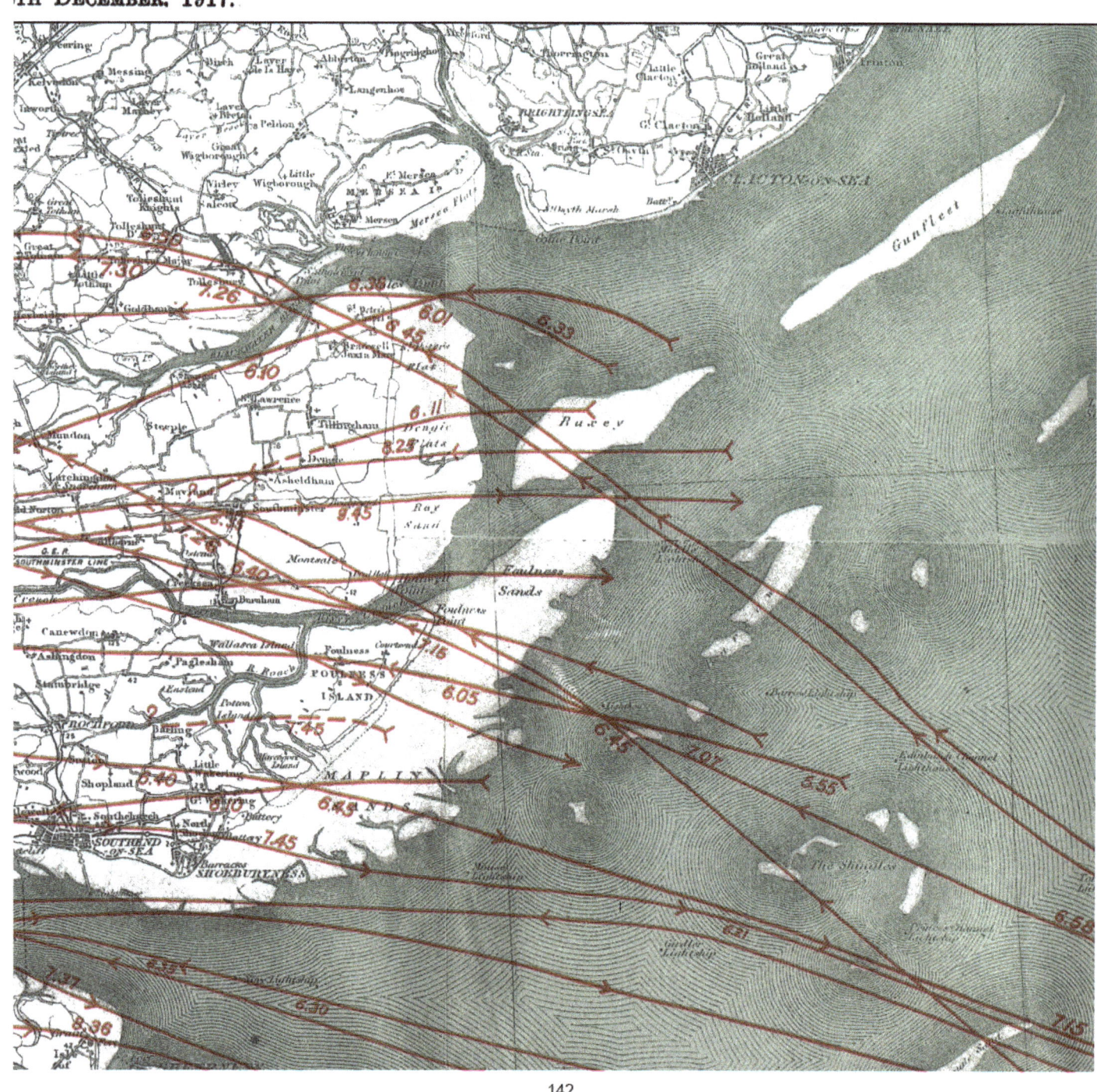

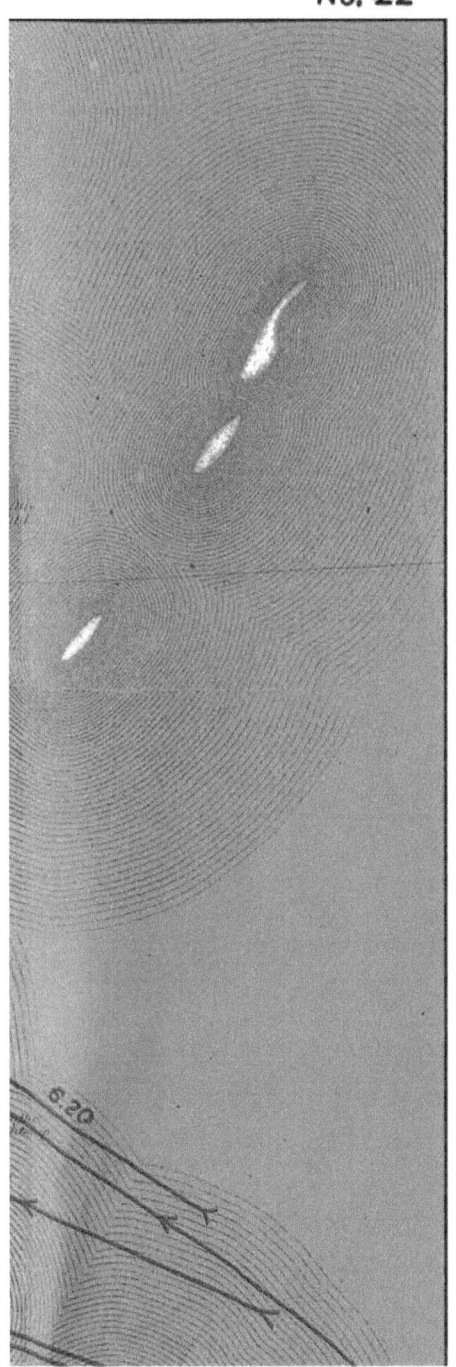

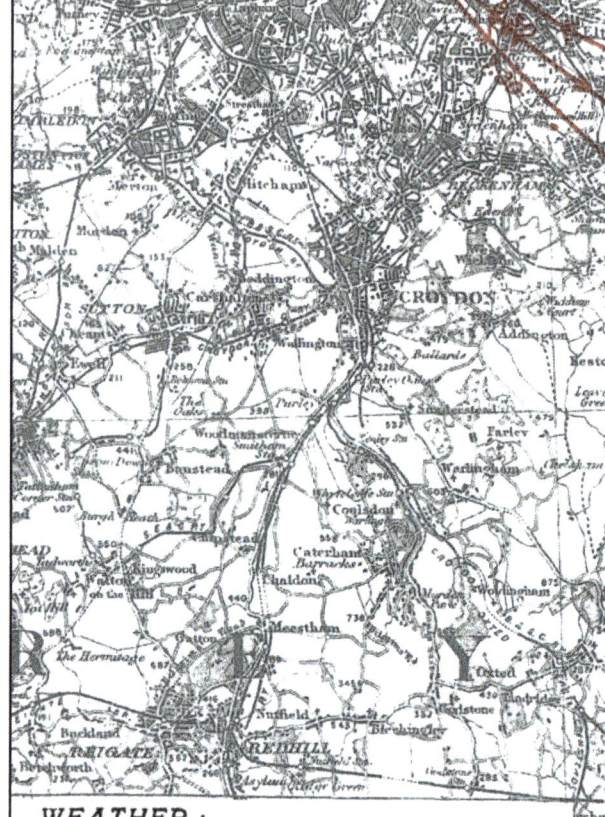

WEATHER :
  Moderate N.E. wind.
  Fine. Country under snow.

BOMBS : 145.

CASUALTIES :
  14 killed, 83 injured.

MONETARY DAMAGE : £238,861.

  Note. This map shows the paths of the hostile aeroplanes according to observations made at the time. It was thought that two, or even more bombers, sometimes came in together. German semi-official accounts say fifteen Gothas and one Giant bomber took part in the raid.

Ordnance Survey, 1935.

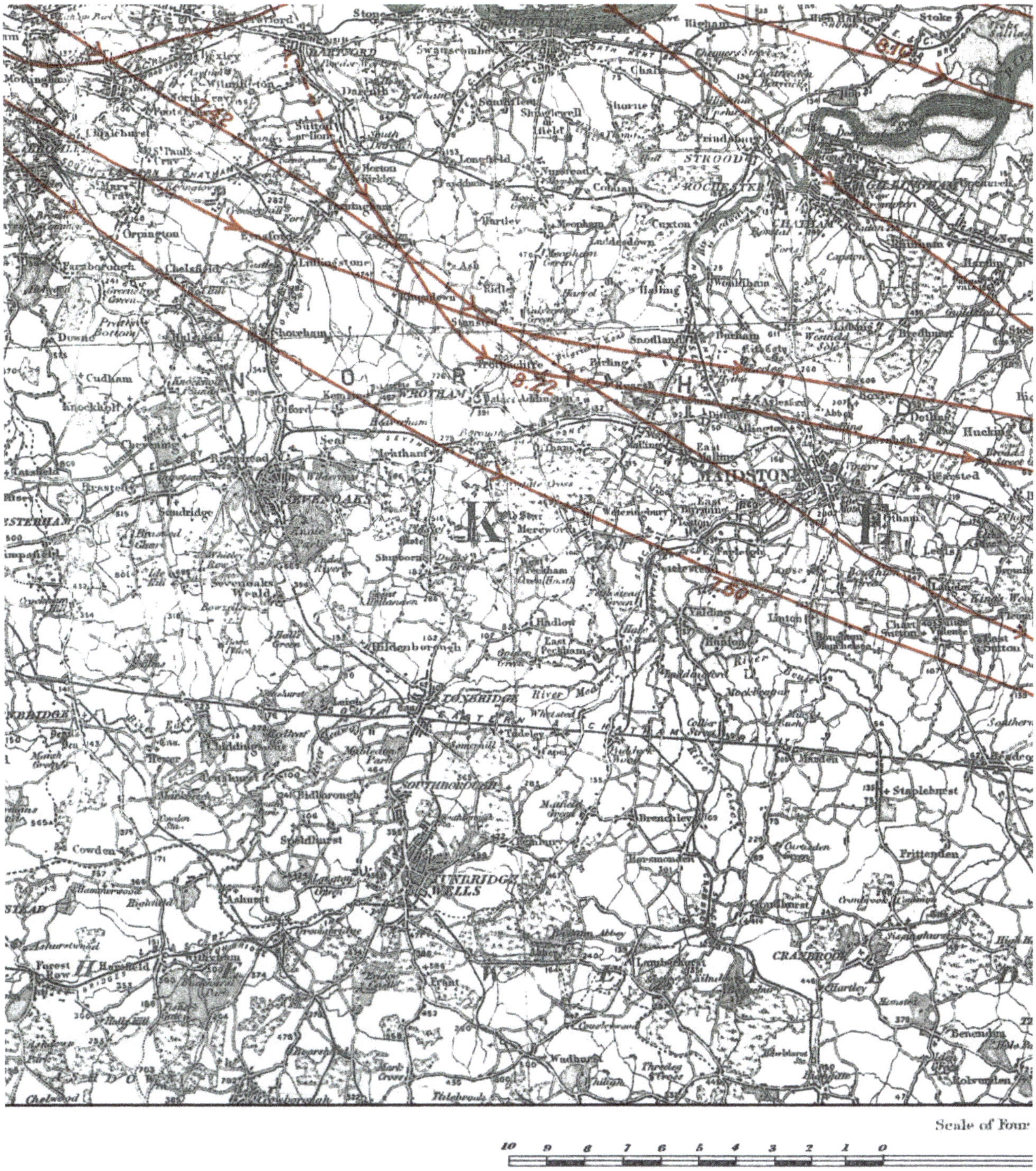

Spread 3

Spread 4

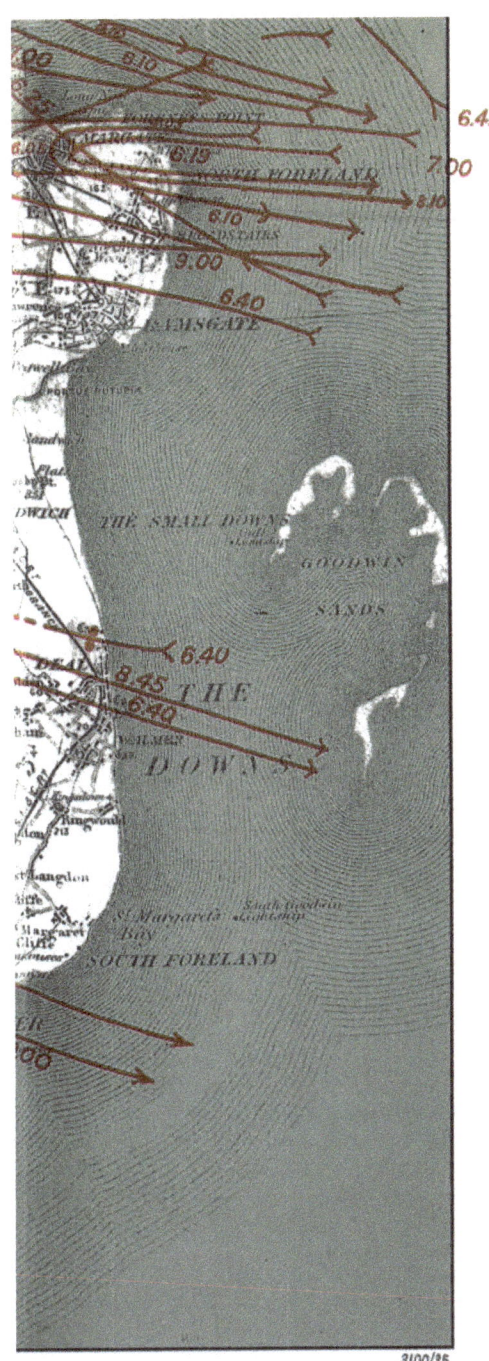

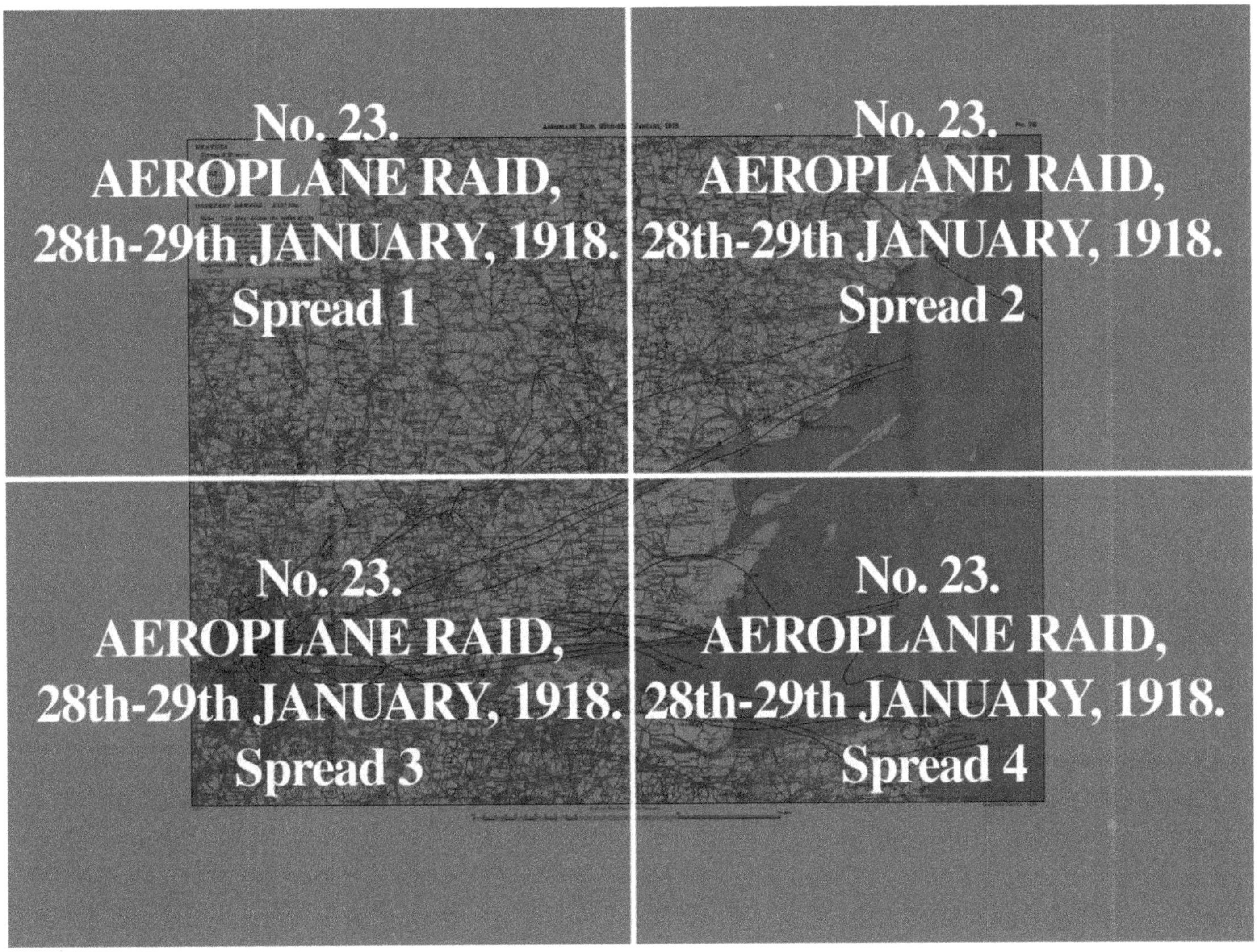

No. 23.
AEROPLANE RAID,
28th-29th JANUARY, 1918.
Spread 1

No. 23.
AEROPLANE RAID,
28th-29th JANUARY, 1918.
Spread 2

No. 23.
AEROPLANE RAID,
28th-29th JANUARY, 1918.
Spread 3

No. 23.
AEROPLANE RAID,
28th-29th JANUARY, 1918.
Spread 4

Spread 1

WEATHER:
 Strong S.W. wind.
 Cloudy sky.

BOMBS: 62.

CASUALTIES:
 67 killed, 166 injured.

MONETARY DAMAGE: £187,350.

Note. This map shows the paths of the hostile aeroplanes according to observations made at the time. It was thought that two, or even more bombers, sometimes came in together. German semi-official accounts say 13 Gothas and 1 Giant bomber set out, but 6 turned back owing to bad visibility. Same source reports London bombed by 3 Gothas and 1 Giant.

Aeroplane Raid, 28th-29th

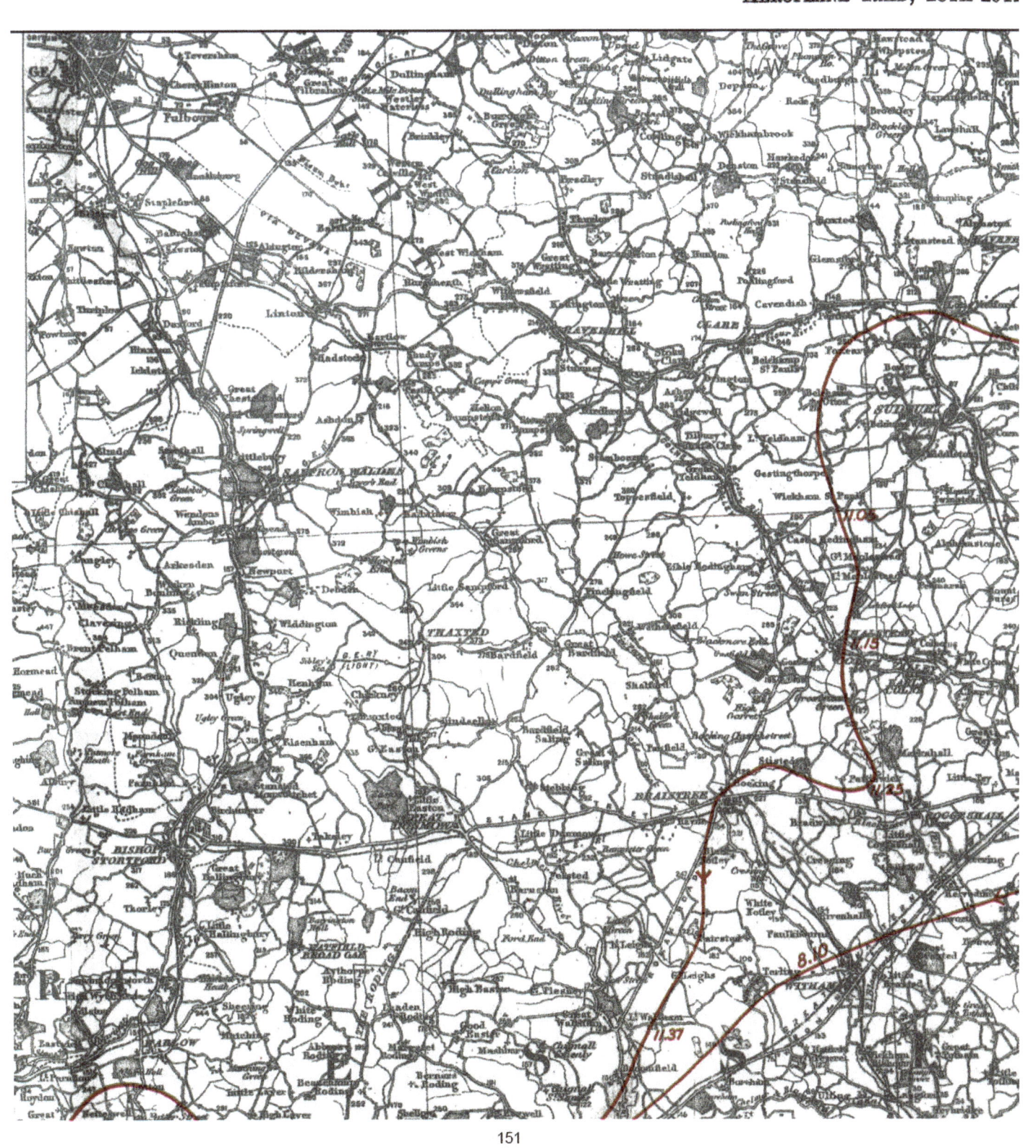

Spread 2

JANUARY, 1918.

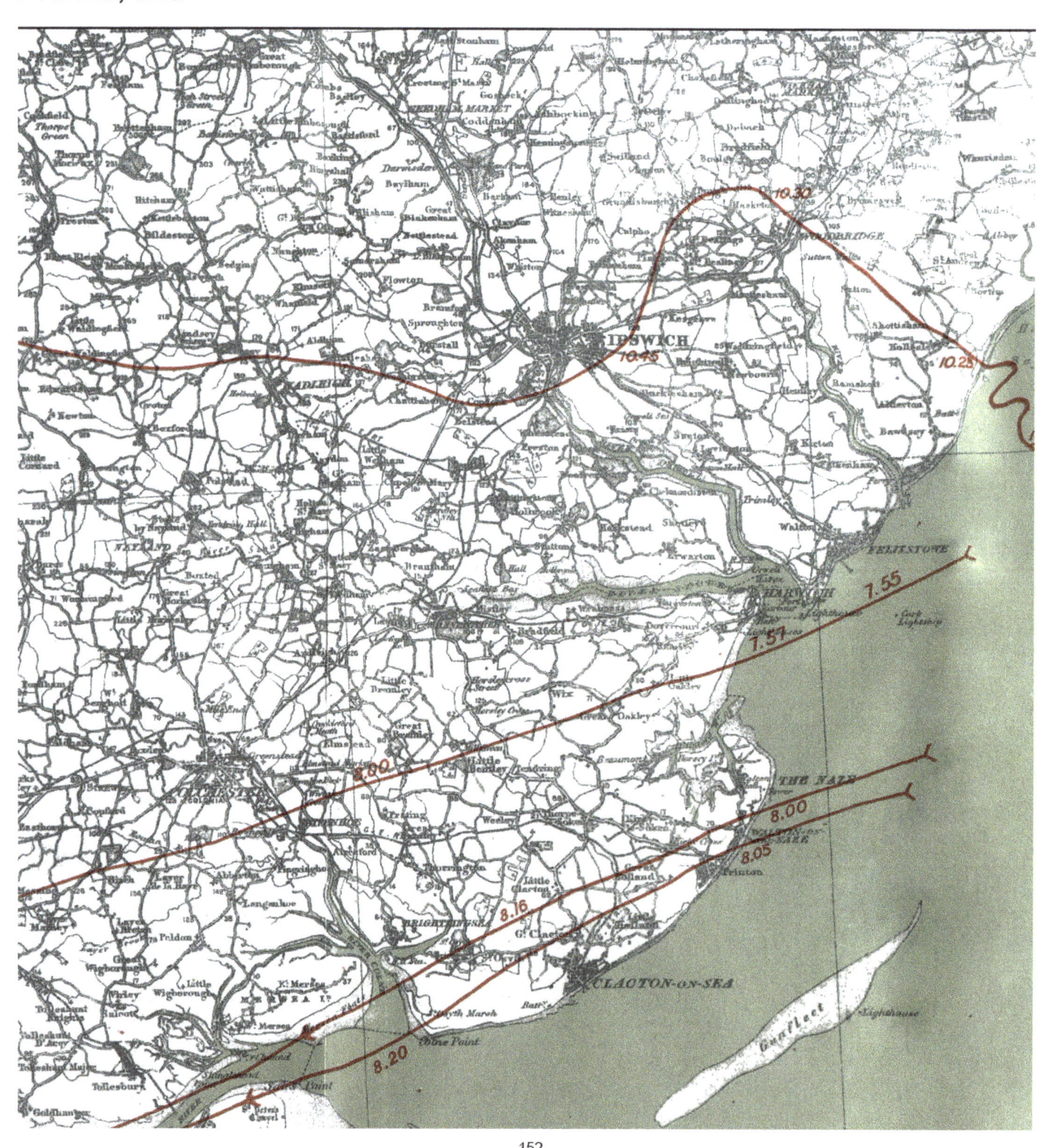

No. 23

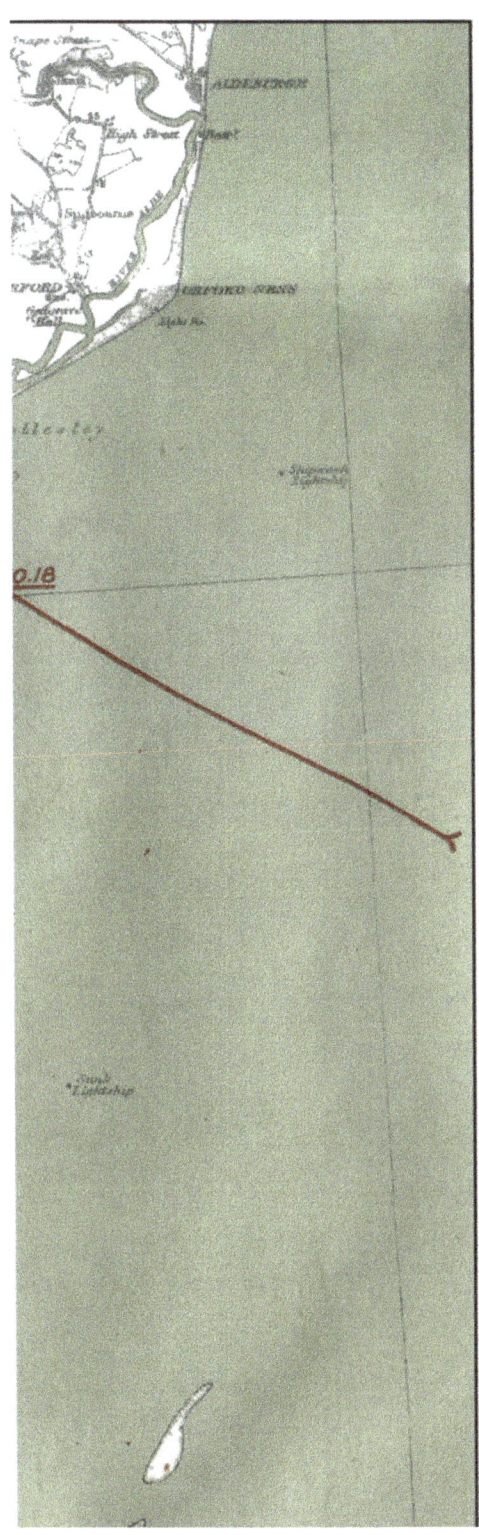

Spread 3

Spread 4

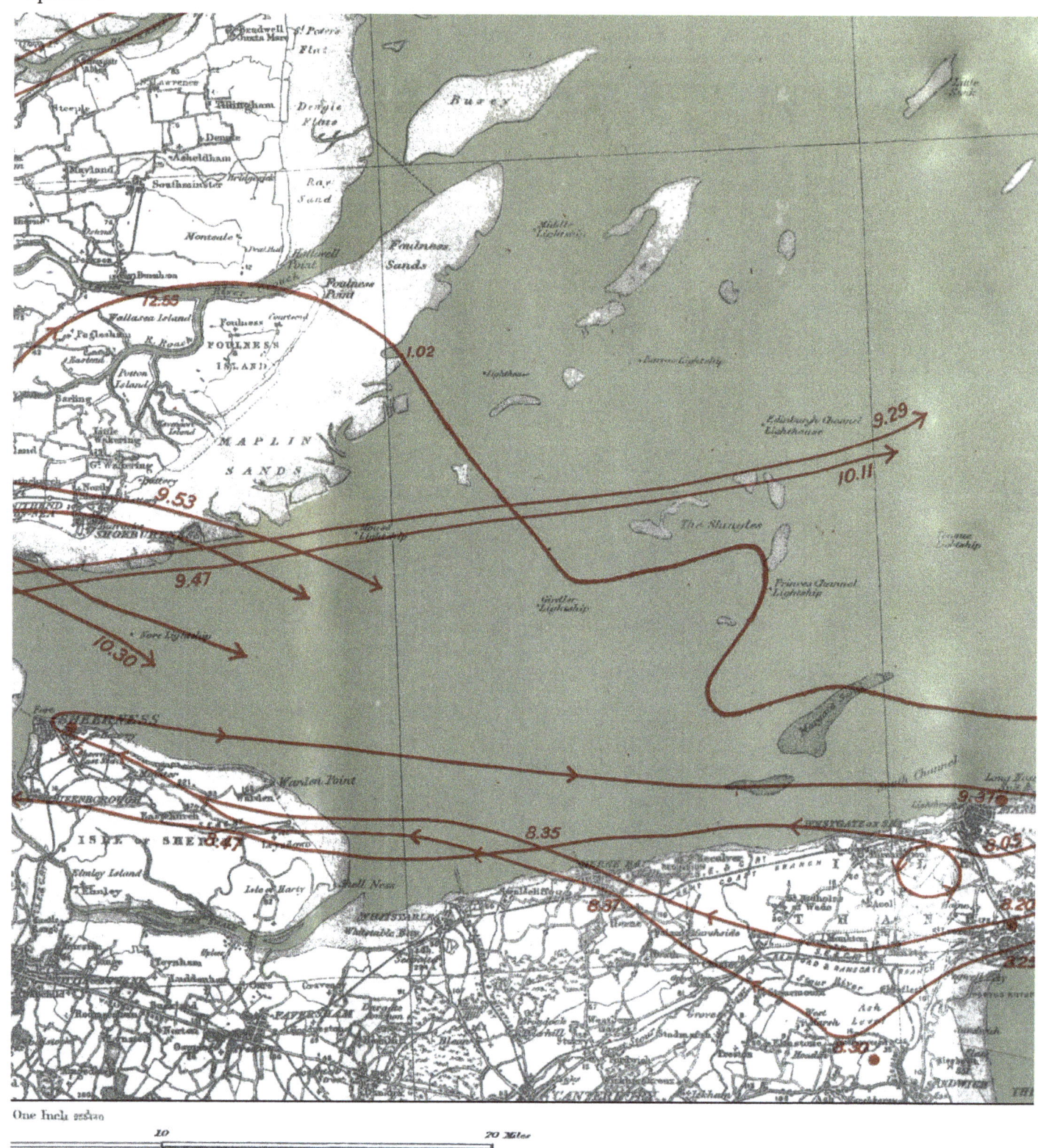

Ordnance Survey, 1935.

No. 24. AEROPLANE RAID, 29th-30th JANUARY, 1918.
Spread 1

No. 24. AEROPLANE RAID, 29th-30th JANUARY, 1918.
Spread 2

No. 24. AEROPLANE RAID, 29th-30th JANUARY, 1918.
Spread 3

No. 24. AEROPLANE RAID, 29th-30th JANUARY, 1918.
Spread 4

Spread 1

Spread 1

Aeroplane Raid,

29th-30th January, 1918.

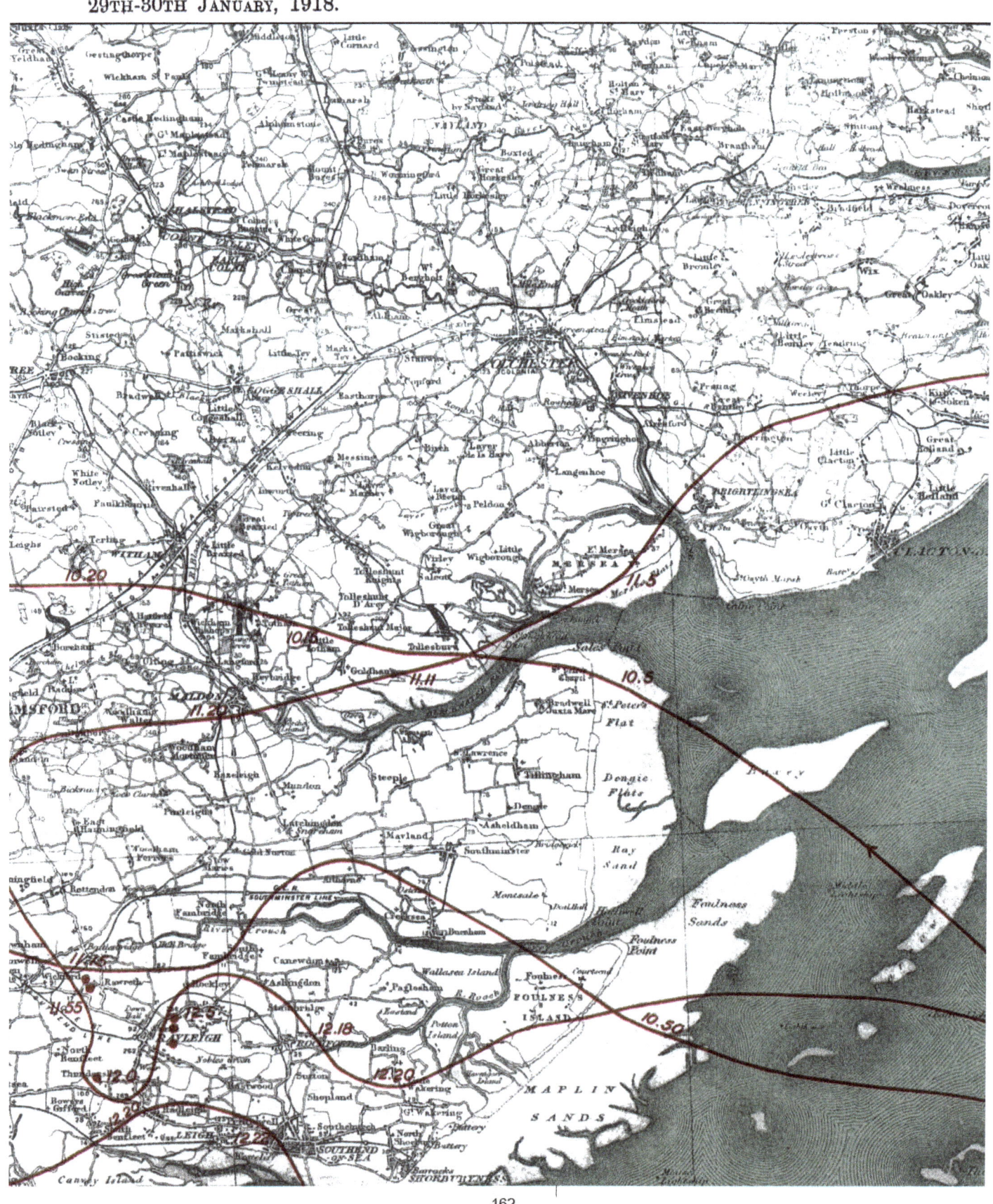

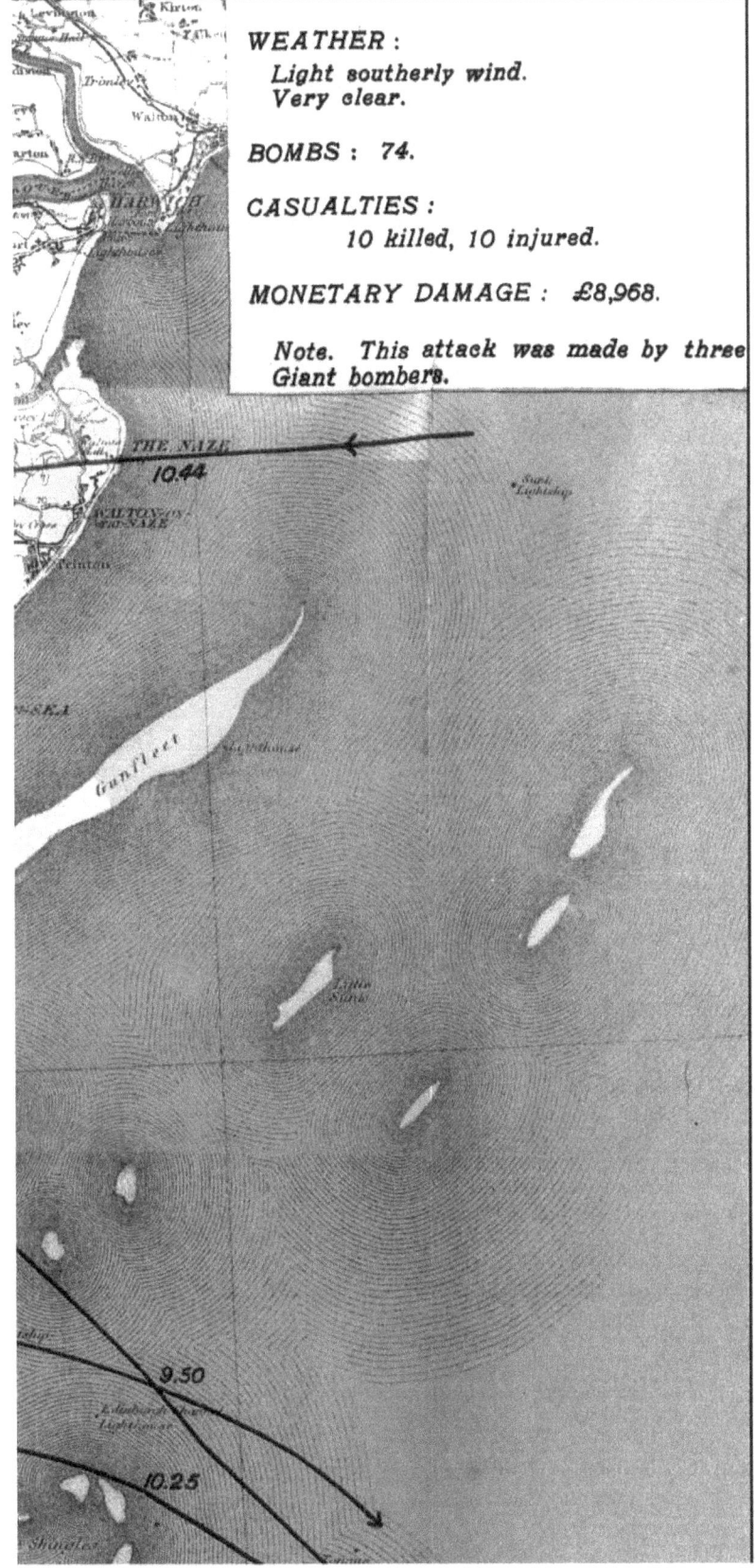

No. 24

WEATHER:
  Light southerly wind.
  Very clear.

BOMBS: 74.

CASUALTIES:
    10 killed, 10 injured.

MONETARY DAMAGE: £8,968.

Note. This attack was made by three Giant bombers.

Spread 3

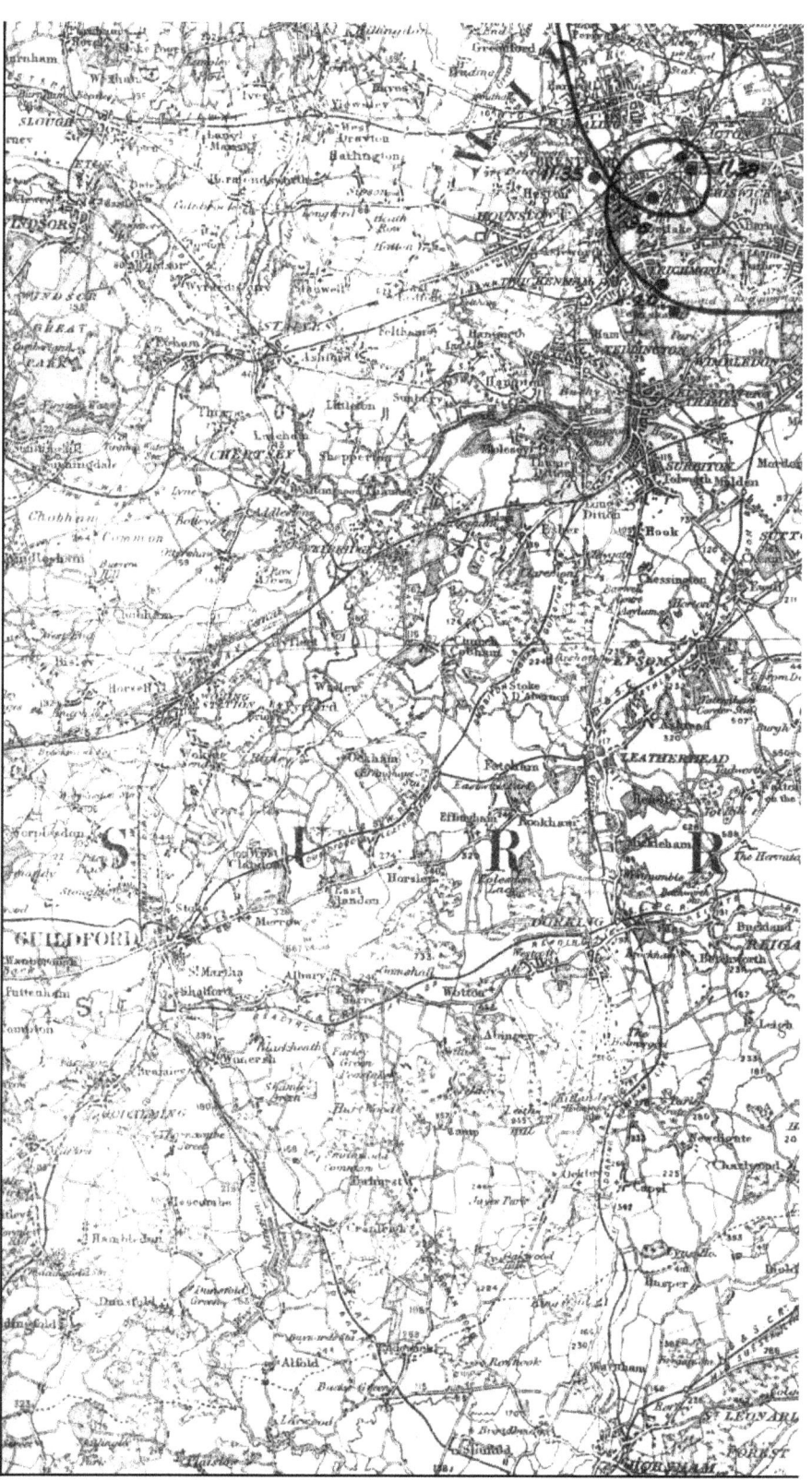

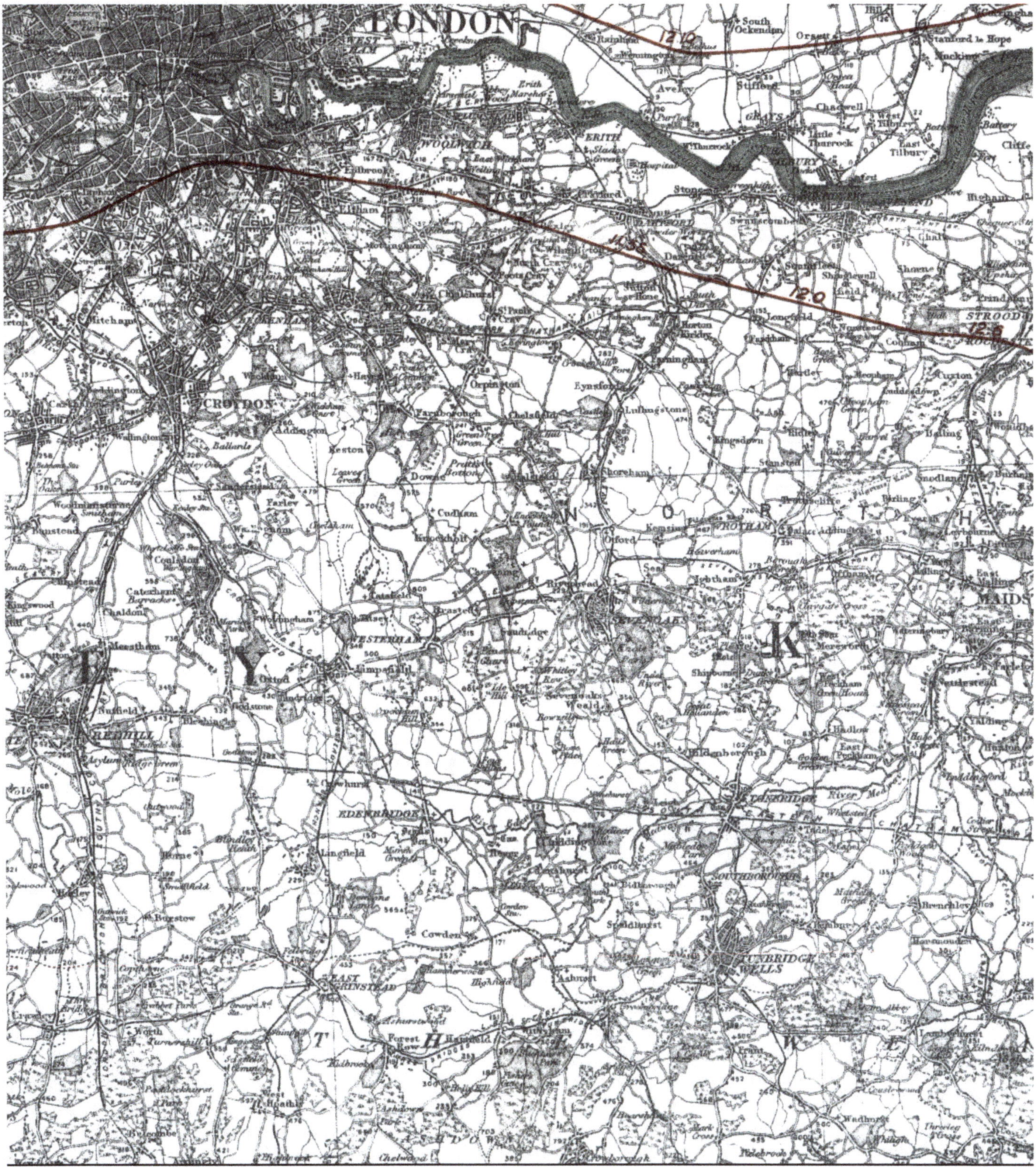

Spread 3

Scale of Four Miles to One

Spread 4

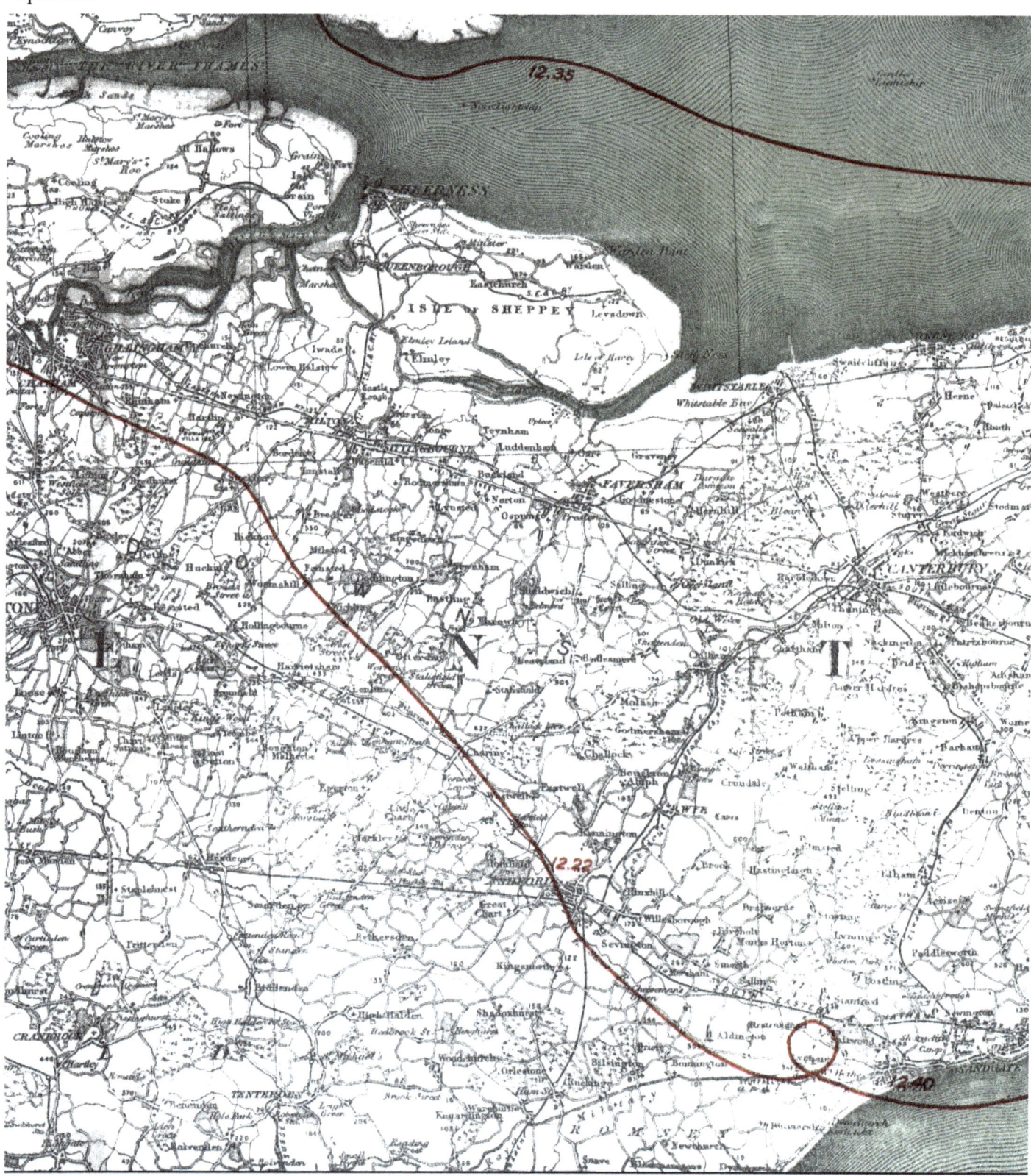

Spread 4

Ordnance Survey, 1935.

Spread 1

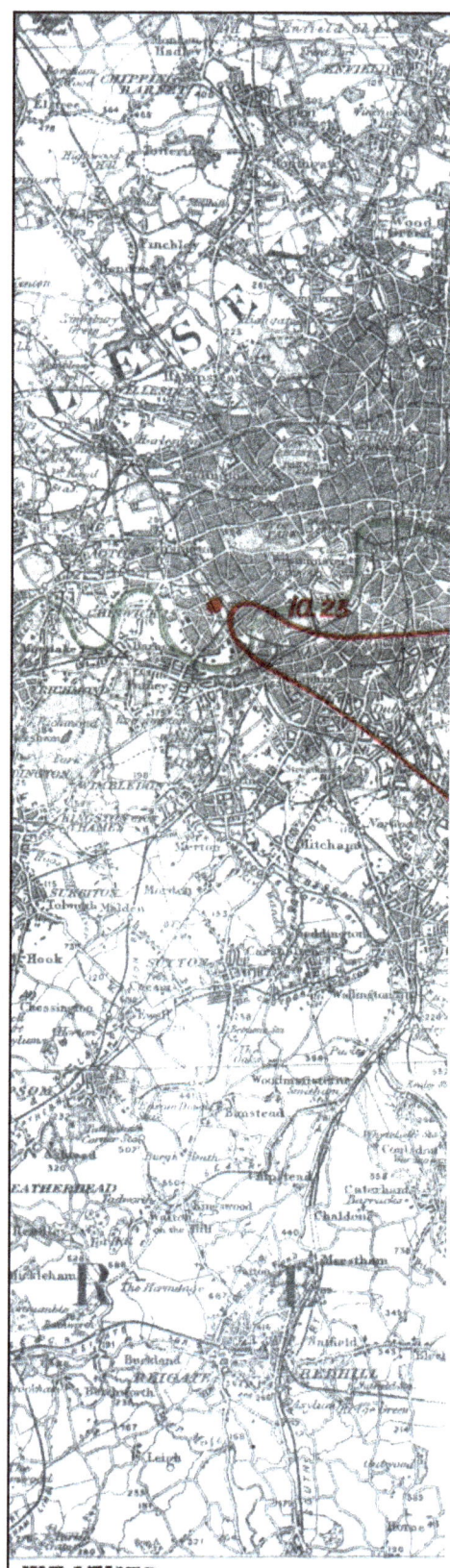

WEATHER :
  Moderate S.E. wind.
  Fine and clear.

BOMBS : 29.

CASUALTIES :
       12 killed, 6 injured.

MONETARY DAMAGE : £19,264.

  Note. Five Giant bombers took but only three came overland.

Aeroplane Raid,

Spread 2
16TH FEBRUARY, 1918.

No. 25

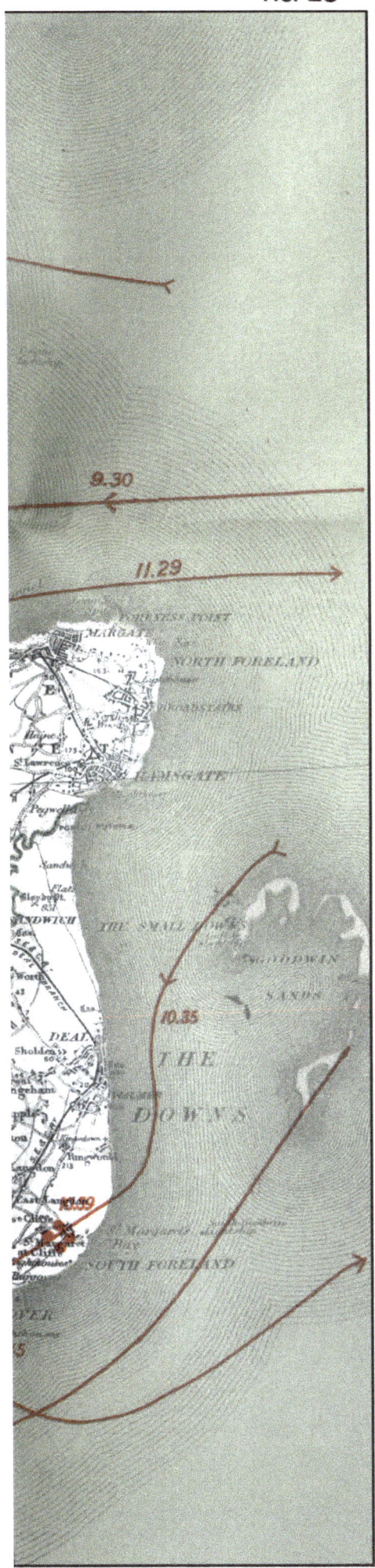

Ordnance Survey, 1955.

No. 26. AEROPLANE RAID, 17th-18th FEBRUARY, 1918.
Spread 1

No. 26. AEROPLANE RAID, 17th-18th FEBRUARY, 1918.
Spread 2

No. 26. AEROPLANE RAID, 17th-18th FEBRUARY, 1918.
Spread 3

No. 26. AEROPLANE RAID, 17th-18th FEBRUARY, 1918.
Spread 4

Spread 1

17TH-18TH FEBRUARY, 1918

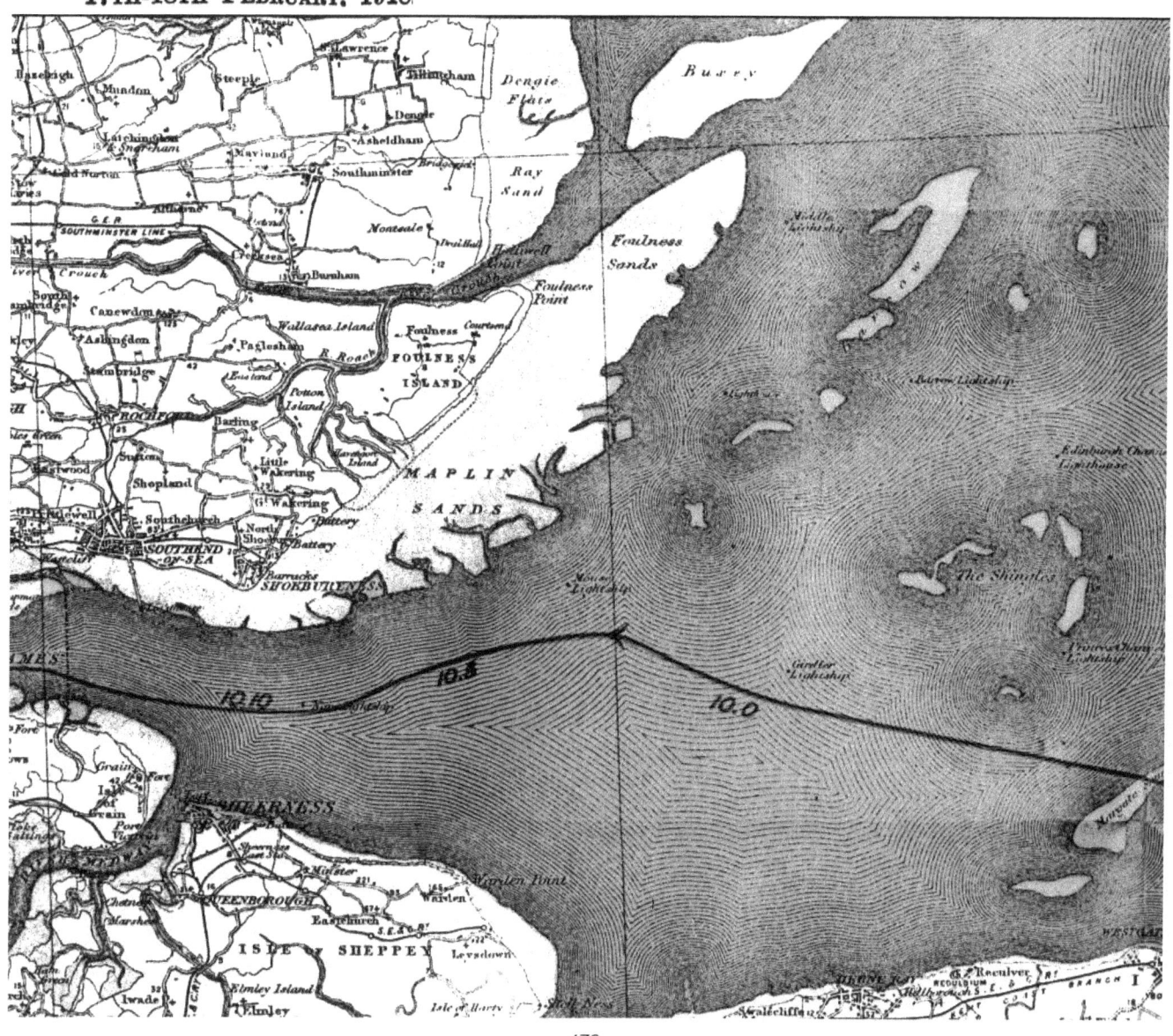

No. 26

WEATHER:
Moderate S.E. Wind. Fine, some clouds, slight fog.

BOMBS: 19.

CASUALTIES:
21 killed, 32 injured.

MONETARY DAMAGE: £38,922.

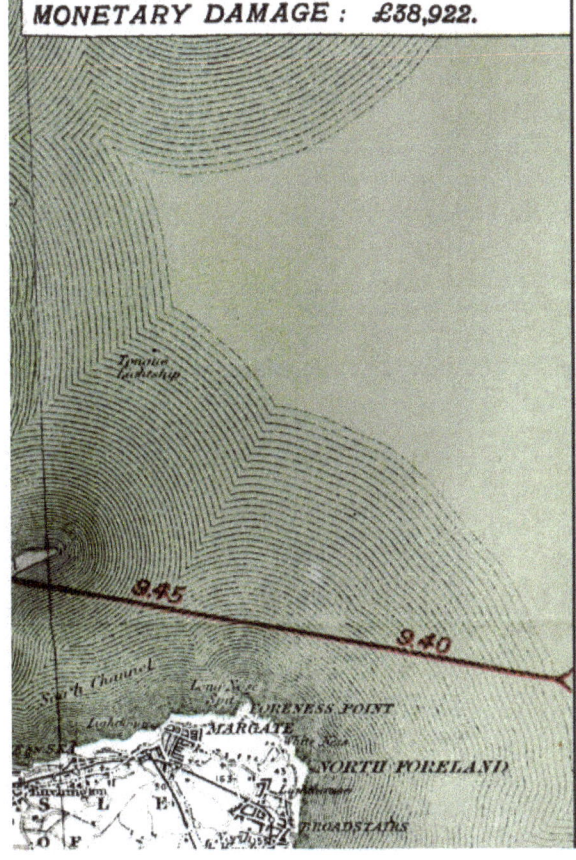

Spread 3

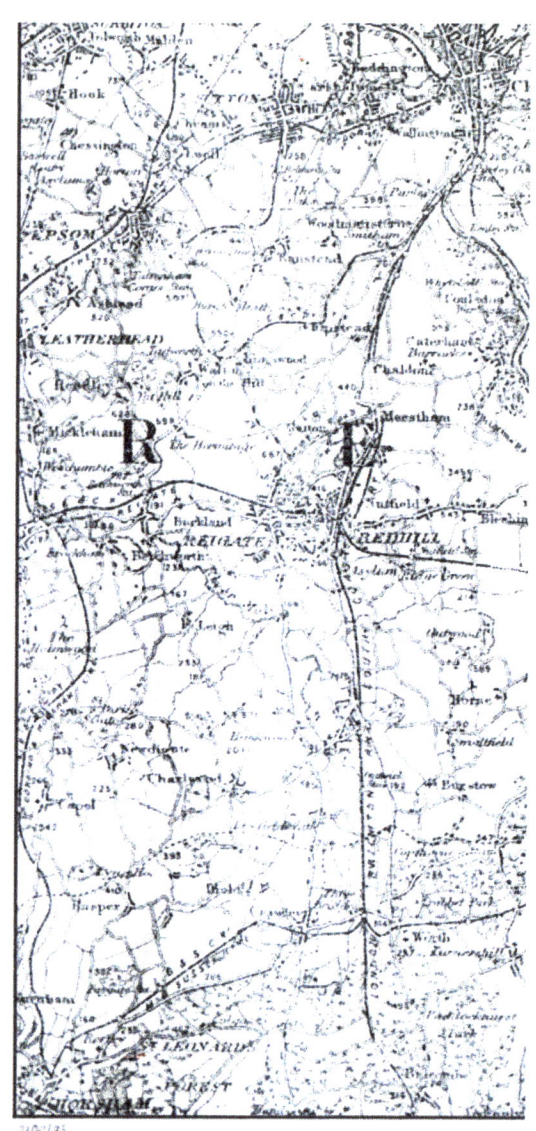

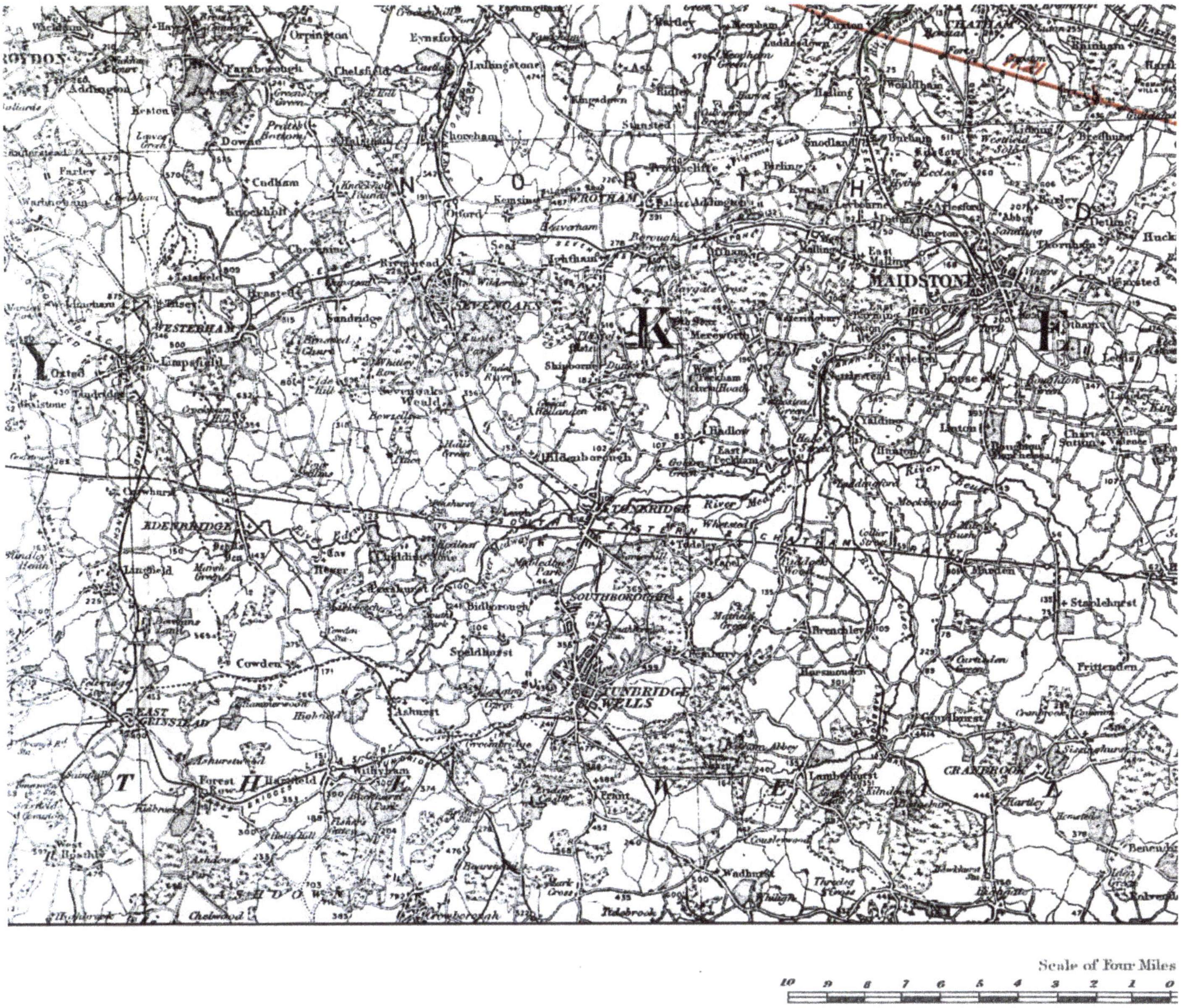
Orpington
Farnborough
Chelsfield
Lullingstone
Eynsford
Westerham
Sevenoaks
Edenbridge
Cowden
Tonbridge
Southborough
Tunbridge Wells
Maidstone
Staplehurst
Cranbrook
Frittenden
Scale of Four Miles
10 9 8 7 6 5 4 3 2 1 0

Spread 4

Ordnance Survey, 1935

No. 27.
AEROPLANE RAID
7th-8th MARCH, 1918.
Spread 1

No. 27.
AEROPLANE RAID
7th-8th MARCH, 1918.
Spread 2

No. 27.
AEROPLANE RAID
7th-8th MARCH, 1918.
Spread 3

No. 27.
AEROPLANE RAID
7th-8th MARCH, 1918.
Spread 4

Spread 1

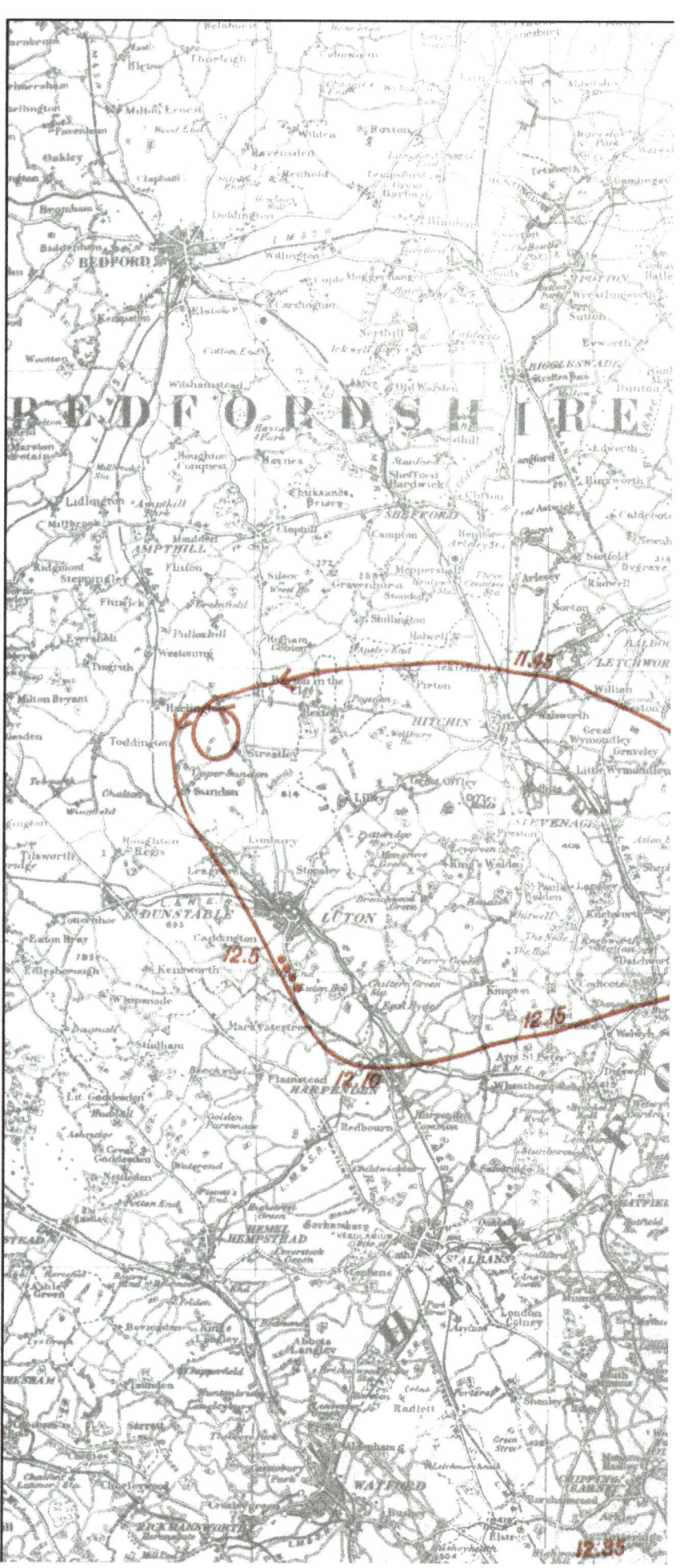

Spread 1

Aeroplane Raid,

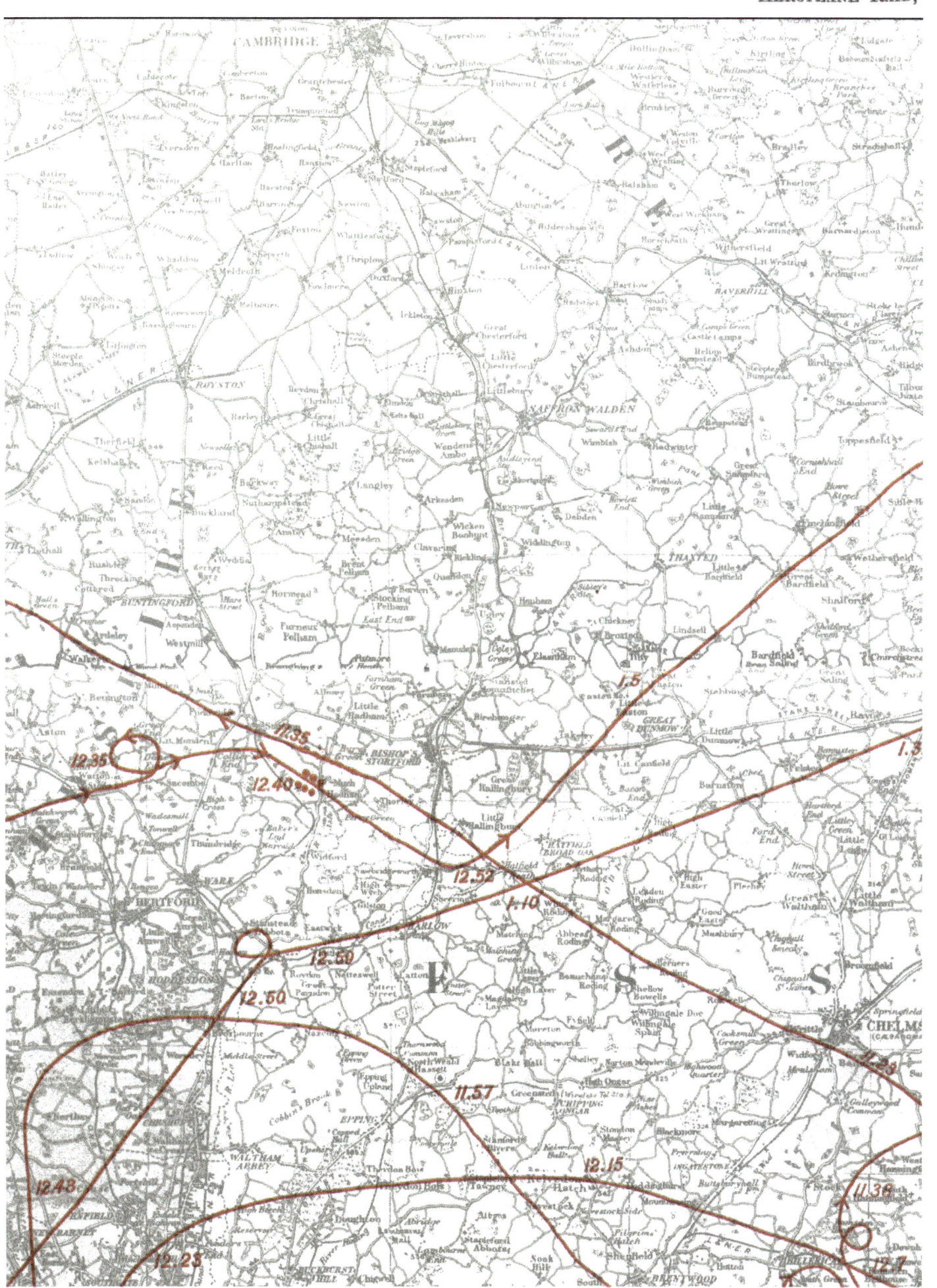

Spread 2

7th-8th March, 1918.

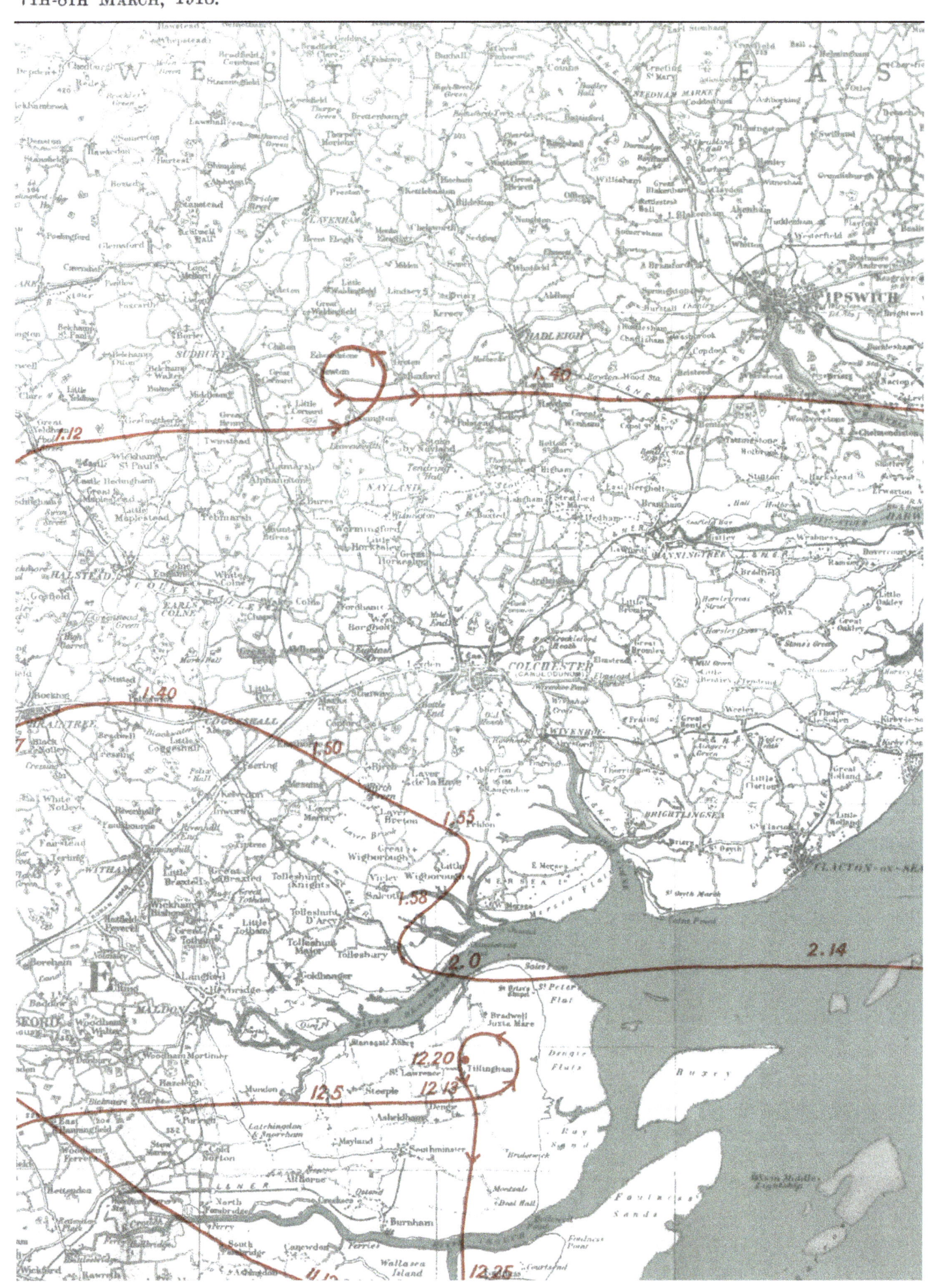

No. 27

WEATHER
 Moderate E.N.E. wind.
 Fine and clear.

BOMBS: 35.

CASUALTIES:
 23 killed, 39 injured.

MONETARY DAMAGE: £42,655.

Note. This raid was made by five Giant bombers.

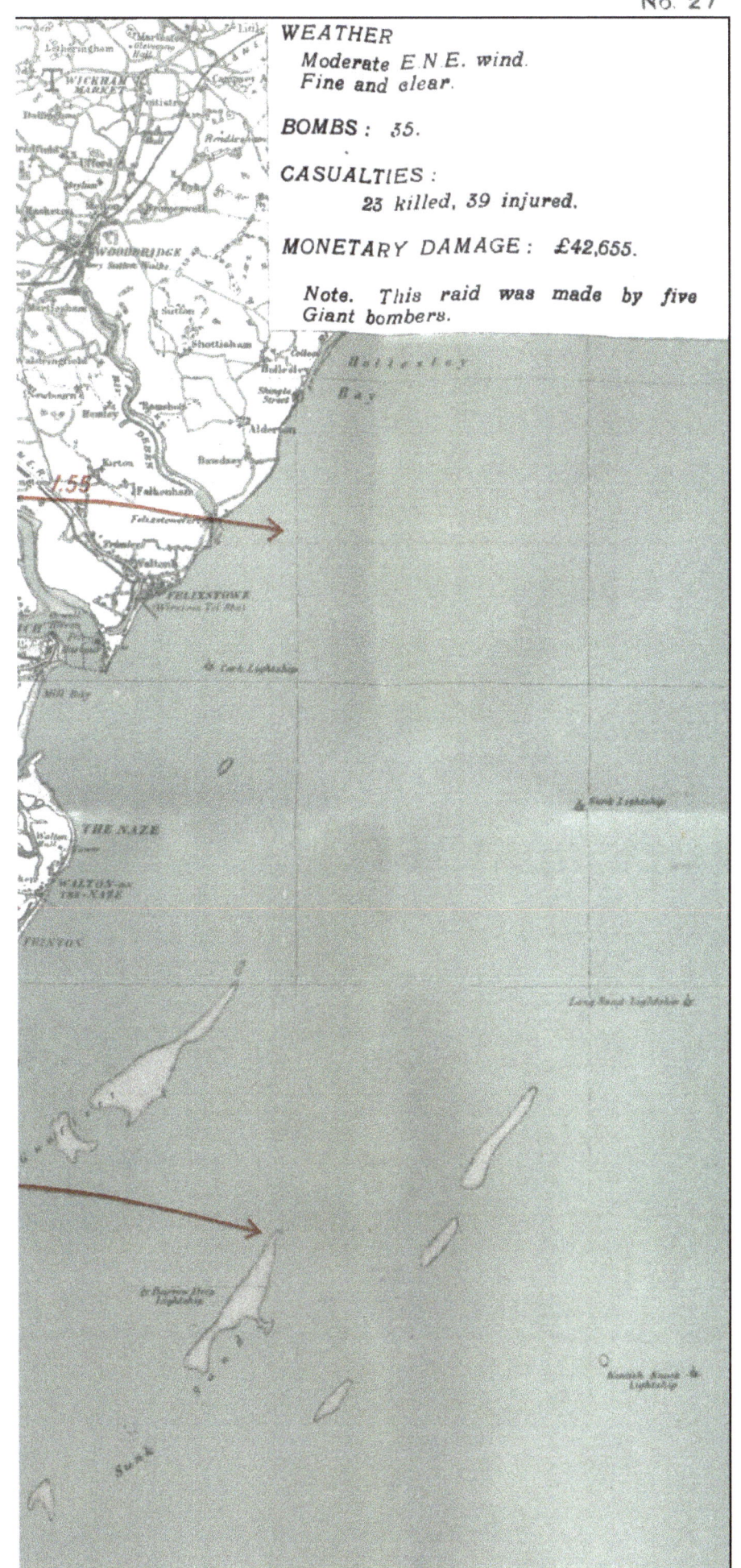

Spread 3

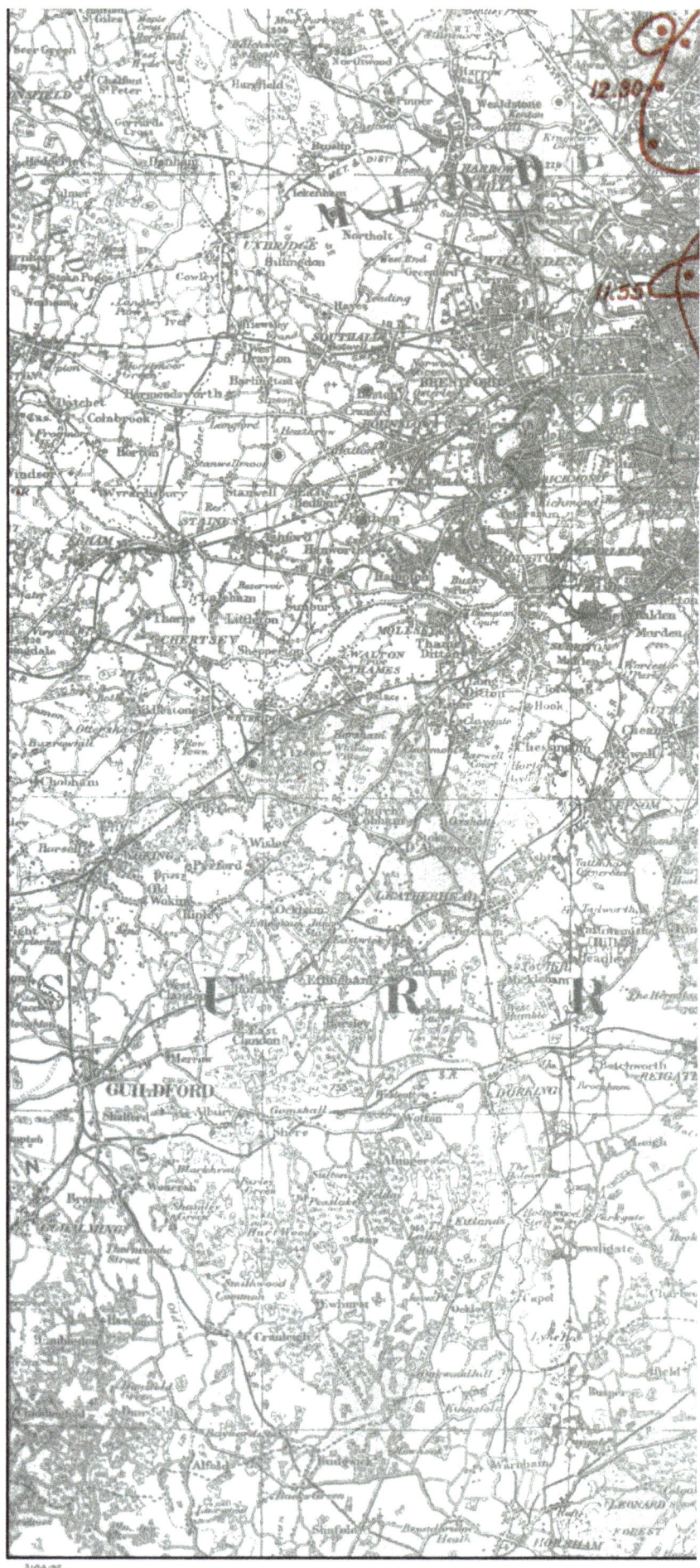

Spread 3

Spread 4

Spread 4

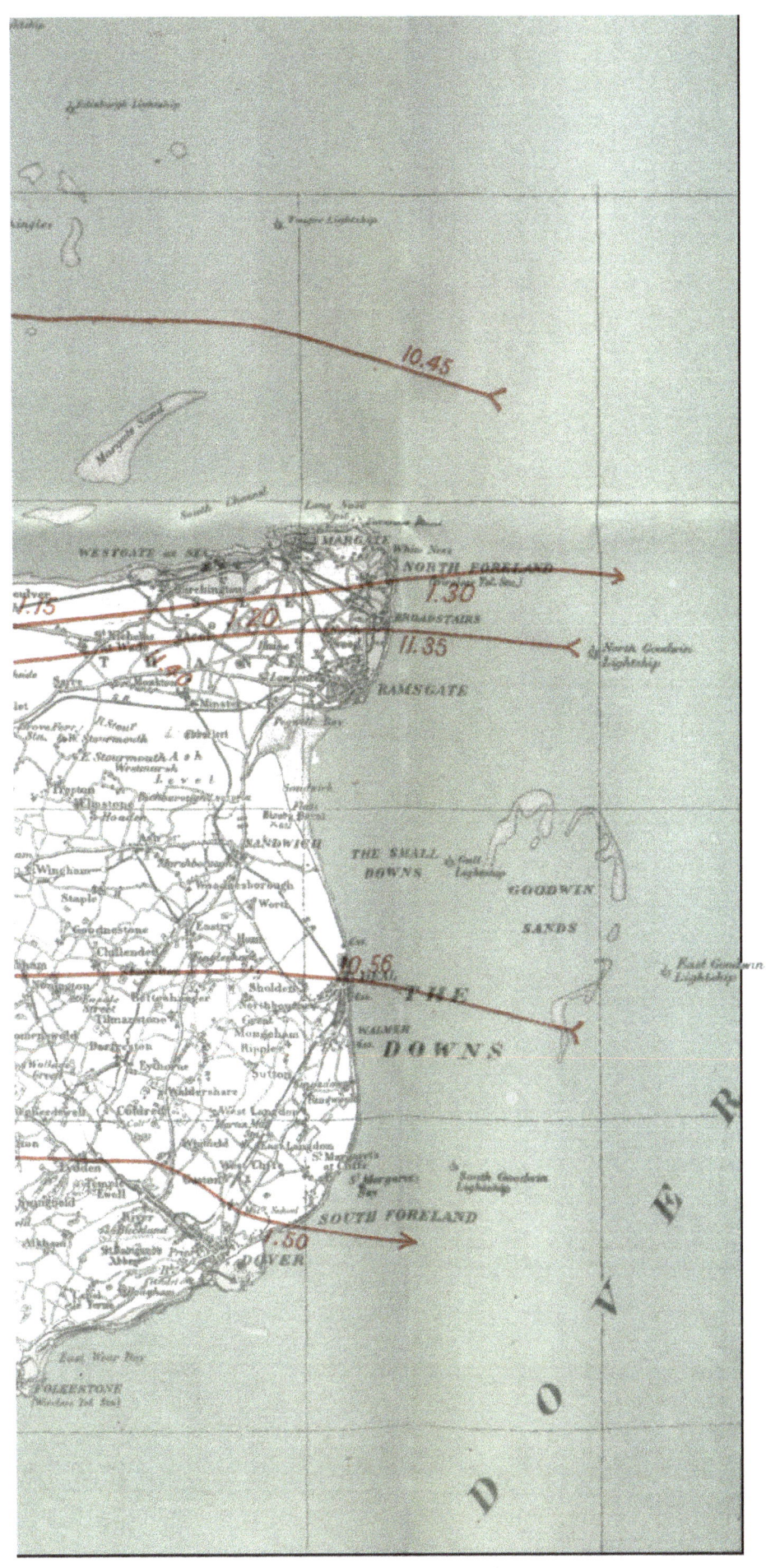

Ordnance Survey, 1935.

No. 28. AEROPLANE RAID, 19th-20th MAY, 1918. Spread 1

No. 28. AEROPLANE RAID, 19th-20th MAY, 1918. Spread 2

No. 28. AEROPLANE RAID, 19th-20th MAY, 1918. Spread 3

No. 28. AEROPLANE RAID, 19th-20th MAY, 1918. Spread 4

Spread 1

WEATHER:
Light E.N.E. wind.
Fine and clear.

BOMBS: 157.

CASUALTIES:
49 killed, 177 injured.

MONETARY DAMAGE: £177,317.

Note. This map shows the paths of the hostile aeroplanes according to observations made at the time. It was thought that two, or even more bombers, sometimes came in together. It appeared that thirty-four bombers crossed the coast and that thirteen attacked London. German semi-official accounts say thirty-eight Gothas, three Giants, and two smaller type bombers took part and that nineteen reached London.

AEROPLANE RAID,

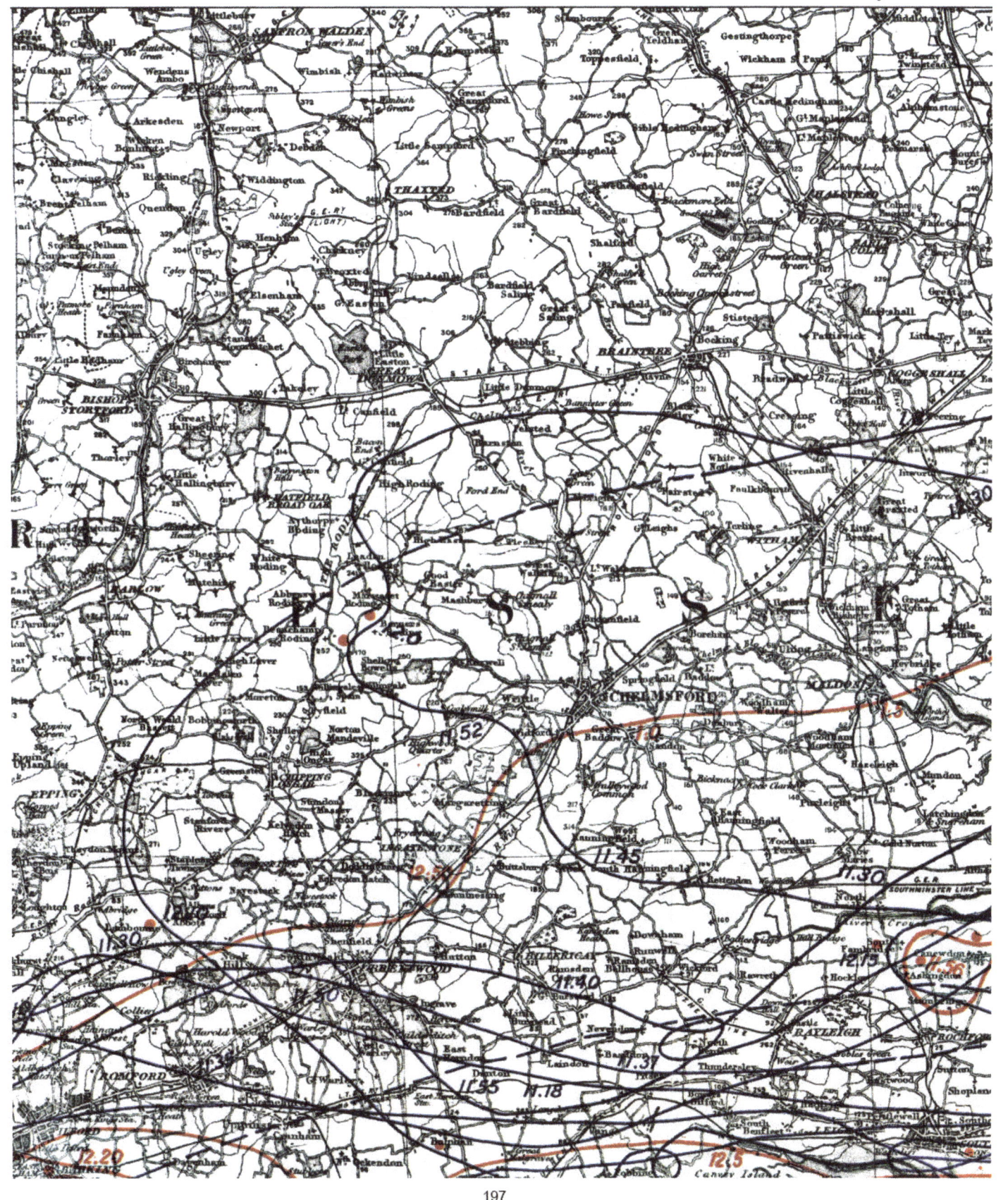

19th-20th May, 1918.

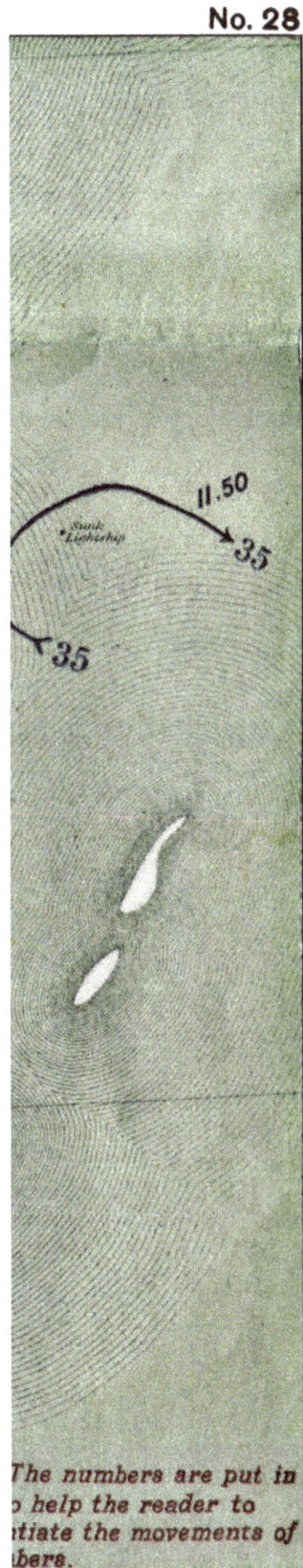

Spread 3

Spread 3

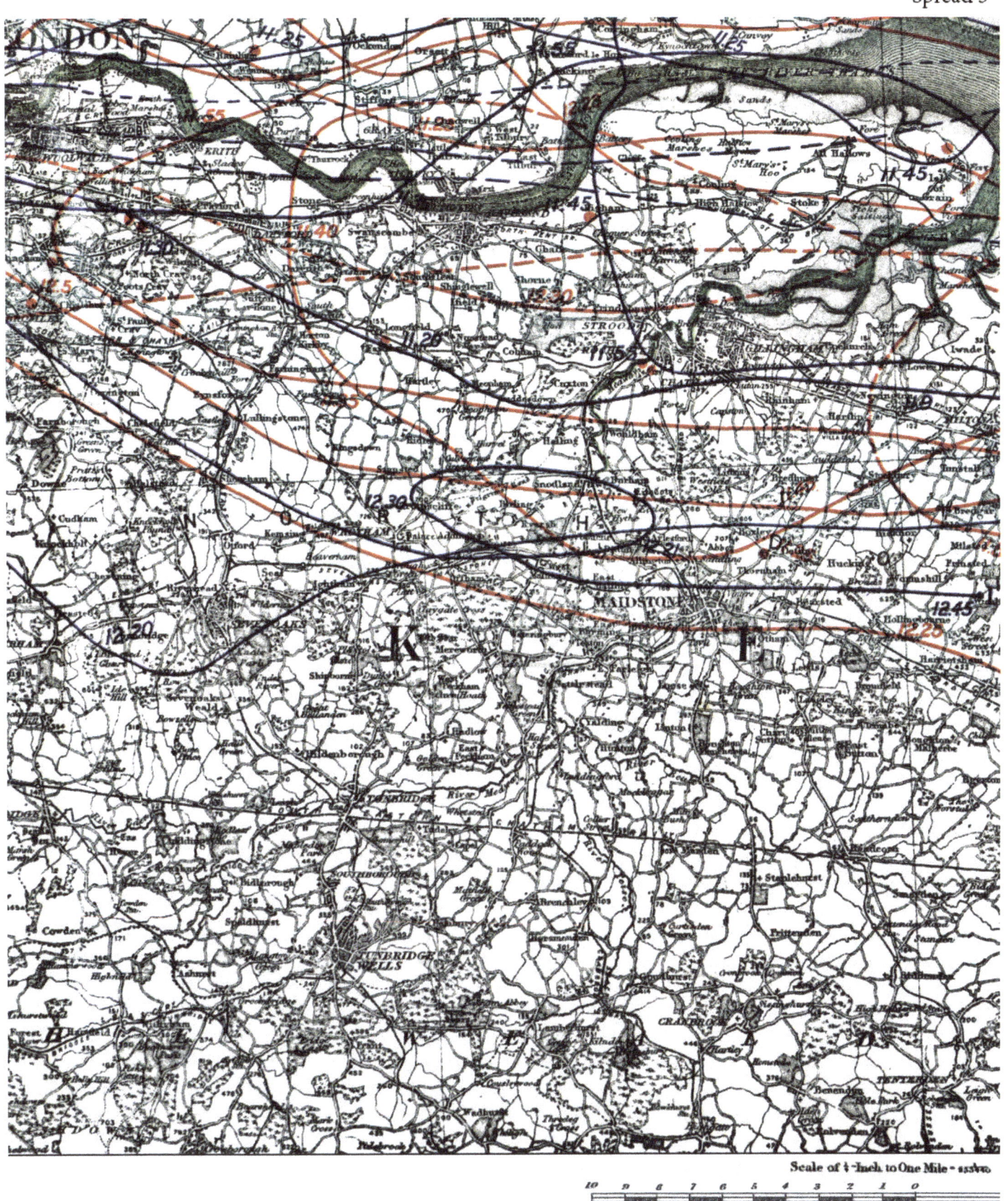

Spread 4

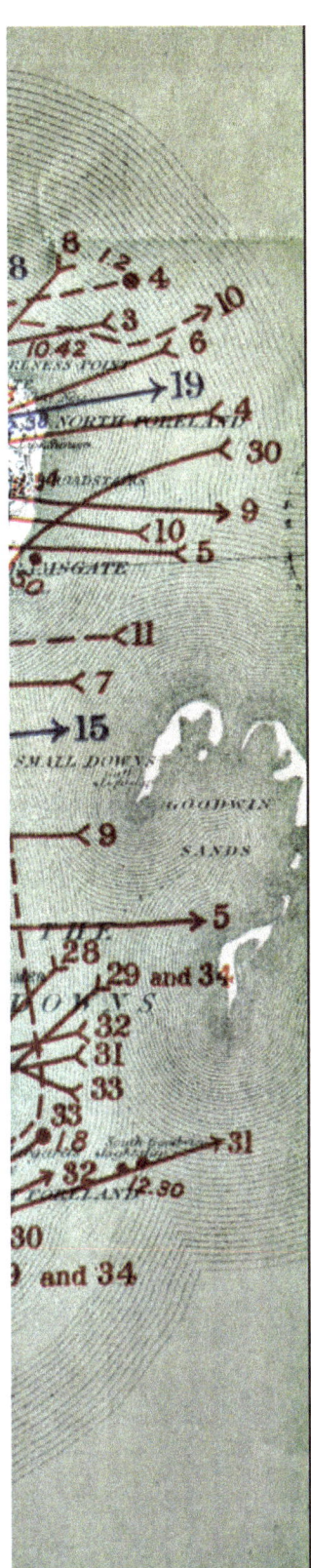

Ordnance Survey, 1935.

www.ingramcontent.com/pod-product-compliance
Lightning Source LLC
Chambersburg PA
CBHW061538010526
44111CB00025B/2961